Public Opinion and the Political Future of the Nation's Capital

Public Opinion and the Political Future of the Nation's Capital

EDWARD M. MEYERS

GEORGETOWN UNIVERSITY PRESS / WASHINGTON, D.C.

Georgetown University Press, Washington, D.C. 20007

Printed in the United States of America.
10 9 8 7 6 5 4 3 2 1 1996
THIS VOLUME IS PRINTED ON ACID-FREE OFFSET BOOKPAPER.

Library of Congress Cataloging-in-Publication Data

Meyers, Edward M.
Public opinion and the political future of the Nation's Capital / Edward M. Meyers.
p. cm.
Includes bibliographical references.
1. Washington (D.C.)—Politics and government—1967– 2. Washington (D.C.)—Economic conditions. 3. Washington (D.C.)—Social conditions. 4. Washington (D.C.)—Politics and government—1967—Public opinion. 5. Public opinion—United States. I. Title.
JK2716.M49 1996
975.3'04—dc20
ISBN 0-87840-622-0 (cloth).
ISBN 0-87840-623-9 (pbk.)

To Karen, Ken, Kathleen, my Mom, and all D.C. residents, whether they want political equality or not.

Contents

Acknowledgements

I greatly appreciate the advice and insights of several researchers. Professor Clyde Wilcox of Georgetown University's Department of Government gave me a full appreciation of qualitative research and the ways it can be used to explore an evolution of public opinion on insufficiently discussed issues in American politics. Professor Wilcox provided thorough guidance on the research design. Professor James I. Lengle, also of Georgetown University's Department of Government, provided superb suggestions on organizational improvements and uses for the data. Professor Jamin B. Raskin, Washington School of Law, the American University, is a widely acknowledged expert on D.C. policies and provided substantive guidance on this topic. Dr. Alice Rivlin, Director of the U.S. Office of Management and Budget, was instrumental in the selection of the research topic and in conceptualizing how the research could be implemented.

I would also like to thank each of the sixty-one panelists who participated in the qualitative research, as well as their recruiters and coordinators: Bruce Lawhead and Jan Shapiro, Van Nuys, California; Lisa Chalstrom, Des Moines, Iowa; Kathleen Burke, Bethesda, Maryland; Diane Dusman and Laura Goldman, Harrisburg, Pennsylvania; and Luz Preito, Austin, Texas. They all came through when I needed them the most. I appreciate the audiotechnical advice of my son, Ken Meyers, who planned the taping sessions. I especially appreciate the administrative assistance of Suzanne Jones, Catherina Hampton, and Melvena Avent.

Finally, I appreciate the energy and time of U.S. and D.C. leaders who provided their insights for this work.

1

Six Hundred Thousand Loose Threads in the Tapestry of American Democracy

> *"You have a collapsing and extraordinarily self-destructive government in the city. It is one of the great problems of our time."*
>
> Newt Gingrich
> (*Washington Post,* December 12, 1994, A24)

Most Americans have some image, personally experienced or media-fed, of their nation's capital. To many, Washington, D.C.[1] is the red-taped home of lazy, self-centered, overpaid federal government bureaucrats who could not relate to Americans' real-life concerns even if they wanted to—which they don't, it is felt.

The nation's capital also has a nebulously defined local government, a "crippled experiment of limited home rule," as described in *Dream City: Race, Power, and the Decline of Washington, D.C.* (Jaffe and Sherwood 1994, 180), a book that chronicled corruption, ineptitude, and abject failure of a people attempting self-government. Another book, *D.C. by the Numbers: A State of Failure* (Edmonds and Keating 1995), statistically demonstrated the District's last place finish in America's socioeconomic standings. A *Washington Post* editorial (February 8, 1996, A24) called D.C. "the region's most heavily taxed, least served and most financially embarrassed jurisdiction."

1. The names Washington, D.C., District, and District of Columbia are used interchangeably in common parlance and are treated as such in this work as well. The District's constitutional convention chose New Columbia as the prospective state's new name.

Even many D.C. residents speak of a "third world government," a motley assemblage of misfits hiring megatons of other misfits whose only discernable purpose, it is said, is to plunder what remains of this jurisdiction's dwindling resources so that they can take long lunch hours, mistreat the local citizenry, and figure out how to bring their cousins on the payroll. Those District residents who have not maneuvered their way into federal or local government employment are said to feed from another public trough—welfare, food stamps, or some grant—or are the plunderees who are expected to foot the bill for this deplorable fiasco. Thousands, black and white, are getting out of Dodge, fleeing D.C.—Dodge City—and its desperate, dangerous streets. Escapees see what they leave behind not so much as distorted New Deal liberalism, but, for them, a raw deal. Since many conclude that D.C. cannot take care of itself, the main task becomes: Who will take D.C.? Congress? Maryland or some other state? Or maybe some huge orphanage in the welfare reform movement? Were the District's sorry plight a little less tragic, it would be a capital joke, a regular riot.

Few works have attempted to focus Americans' attention, as this research does, on the nation's capital beyond the above stereotypes. Can Americans envision D.C. residents as fellow citizens, with commonly shared political, social, and economic goals, or after examination, are D.C. residents truly a bizarre breed apart, richly deserving of the inferior political status handed down to them by our nation's founders?

While a financial control board has been formed by Congress to recommend how the District can overcome its financial crisis and serve the local citizenry, this work is primarily an assessment of D.C. residents' political rights. These rights have been on hold not only while the District's financial structure is resolved but for the more than two hundred year history of this unique entity. This research is also a journey in political cognition, adding to our understanding of how people process new information, match it against a storehouse of prior knowledge, and arrive at reasoned policy judgments on an issue to which they may not have previously given a moment's notice. Average Americans thus contribute, through this work, to the discussion of D.C. residents' political future.

THE WINDS OF CHANGE

D.C. residents do not share in the full self-government and congressional representation enjoyed by their fellow Americans. Thus unprotected, they are buffeted by the larger political winds sweeping over their sixty-nine square mile landscape. The residents cannot control their own laws, budgets, and resources, and they even lack a single vote in the U.S. House or Senate, the bodies that shape their destiny.

In recent times, D.C. residents' hopes for equal political rights with other Americans and D.C.'s full self-government aspirations were raised by an incoming progressive Democratic administration. These hopes were soon dashed, however, by their local government's financial collapse and by a Republican–controlled Congress' imposition of a presidentially appointed financial control board to scrutinize and potentially overrule any local decision, large and small. Moreover, social and economic winds have swept tens of thousands of D.C. residents into the more affluent, more stable, and safer suburbs. This flight of people and resources knocked the props from a dinosaurian government which then collapsed under its own weight. A fiscal gap of three-quarters of a billion dollars could not be closed by the resources of the remaining D.C. residents and businesses. Therefore, Congress and the local government reverted to stereotypes, with Congress imposing stern external discipline and the District government depending upon greater federal aid.

The options of structuring D.C.'s political future remain wide open. Once the work of the financial control board is complete, a plan for more extended federal control of the District could be developed. One could also envision District residents obtaining some voting rights in Congress while Congress retains oversight over D.C. laws and budgets. Alternatively, the whole territory could be retroceded to Maryland if the state is given sufficient financial inducement to take D.C. At the far and of the control vs. independence continuum, D.C. would achieve full self-government and equal political rights, which by logical extension would mean statehood.

The status quo appears to be the least likely option. Few national or local political leaders believe that the District does, or is able to, function well under its current structure. Moreover, as this research demonstrates, the status quo makes no sense at all to average Americans, a conclusion drawn from in-depth discussions held around the nation. The District's political transmission is due for an overhaul.

THE "MAYOR-FOR-LIFE"

District residents were disgraced internationally when their leader, Marion Barry, was seen smoking a crack pipe on perhaps the world's most widely viewed videotape. But scarcely four years later, the residents once again tied their hopes to a resurrected Barry, the subject of so much scorn both outside and inside D.C. who was nevertheless viewed by local voters as the best among those running for mayor to heal their many urban ills—just as he was healing himself.

Like gamblers hounded by dozens of creditors, D.C. voters felt that they could not sink much lower in the eyes of the nation, so they bet their political mortgage on their longshot hunch. If Barry could re-energize his talents, perhaps the District's fortunes would also rise. While Barry was portrayed around the nation as a demagogue who tricked the jobless, druggies, and criminals into voting for him, during the 1994 election it was hard to find working people—cab drivers, waiters, and clerks—who were not pro-Barry. Moreover, at least some of the business community recalled his ability to revitalize an economy and covertly supported him (*Washington Post*, September 15, 1994, B10, B12).

Barry was also viewed by much of D.C. as the best among the candidates to voice D.C. residents' independence from congressional overrule. Citizens seemed cognizant of the potential for congressional punishment of the District over their choice for mayor. As Representative James Moran (D–Va.) put it, "There's a lot of members who are gleeful because it makes the District such an easy target" (*Washington Times*, September 15, 1994). However, D.C. residents did not view puppy-dog devotion to Congress as ever having won much favor, and besides, Barry at his best was a skilled negotiator, bargaining with Congress not in supplication but on equal footing. The voters were aware of the downside, but voted the upside thinking that a true Barry and D.C. resurrection would win warmer, more sustained pro-D.C. treatment down the road than would a predictable, subservient life under a docile leader. D.C. residents sought a storybook rescue.

During the election, conspiratorial theorists had it that Barry would win and, as a result, Congress would swoop down on D.C. and reclaim what little power it had given the city two decades previously under limited home rule. After the election, the theorists muttered: "See, we told you."

THE FINANCIAL CONTROL BOARD

The federal imposition of a financial control board—the D.C. Financial Responsibility and Management Assistance Authority—in the first year of Barry's new term at least partly supplanted the mayor and the legislative body in the Congress-D.C.-people chain of command. Pre-election concerns that Barry would run amuck were soon replaced by conjecture that Barry and the other elected officials were largely irrelevant. Barry insiders counter that the mayor is far from irrelevant, that he is in frequent contact with control board members, influencing their decisions, not to mention the thousands of tasks of running the District that are outside the control board's areas of interest.

The control board's initial public hearings drew the ire of some D.C. residents and employee union members, since they saw the board slash the government payroll, control leases, and determine which kinds of D.C. bills were paid first. One resident fulminated that the authority "will never be legitimate in any moral or ethical sense of the term" because it is "beyond the reach of our votes." He called the board merely another "instrument in the 200-year history of congressional abuse of the rights of District citizens" (*Washington Post,* August 13, 1995, B1). Most D.C. citizens seemed too dispirited to protest the board's actions in an era when even Americans who have congressional representation and self-government feel that no one listens to them. Congressman Jack Kingston (R–Ga) summed up who was in charge around D.C. anyway: "It's the city of the United States of America. It would be a mistake to say it's their [residents'] city" (*Washington Times,* July 28, 1995, C9).

HISTORIC HOUSE VOTE ON D.C. STATEHOOD

Less than a year but a political eon before Republicans assumed congressional control, before Barry's return to local power, and before revelations of the District's massive fiscal hemorrhage, Congress confronted the District's political status. In late 1993, by a count of 277 to 153, the U.S. House of Representatives denied statehood to the residents of the District of Columbia. With one exception, all Republicans joined in the opposition to D.C. statehood, and 40 percent of House Democrats also voted to defeat the measure. The Democrats did so despite the support of President Clinton for statehood as well as their own advocacy of it in the previous three Democratic party platforms. After leading a vigorous debate on the floor of the House, D.C.'s delegate to the House, Eleanor Holmes Norton, was "forced to stand by voteless" (noted a *Washington Post* editorial of November 23, 1993) as the count proceeded—simply because D.C. residents lack the voting representation in Congress that is routinely afforded to other Americans.

The defeat was an indication of the boundless distance D.C. advocates must travel. Nonetheless, this was the first time that D.C. statehood was debated and voted upon in Congress. A longer view of the District's political struggles yields the realization that Congress, whether controlled by Republicans or Democrats, will at some point decide upon an improved structure for the nation's capital, one that meets the twin goals of assuring not only financial stability of its governing entity but political rights for its citizenry.

DEMOCRACY IN D.C.: OUT OF SIGHT, OUT OF MIND

D.C.'s political status is not a salient issue in America. Most people have not thought about the fact that there are nearly six hundred thousand people living in the United States, nestled among the thirteen original states, who have no U.S. senators or voting representatives to speak for them in a debate over whether to send their sons or daughters off to war. Most people do not give thought to the fact that Congress has control over all bills and budgets of the District even though Congress could never exercise such control over Arizona or New Jersey. Many have heard that a financial control board was legislated by Congress to put the District's financial house in order, but Americans have little idea of what the District's structure was before the control board was imposed.

D.C. residents often refer to their jurisdiction as the "last colony." Indeed, D.C.'s political status is about the same as that of American Samoa except for the fact that the people of the latter territory, as U.S. nationals, pay no income taxes to the U.S. Treasury, unlike the District's residents. While the matter of taxation without representation was resolved over two hundred years ago, it is a daily occurrence in Washington, D.C., the capital of the free world. These are forgotten people, six hundred thousand loose threads in the tapestry of American democracy.

The District's inferior political status would remain in oblivion were it not for several factors. First, as the District's financial collapse illustrates, the status quo is unworkable. It has become apparent in both national parties that the District cannot function within its current structure and that the problem lies not only within but also beyond local management problems. *Something* must be done. Second, as this research demonstrates, average Americans, once they explore the topic in depth, regard the District's status as unjust. Third, inside the District, opinions about the topic are often divided along racial lines, adding a human rights flavor to the issue. In opinion polls and the voting booths, blacks by wide margins prefer self-government, and by equally wide margins, whites prefer congressional control over D.C. and its predominantly black government. Fourth, the lack of representation of citizens of the nation's capital in the national legislature is unique among the world's democracies. Considering all of these factors, the issue has sufficient appeal at this point to lift it from torpidity.

VOICES, PAST AND PRESENT, ON D.C.'S POLITICAL STATUS

The District's political standing has been debated at least as far back as 1800, when Representative John Smilie of Pennsylvania said in a House debate (Noyes 1951, 118):

> Not a man in the District would be represented in the Government, whereas every man who contributed to the support of a government ought to be represented in it; otherwise his natural rights were subverted and he was left not a citizen but a slave. It was a right which this country, when under subjection to Great Britain, thought worth making a resolute struggle for and evinced a determination to perish rather than not enjoy.

Since that time numerous resolutions have been proposed in the House and Senate to improve political rights for District residents (ibid., 111–55, 164–78, 191–245). In 1922, Senator Wesley L. Jones of Washington advocated a constitutional amendment to provide voting representation for the District in Congress, and asked (ibid., 233):

> What is there in our scheme of government that requires that the Capital of the United States should be the one capital among the civilized nations, the inhabitants of which are excluded, deliberatively and of set purpose, from all participation in their government?

Jones (ibid.) viewed his amendment as necessary to "relieve the Nation of the shame of un-Americanism at its heart. . . ." The remarks of Representative Hatton W. Summers of Texas in 1945 epitomized the views of many over the decades (ibid., 240):

> Looking into this matter from a national standpoint, these people [District residents] are a part of the Nation's citizenship. They contribute with their taxes, they make contribution of their young men in times of war, they have a share of all the Nation's burdens. It seems to me they ought to be permitted to participate in the selection of those persons who bespeak the voice of the Nation.

The arguments for full democratic participation and statehood continue, as a sampling of recent editorial opinion from some leading newspapers indicates:

> It is time to right a great historic wrong. Since 1800, the residents of Washington, D.C. have been the only taxpaying U.S. citizens denied representation in Congress. With the election of Bill Clinton, it has become politically possible to give them the status that is their due. We believe now is the time to begin defining and then putting in place an arrangement that puts District residents on an equal footing with all Americans. . . . The only achievable alternative, if citizens are to enjoy the full political participation that is their due, is statehood.
>
> *The Washington Post*
> January 13, 1993

> The District's treatment is a scandal, albeit one with a long history. The Federal Government runs the city like a plantation, denying it a voting representative in Congress, forbidding it even rudimentary self-rule and limiting severely its ability to raise revenue. . . . Those who oppose statehood typically offer weak constitutional arguments against it. It seems fairly clear, however, that Republicans who oppose statehood do so because the District would send two more Democrats to the Senate. . . . The issue of statehood raises an obvious question: How can we justify championing democracy abroad while inflicting second-class citizenship in the nation's capital? The answer is obvious, too: We can't.
>
> *The New York Times*
> November 25, 1991

> Those who oppose statehood often claim that the Constitution forbids creation of a state in the District. That claim is without merit. The Constitution says only that Congress will exercise control over a seat of Government that does not exceed 10 miles square. A state could be created that would reduce the size of the Federal enclave but not eliminate it. The real objections to statehood are political. . . . The Democrats also have acted spinelessly, giving statehood little more than token support.
>
> *The New York Times*
> October 5, 1991

> Congress has long kept the city in a degree of thralldom that suited the convenience of representatives and senators who legislate matters as trivial as taxicab rules. The problem was exacerbated by longtime bigotry against the city's large black population from a Congress often dominated by members from the old South. . . . The political question of D.C. statehood has been complicated by its predominately Democratic voter registration, making the matter unpalatable for Republicans when the balance of power would hinge on just a few votes. That is a weak excuse for perpetuating political inequity in a country launched on a cry of "no taxation without representation." Make the District a state.
>
> *Boston Globe*
> December 2, 1992

Even *USA Today*, a newspaper that helps define the American mainstream, has editorialized in favor of strengthened political rights for D.C. residents without taking a stance on statehood:

> . . . [W]hatever the Founding Fathers had in mind when they prescribed a federal city, it wasn't to create a constitutional ghetto whose

> residents are denied their rights by lawmakers who sometimes revert to carpetbagging and demagoguery. . . . District residents are full citizens. One way or another, they deserve full representation.
>
> *USA Today*
> July 8, 1993

And from the deep South:

> Congress needs to find a sensible solution. D.C. residents are being denied basic rights of representation. And the current setup in which the District is governed partly by local elected officials and partly by Congress is the worst of all possible worlds. Nobody's completely in charge, so nobody acts like they're in charge—and our nation's capital, which should be a wealthy, growing city, is a bankrupt disaster.
>
> *Birmingham (Ala.) News*
> August 8, 1994

Notwithstanding such newspaper editorials and occasional anguished outbursts from D.C. residents, the critical factor today, as it seemingly always has been in the two-century history of this issue, is the level of interest in full democratic rights for District residents among average Americans and their national elected representatives.

SURVEYS INTO D.C.'S POLITICAL FUTURE

As long as a federally imposed control board makes financial decisions for the District, D.C. residents cannot expect to expand their self-government authority. Even in less turbulent times, however, D.C.'s standing among Americans was low compared to the prospects of other territories seeking full political rights. For example, the lack of support for D.C. statehood among Americans, in comparison to much higher levels of American support for the statehood drives of Hawaii and Alaska, has been traced by opinion polls. The *Washington Post* has conducted two quantitative national surveys into public opinion on D.C. statehood (Roper Center 1994). In March of 1989, Americans opposed D.C. statehood by a 56–to–30 percent margin, with 14 percent "don't knows." Then in October of 1992, a *Post* survey of Americans indicated opposition to D.C. statehood by a 57–to–20 percent margin, with 24 percent "don't knows." Some of those favoring D.C. statehood in the earlier pool may have sought shelter as "don't knows" in the wake of adverse press accounts following the arrest of Marion Barry. Also, the question in the latter poll, unlike the earlier query, asked if D.C. should be made a "separate state" instead of just a state. The question design could have added to the confusion. Additionally, a *U.S. News and World Report* survey (Tooley 1991) found a 50–50 split among Americans polled about their support for D.C. statehood.

The *Washington Post* surveys indicate low popular support for D.C. statehood, especially when compared to polls conducted prior to the admission of Hawaii and Alaska in 1959. The Roper Center for Public Opinion Research (1994) reports that there were sixteen Gallup polls conducted between 1940 and 1958 on the admission of Hawaii. After 1946, a majority of Americans polled favored admission, and after 1950, at least 60 percent of those surveyed favored admission. Much the same results are found in twelve polls conducted by Gallup from 1946 to 1958 on the question of Alaskan statehood. In no instance did fewer than 64 percent of those polled favor statehood, and after 1950 the lowest favorable percentage was 71. Because D.C. statehood is garnering nowhere near the acceptance achieved decades ago by Hawaii and Alaska, political options other than statehood are more likely to be voiced by national leaders.

HAWAII AND ALASKA

While statehood is dormant in the array of current D.C. structural considerations, it may be useful to see what has accounted for the District's low levels of popular support for statehood over the years in comparison to Americans' support for Hawaii and Alaska. The District has a host of unusual circumstances and problems—but so did the last two states to gain admission to the Union in 1959, Alaska and Hawaii. Both Hawaii's and Alaska's statehood efforts took decades to bear fruit; both were thwarted by the territories' small population sizes, by the transient nature of their populations, and by partisan political concerns. In both cases, statehood led to growth which helped overcome some structural economic problems in these territories.

Hawaii's statehood efforts were delayed by a widespread concern in the mainland, during an extended post–World War II era, over the racial composition of the Hawaiian population. Hawaii was thought of as a territory unsafe for whites; moreover, most white Hawaiians preferred U.S. government control to self-government by a minority–controlled population.

While Alaska was not troubled by extraordinary racial concerns, its statehood drive also bore similarities to those currently faced by the District. Alaska's economy was excessively dependent upon federal "handouts" and was not thought of as self-sufficient. The territory had high tax rates, attributed to fiscal mismanagement by the territorial government.

Hawaii

Hawaii's statehood process began shortly after U.S. annexation in 1898. Hawaii was said to be "the most thoroughly studied, the most exhaustively investigated, and the most frequently rejected by the Congress" of all the states ultimately gaining admission (Bell 1984, 4). Because of this precedent, actors in the District's statehood drama are often advised of the need for unearthly patience.

A characteristic of Hawaii's efforts, similar to the District's, involved the composition of Hawaii's population. Bell (1984, 295) stated: "The unique ethnic composition of Hawaii's community . . . was for sixty years the underlying barrier to its attempts to emulate all other incorporated territories and gain statehood." As Hawaiian statehood proponent Robert Hale (R–Maine) stated (ibid., 135) in congressional debate:

> Let us be frank about it. The opposition to this measure arises primarily from the fact that the racial strains in Hawaii are more Asiatic than European. The opposition springs from a dangerous form of racism.

Whether the District continues to be subject to similar racial attitudes, or whether Congress and the general public are now more enlightened, is debatable. Nonetheless, at the time the evidence was clear. Six national Gallup polls from 1950 to 1958 revealed greater opposition to Hawaii's admission than Alaska's. Both territories were noncontiguous to the mainland, both were important strategically, both had been incorporated as territories for long periods, and both had small populations (even though Hawaii's population was more than double Alaska's). However, "the only significant variable which might have influenced the differences in mainland opinion was the composition of Hawaii's population" (ibid., 253). The opposition to statehood for Hawaii increased as the nature of its mixed population became more widely known. Ironically, this increased knowledge was gained as a result of the vigorous publicity campaign conducted by statehood supporters.

Unlike today's situation with the District, people were not reluctant to make their views about Hawaii's racial composition known publicly. As late as 1957, the *Tulsa Tribune* asked rhetorically, "Do we want to put a couple of Japs in the Senate of the United States?" (ibid.). From another source: "In 1917 the births of the two races were: Americans, 295; Japanese 5,000! Comment is superfluous" (ibid., 49). As is the case with the District, crime was cited as a reason to oppose statehood, and many commentators expressed alarm that Hawaii was "unsafe for white Americans" (ibid., 58).

Members of Congress were not innocent bystanders; many led the rhetorical charge. In 1947, still in the era of Pearl Harbor, Representative Prince Preston (D–Ga.) said, "When you give these people the same rights we have today, you will have two Senators speaking for these 180,000 Japanese." Moreover, opponents of statehood seemed concerned that Hawaii's senators would be nonwhite and would be liberal on civil rights issues (ibid., 134, 236). As Senator James Eastland (D–Miss.) said, statehood would mean ". . . two votes against all racial segregation and two votes against the South on all social matters" (ibid., 134). Opponents of statehood for the District also point to the likelihood of an additional two liberal senators (Schrag 1990, 345, n. 167).

Hawaii's prestatehood condition was similar to the District's in other respects. Many congressman were influenced by the calculation that, as of the 1950s, one senator would represent 223,000 citizens, while the congressional average was one per seventeen million. House debaters cited the warnings of Daniel Webster that adding new, small states "deranges and disturbs the proper balance between the Senate and the House of Representatives" (Bell 1984, 256).

As is the case with the District, statehood for Hawaii was entangled in partisan concerns. Democrats delayed their support for statehood until it became clear, after the 1956 elections, that Hawaii, like Alaska, would often vote Democratic (ibid., 236, 335 n. 4). President Eisenhower and Republican congressional supporters did not desert Hawaii once Hawaii turned Democratic (ibid., 2343, 272).

Also similar to the District's situation, there is some indication that many of Hawaii's white minority and business interests opposed statehood initially. The possibility of a veto by a presidentially appointed governor had some appeal, especially as a tool in defeating radical tax structure changes (ibid., 257–60, 294). Ultimately, Hawaiian statehood won the overwhelming support of all of the islands' racial groups, thereby aiding the statehood drive. Hawaii's status as "America's stepchild," in the words of a statehood leader, was finally over (ibid., 294).

Alaska

Similar to the case of Hawaii, statehood for Alaska was also years in the making. Alaska's first statehood bill was proposed in 1916 (U.S. Congress 1957, 2936). Unlike Hawaii, Alaska's racial composition in the years immediately preceding statehood was largely white, with substantial numbers (nearly 34,000) of Eskimos, Indians, and Aleuts (U.S. Senate 1957, 2949). Nonetheless, Alaska's prestatehood conditions were uncannily like the District's in many ways.

Most residents of Alaska had moved there from somewhere else in the United States and were accustomed to voicing their opinions to their congressperson and registering their protests in the voting booth. However, during Alaska's territorial years, the new residents only had one nonvoting delegate to represent them in Congress. As Bowkett (1989, 9) summarized, "The situation was particularly galling to Alaskans because they were U.S. citizens and paid taxes and served in the armed forces just as their fellow citizens in the states. Without the leverage of a full-fledged congressional delegation, they could rarely . . . have any real influence" over federal policies and programs. Many Alaskans felt that the Washington bureaucracy which ultimately governed them was "not particularly sensitive to the needs of the residents of the Territory" (ibid.). As an Alaskan delegate said in 1946 (ibid., 13), "The whole form and fabric of our [U.S.] free government is based on the assumption that people can govern themselves in better fashion than they can be governed by anyone else."

Alaskan independence was complicated by the federal government's extensive ownership of land in the territory, as is the case in the District. As of 1990, 81.1 percent of Alaska's land remained in federal government ownership, almost double the federal proportion in the District (U.S. Census Bureau 1991, 203). Prior to achieving statehood, over 99 percent of Alaska's land was owned by the federal government. This land consisted of federal wilderness or reservations, glaciers, mountains, and what a congressional report (U.S. Congress 1957, 2938) called "worthless tundra."

Alaska's small population, like the District's, was an obstacle. At the same time that statehood was being considered for Alaska, its population, estimated at 161,000, was only 27 percent of the District's 1990 population. Opponents of Alaskan statehood asserted in a congressional report (U.S. Congress 1957, 3009) that Alaska's population, minus fifty thousand transitory military personnel and minus twenty thousand people who were under voting age, totaled "less people than the capacities of many college football stadiums."

A minority report (U.S. Congress 1957, 3007–8) filed in opposition to the Alaskan statehood bill noted that only 28,767 people voted in the previous year's 1956 Alaskan general election. This compares to 228,000 District voters in the 1992 general election (U.S. Bureau of the Census 1994b, 271). Alaska's small population gave residents of the new state a six-to-one advantage in the effectiveness of their votes compared to residents of the lower forty-eight states, and Alaskans had one senator for each 80,500 of population (ibid.). The Committee's majority report (U.S. Congress 1957, 2944) stated that the low population argument was without merit, noting that Alaska's population at the time was "greater than at least one of the present States."

This low level of population, at 161,000, was supported primarily by federal defense construction booms associated with World War II, and then by the Korean War (Bowkett 1989, 14–16). In fact, similar to the District's case, Alaska's efforts to achieve statehood were questioned on grounds of excessive dependency on the federal government. A House Interior Committee minority report (included in U.S. Congress 1957, 3008) on an Alaskan statehood bill indicated that Alaska's economy "is an artificial one, bolstered by huge Federal handouts." Alaska's 1958 budget provided for a federal civil expenditure of $122 million plus a military defense and construction expenditure of $350 million, for a total of $472 million. The total income from all private industry at the time was $160 million. Therefore, this report stated, "The economy is dependent to the extent of more than two-thirds of its income upon Federal expenditures."

Opponents of Alaskan statehood were concerned that Alaska's own resources were "as yet insufficiently developed to permit private enterprise based on such resources to take up the slack in employment and tax revenue which would be needed if Federal spending comes to an abrupt end" (ibid., 2944). However, the House Interior Committee (ibid., 2946) dismissed such a concern, stating that "there is no reason to expect any immediate cessation of such expenditures," and that, even after the completion of a large federal construction program taking place in Alaska at the time, "the complement of Federal personnel, both military and civilian, in the Territory will remain large." The same comments could be made about prospects for federal employment in the District in the years ahead.

The House Interior Committee also expressed concern that Alaska, as a state, would not be able to finance the basic functions of state government, especially road construction and maintenance (ibid., 2938). It was feared that private sector taxable resources might not be sufficient. This argument as well has a familiar ring as one reviews obstacles currently faced by the District. In summary, it is likely that at the time Alaska achieved statehood, its economy was dependent upon the federal government to a much greater extent than the District's is currently. The proportion of its own land owned by the federal government was much greater than is the case with the District, and its population was considerably smaller than the District's. Alaska, along with Hawaii, had the additional consideration of noncontiguity with the lower forty-eight states, which at the time was termed a "questionable precedent" (ibid., 3009).

Despite all of these drawbacks, there was "nothing presumptuous about asking for admission to the Union," according to one writer (Bowkett 1989, 14). With Alaska's "problems and needs rapidly mounting and the shortcomings of territorial status glaring, it became clear that nothing less than statehood would do" (ibid.).

As is the case with the District, partisan concerns played a large role in Alaska's statehood drive. Both major parties were strong in Alaska; however, the territory's delegates to the U.S. Congress since 1932 had been Democrats (ibid., 17). President Truman, a Democrat, had proposed statehood for Alaska in 1946 and 1948. However, Eisenhower, a Republican, initially ignored Alaska in his early messages to Congress, favoring instead Hawaii, which during the early 1950s appeared to be more solidly Republican (ibid., 16–17). Ironically, in eight poststatehood elections for president, Hawaii voted Republican twice while Alaska voted Republican seven times. In recent years, Hawaii has sent two Democratic senators to Washington and Alaska has sent two Republican senators (U.S. Bureau of the Census 1991, 251, 262).

Alaska's reputation was burdened by a territorial legislature said to be the "worst ever" in 1947 by Ernest Gruening, the territory's governor at the time. The legislature seemed excessively influenced by absentee commercial interests, and its failure to enact sufficient taxes precipitated a financial crisis in the territory. However, by 1949 a legislature rated one of the best restored the territory to solvency. As a result of this turnaround in performance, statehood for Alaska could once again be "legitimately pursued" (ibid., 15–16). However, as late as 1957, congressional opponents of Alaskan statehood (U.S. Congress 1957, 3008) pointed to Alaska's highest-in-the-nation tax rates and stated that "Alaska's development is being retarded by its unsound economy and fiscal management." The District's reputation was also tarnished severely in the latter years of Mayor Marion Barry's past tenure in office (Raven-Hansen 1991, 161), and by the mid-l990s financial crisis and excessive D.C. tax rates. Concerns still abound in the broader population over the District's "readiness" for statehood—or any other form of political autonomy—and its sufficiency of resources to cope with statehood's demands.

PUERTO RICAN STATEHOOD

Statehood for Puerto Rico, were it to be considered, is thought by some in D.C. to boost D.C.'s statehood chances. After all, congressional debates on statehood for Puerto Rico could cast greater attention on D.C.'s political inequalities. In both Puerto Rico and D.C., residents fought and died in U.S. wars, although the people of D.C. did so for more than a century longer. The citizens of both jurisdictions are U.S. citizens, Puerto Ricans having attained that status in 1917. Both jurisdictions have racial and ethnic minorities as their predominant population groups. Both jurisdictions have heavy concentrations of poverty, although Puerto Rico, with nearly 60 percent of its population living below the federal poverty line (*Washington Post*, November 13, 1993, A4) has triple the proportion of poverty as found among the District's population. Both have high unemployment, although Puerto Rico, with 17 percent unemployment in the autumn of 1993 (ibid.), has double D.C.'s proportion.

There are significant distinctions. The Puerto Rican population of 3.6 million is considerably larger than D.C.'s. Moreover, unlike D.C. residents, Puerto Ricans do not pay federal income taxes. Mainland U.S. companies also receive a lucrative tax break if they locate plants in Puerto Rico (*Washington Post*, November 18, 1993, A22).

Most significantly, D.C. residents have voted favorably on statehood, while Puerto Ricans have not. By a 48–to–46 percent margin, with the remainder favoring complete independence, Puerto Ricans voiced their preference in a plebiscite of November 14, 1993 to retain their commonwealth status over statehood (ibid.). Undoubtedly, loss under statehood of their federal tax advantages weighed heavily in the Puerto Ricans' vote.

In summary, the District has social, economic, and political conditions that are not wildly different from those of Alaska and Hawaii in 1959. Whether the District's goal is statehood or some alternative that improves its political standing, it must achieve greater levels of acceptance than it now experiences from the American people as well as from Congress. Because the District's political status is such an unformed issue, in-depth, qualitative research may be needed to examine this acceptance level. Moreover, qualitative research would explore the variety of political options better than would forced-choice surveys, since respondents would have little or no basis for choosing one option over another without a more in-depth understanding of the issues.

QUALITATIVE RESEARCH INTO UNFORMED ISSUES

Issues penetrate the nation's consciousness from time to time. The civil rights movement, a war in Vietnam or Iraq, a presidential tax proposal, and an impeachable offense by a national leader are examples of issues that capture public attention. These are topics of the dinner table, the nightly news, the office elevator chat.

There are numerous issues, such as the District's political future, that receive far less attention. A trade imbalance, an environmental problem that has not reached a crisis stage, and an arcane tax loophole are among many thousands of issues that deserve, but do not receive, the daily attention of the American people. This is understandable. It is tough enough to seek, find, and keep a job, to pay the rent or mortgage, or to pay the kids' medical bills. Besides, political scientists have for several decades concluded that only a small percentage of Americans are ideologically oriented. Most people have an insufficient frame of reference to absorb considerable amounts of new information or issues, organize these thoughts, and develop a coherent public opinion.

Thus the lack of any thoughtful opinion by Americans on D.C.'s political future is typical, not malicious. If a president and other national leaders wanted to gauge public opinion on D.C.'s political status before deciding whether or how fiercely to lend their views, how would they approach this task?

At this early state of public opinion evolution on the issue, quantitative research (i.e., opinion surveys) would surely disappoint. Since Americans have not confronted this issue, it would be difficult even to design forced-choice questions. Even with lucky guesses in designing survey questions, respondents would likely be primed to reply according to how they felt about the District in general or to how the questions were worded. The best, most objectively designed survey would be a status check on the whims of people who took a minute from their daily lives.

We can say that Americans today are responding less favorably to the notion of D.C. statehood than Americans responded decades ago to Hawaiian and Alaskan statehood. However, we cannot say why that is and what the depth is of today's negative responses. Nor can we say how Americans view political options other than statehood for District residents and why respondents may lean one way or another. We also do not know what the opinions would be if respondents prepared themselves prior to answering the polling question—for example, by watching a television debate on the topic or exchanging points of view with others on the issue.

Herbert Asher (1992, 21) asks readers of opinion surveys to determine whether a poll topic is one on which citizens have "genuine opinions." If it is, then "the topic is suitable for a public opinion poll." However, "if the topic is so remote from and irrelevant to citizen concerns that they do not possess real views on it, then any poll on the topic will measure nonattitudes rather than attitudes." Asher (ibid.) states that information obtained about nonattitudes will be suspect, "even if the questions are properly worded, the sample scientifically collected, and the data appropriately analyzed."

Because citizen viewpoints on D.C.'s political options are based on sparse information, the above-referenced surveys likely measure nonattitudes as much as attitudes. Qualitative research is called for. Unlike quantitative research which surveys a large statistical sampling of a population to arrive at data on a political or other matter, qualitative research involves a more in-depth exploration of the thought processes of relatively few research participants. Examples of qualitative research involve the use of extended interviews (Hochschild 1981; McCracken 1988) and focus groups (Morgan and Spanish 1985; Conover, Crewe, and Searing 1990).

This qualitative research into public opinion on D.C.'s political options uses focus groups to capture the interactive effects among participants. In some ways this research simulates what would happen if this issue were discussed and debated across America. Unlike with opinion polls, in qualitative research researchers cannot as easily generalize findings from a statistical sample to the population at large. Nonetheless, qualitative research is able to improve one's understanding of how many Americans are likely to approach the issue if it were to be presented to them.

For this research, focus groups were conducted in Bethesda, Maryland; Harrisburg, Pennsylvania; Des Moines, Iowa; Austin, Texas; and Van Nuys, California. Each group had from eleven to thirteen participants. An effort was made to assure political heterogeneity with a representative mixture of Democrats, Republicans, and Independents. A degree of heterogeneity was achieved in participants' ages, income levels, and occupations. Following focus group research guidelines, some homogeneity in education levels and in the races of participants was provided so that honesty and full interchange of viewpoints would not be restrained.

SUMMARY OF CONCLUSIONS AND ORGANIZATION OF THE RESEARCH

The five lively focus group sessions addressed the long-term issue of D.C.'s political structure and future beyond the immediate financial or management problems. Nearly everyone (57 of 61 panelists) favored voting representation for D.C. residents in Congress, and a majority (35 of 61) provided for D.C. voting membership in the Senate. Significantly, only three panelists, by the conclusion of the focus group sessions, advocated the political status quo for D.C. Over two-thirds (42 of 61) favored reduced congressional control over D.C. bills, budgets, and other affairs, while 25 supported full self-government. Statehood was advocated by 16 panelists, with most of the others favoring either nominal statehood—whereby D.C. would gain representation in Congress and reduced congressional control—or, to a lesser extent, favoring using Maryland as a means through which D.C. could vote or be governed.

In the next chapter, this work discusses the District's social and economic conditions, thus providing a context for analyzing the options that will shape the District's future. Because race is routinely assumed by many D.C. residents as a reason why D.C. is excluded from the federal political system, chapter 4 provides a framework for analyzing data for racial content and influence. The methodology appendices (F and G) establish a theoretical basis for qualitative research, with an emphasis on political cognition and schema theories, and provide a structure for analysis of focus group "data" or raw information. The focus group data are then evaluated against this theoretical backdrop, and research conclusions are developed. Chapter 5 discusses policy options that emerged from the five focus groups sessions.

In the sessions, average Americans were able to grasp the District's arcane political structure and offer their insights. Chapter 6 describes the schematic framework that enabled the public opinion evolution to take place. Six schemata or conceptual references used by the focus group panelists guided and facilitated public opinion development. The strongest was a democracy schema which fostered the view that all Americans should participate fully and equally in the federal political system. A state schema enabled panelists to match what they knew about D.C. against their concepts of what a state is or should be like. Their D.C. schema contained a variety of often negative conceptions about the District. Panelists' special treatment schema placed them on guard against groups which they believed may be attempting to take unfair advantage of a social, economic, or political system. Their anti-big-government schema produced wariness over excessive federal government control, while their founding fathers schema produced a profound respect for the framers of the Constitution. The manifestations and relative strengths of these schemata varied among the participants, as explored in chapter 6. Finally, chapter 7 includes the views of national and local leaders shaping the District's political future.

2

The Political, Social, and Economic Status of Washington, D.C.

"We have been conditioned to look at ourselves as slaves and to accept it. We have to be willing to show Congress that, as much as they may try to shackle us, we still know how to break loose."

Josephine Butler
D.C. resident and statehood activist
(*Washington Post*, November 13, 1994, B5)

THE DISTRICT'S POLITICAL STATUS

The District's origins date from those of the nation. Article 1, section 8, clause 17 of the U.S. Constitution provided for Congress to have the power

> to exercise exclusive legislation in all Cases whatsoever, over such District (not exceeding ten Miles square) as may, by Cession of particular States, and the acceptance of Congress, become the Seat of the Government of the United States . . .

In *Federalist* number 43 (Hamilton, Madison, Jay [1788] 1961, 272), Madison wrote of the "indispensable necessity of complete authority at the seat of government" of the national government by virtue of the latter's "general supremacy." Without this complete authority, the national government's public authority "might be insulted and its proceedings interrupted with impunity."

Madison further wrote that the states ceding the land for the nation's capital "will no doubt provide in the compact for the rights and the consent of the citizens inhabiting" the ceded land (ibid.). Madison did not waiver, in the District's special case, from his insistence on consent in the government of those governed, and thought that the District residents' consent could be obtained by means of "sufficient inducements"—namely, "their voice in the election of the government which is to exercise authority over them" and the authority to establish a municipal legislature.

At this stage of American history, one has to wonder whether the compact between the governed and the governing remains intact. D.C. residents lack a voice in the Congress that exercises authority over them, and their local government, subject to Congressional overrule at any level of detail, no longer provides for many residents a "sufficient inducement" to comply willingly with the special arrangement.

What is now considered the District's status quo was not set in stone at the nation's beginning to remain inert for two centuries. Rather, its evolution has had several dynamic phases. In the District's earliest years, the residents simply were required to adhere to either Maryland or Virginia laws, depending upon where in the District a case was tried. Shortly after the turn of the nineteenth century, Congress provided for a city council to be elected by the vote of all white male property holders in the District (Smith 1991, 6–7). Then in 1820, Congress provided for a popularly elected mayor. In 1846, Congress allowed all white males who paid a one dollar school tax to vote (ibid.). There was an attempt to expand enfranchisement to blacks in the mid-1860s; however, 99.1 percent of District voters opposed the referendum (apparently, one voting resident of Georgetown liked the idea) (ibid., 7). In 1866, Congress permitted black males to vote in D.C. elections (Edmonds and Keating 1995, 240), and for the next five years the District enjoyed a measure of self-rule.

This restrictive experiment in D.C. democracy was diluted in 1871 when locally elected officials were replaced by a federally appointed governor and council, with only the House of Delegates, the lower branch of the legislature, remaining popularly elected (Schrag 1990, 312; Smith 1991, 7). Smith (1991, 7) attributed the District's diminished political status largely to white concern over excessive influence by blacks over local affairs. Shortly after Congress approved black suffrage, a mayor sympathetic to black needs was voted into office. This mayor, Sayles Bowen, was thought to have hired excessive numbers of blacks, apparently for make-work projects, and in the process added substantially to the District's debt (ibid.).

After the 1871 self-rule restrictions, social welfare costs remained high, since the District was a magnet for forty thousand freed people with few job skills. Moreover, Alexander "Boss" Shepherd, who headed public works for the District, embarked on a massive infrastructure program—including new gas and water mains, roads, sidewalks, and sewers—that rebuilt an underdeveloped, war-scarred city and literally paved the way for future economic growth. In the process, however, the District accumulated massive debt and lost whatever trust Congress had in it. This crisis and its resolution are strikingly similar to the situation in which the District finds itself today—namely, in its own judgment or misjudgment, the District provided for its citizenry in ways for which it lacked the means. By 1874, the federal government had taken complete control over the District in replacing the vestiges of self-rule with three presidentially appointed commissioners (Schrag 1990, 312; *Washington Post*, January 9, 1995, D1, D5).

This structure remained for nearly a century. During this time, U.S. presidents appointed about a hundred commissioners to run the District. All but one was white and all but one was male (*Washington Post*, April 17, 1995, B3). During the entire time between 1874 and limited self-government in 1975, the white, affluent areas of D.C. received the best in educational and municipal services (ibid.), and the legacy of this protracted era of federal control is massive (while unmeasurable) today. During the many decades of federal control, the District Suffrage League worked toward a constitutional amendment for voting representation in Congress and in the electoral college, while a variety of self-rule resolutions were introduced and defeated in Congress (Edmunds and Keating 1995, 243). Mostly, however, residents seemed to accept their inferior status along with the variety of other hardships confronted in daily life simply because, unlike other Americans, they had no choice in the matter.

A breakthrough in improved political standing came in 1961, when District residents were granted the authority to vote in presidential elections by means of the Constitution's twenty-third amendment. The amendment limited the District's electoral college votes to the size of that of the smallest state. Future D.C. population upturns could create an inequity. Also, there was no provision for the District's participation in contingent presidential elections in the House of Representatives in the event that no candidate wins a majority of the electoral college, as could easily have happened in the election of 1992 given Ross Perot's strong candidacy. Moreover, the twenty-third amendment is dependent upon implementing legislation by Congress which could remove the District's participation in the electoral college at any time (Raskin 1993, 5–6). Thus, under the Constitution, District residents are by no means guaranteed equal political footing with other Americans in presidential elections.

As another step forward, in 1967 President Johnson and Congress reorganized the District, providing for a council and mayor that were appointed by the president, but which had a greater local flavor than experienced under previous arrangements. However, many on Capitol Hill still referred to the mayor as "commissioner" (Jenkins 1993, 22), and it became clear that a more genuine advance was needed.

Then in 1973, Congress adopted and the president signed the District of Columbia Self-Government and Governmental Reorganization Act, often termed the Home Rule Act. This act, which is currently in effect, provided for an elected council and mayor while reserving to Congress several powers. The act was an attempt to achieve the vision of self-government voiced by Madison and other founders. President John Adams, upon moving to the new capital in 1800, said, "In this city . . . may self-government which adorned the great character whose name it bears be forever held in veneration" (Smith 1991, 6). Adams added that it was at Congress' discretion whether Congress' constitutional powers over the District should be exercised (ibid.). Nonetheless, Congress retained authority over District laws and budgets both before and after the Home Rule Act.

By 1990, Congress had attached more than seventy-five riders to the budgets since limited home rule was enacted, restricting the District government in various ways (Schrag 1990, 314–16, 355–71). According to Schrag (ibid., 314–15), "Congress has shown particular interest in the regulation of morality." Its members can take a "highly visible stand" on D.C. issues without affecting voters back home. The members are thus able to "win the approval of their conservative constituents without incurring as much wrath from their liberal constituents as they would attract if those constituents were themselves being regulated" (ibid.). For example, the District was barred from using its own funds to perform abortions; prevented from decriminalizing consensual, adult sodomy; barred from advertising its lottery on the public transit system; and required to amend its human rights laws "to permit church-related educational institutions to discriminate against people who promote or condone homosexual acts or beliefs," according to Schrag (1990, 315, n.25–n.31). The latter rider was overturned in the courts.

Then in 1995, following election year budgeteering which did not confront collapsing revenues and gaping deficits, the District sunk in a financial morass from which it could not escape through its own means. Congress imposed a financial control board—the D.C. Financial Responsibility and Management Assistance Authority—which is imposing the discipline that D.C.'s elected leaders apparently lacked. The five-member board of presidential appointees remind longtime D.C. residents of the three-commission federally imposed structure of an earlier era. Although the board is similar to state-created authorities in Cleveland, New York City, and Philadelphia, residents of those cities were represented without interruption in their state and national legislatures.

THE DISTRICT'S ILL-FATED EMPLOYEE RESIDENCY REQUIREMENT

The District's employee residency requirement illustrates how easily the U.S. Congress can reverse a routine local prerogative, even in times free of crisis.

Initiated in the late 1970s by then-Council member Marion Barry, the requirement gave D.C. residents improved chances to land D.C. government jobs, kept the expenditure of tax revenues inside D.C. limits to a greater extent, and stimulated the local economy. At the time, the D.C. government was like any federal agency, with 62 percent of its mid-and higher-salaried employees (DS–9 and above) living in the suburbs (Meyers 1987).

The policy accomplished its objectives. By 1987, 60 percent of the D.C. government workforce consisted of D.C. residents. The law pertained to new hires, but even existing employees perceived a need to live in D.C. to increase their chances of advancement. The D.C. government no longer seemed like another federal agency; rather, a D.C. feel and zeal had evolved, a government not just "for" the people but "by" and "of" the D.C. people as well—a workforce that could weather the urban storms. However, many suburban-residing employees did not want to play along. Suburban-residing police officers in particular were effective in reaching their members of Congress, and many had legitimate concerns about their safety during their off-duty hours. After all, the officers not only knew the criminals; the criminals knew about them too, including where D.C.-residing police officers and their families lived.

This writer went to lunch one day with a congressional staffer who formerly worked for D.C.'s delegate in Congress and had shifted over to Representative Stan Parris's staff of suburban Virginia. The staffer inquired about the District's residency requirement and was informed that the District was exploring options that would retain the requirement but make it more palatable to police and fire personnel. He laughed nonchalantly and said, "Don't worry about it. We're going to take that law away from you." And Congress did, quite effortlessly in 1987.

The District's policy office, which this writer directed, conducted surveys for Congress in association with Peter D. Hart Research Associates to attempt to stem the tide. The survey demonstrated that 55 percent of the new hires thought the residency requirement was reasonable, 59 percent felt that the requirement gave D.C. employees a personal stake in the District's quality of life, 63 percent thought it helped D.C. workers stay in closer touch with D.C. people, 73 percent said the requirement helped D.C. finances, and 79 percent said it helped D.C. residents in the job market. Moreover, thirty-two of forty-seven large cities responding to another survey indicated they had a residency requirement to improve their socioeconomic standing in their regions (ibid.).

Today the District is once again evolving more of a suburban flavor in its workforce. By 1995, 70 percent of D.C. government employees were suburbanites (*Washington Post*, August 2, 1995, D1). The District has directly lost approximately $420 million annually (twelve thousand workers times $35,000 salary per worker) from its local economy to its more affluent suburbs—not counting spin-off economic benefits. The blow would be easier to take if the District had the authority to tax the income of its suburban-residing workers, but Congress prohibits the District from enacting that rather standard tax policy as well.

Congress transformed the District with this one policy revision more than it did with all its other post–1975 actions combined. When Congress substituted its wisdom for the judgment of the District's elected leaders, the District lost much of its social and economic infrastructure.

The District's declines did not result from this one policy shift; however, the difference between success and failure in any delicate system often hinges on changes in marginal factors. Fewer strong families remained to run Junior Achievement programs, Little Leagues, or Girl Scout troops. Fewer dollars supported grocery stores, downtown shops and department stores, and local commercial centers. Neighborhoods lost much of their vitality, as many no longer held a critical mass of stable families. Housing values plummeted and so did property tax revenues. Middle-class flight was accelerated by the employee mobility, and most of the twelve thousand workers who moved out took families, including other job holders, with them. With middle-class flight, the public schools were left with greater concentrations of impoverished students from tough learning environments, while administrators and teachers were held responsible for scholastic achievement scores that have been more than 20 percent below national averages (*Washington Post*, August 24, 1995, C1).

Moreover, the D.C. government has had to pay ten percent more, effectively, for each suburban-residing employee, since it could no longer collect income taxes from them. The remaining D.C. taxpayers have coughed up the difference. Congress voted to remove D.C.'s residency requirement alone, leaving standing similar statutes in their home districts' urban centers.

Representative Tom Davis—from a district where 55 percent of the homes were worth more than $200,000 (*Washington Post,* July 10, 1995, A8)—told this writer (1995) that he had a "pro-suburban bias." He said that the District could use more suburban talent, not less, "on how you balance budgets, how you make tough decisions, and how you say no to interest groups." Davis acknowledged that D.C. residents have "some amount of pride in this state [of D.C.]," but said "you want the best people running your city—whether they live in Fairfax [Davis' county], D.C., or Timbuktu—if they can get to work every day." Davis thought that talented D.C. residents "do not want to work for the D.C. government; they can find other jobs in other places."

ARENAE, STADIA, AND TRIVIA

The story of District-congressional relations can also be told through major economic development projects. Congress resembles a big brother to the District, one who seems a bully in some ways but who claims to—and often does—look out for the District's best interests.

Twenty years ago the District sought and gained permission from Congress to construct, with its own funds, a convention center. But it paid a price for the approval. This writer staffed the effort to finance the center and was familiar with the political maneuvering. The District's center would have competed with a large arena in suburban Maryland, and Maryland had plenty of clout in Congress, while the District stood voteless. Thus, as a condition for approval, the District agreed to scale back its center and delete entirely its plan for a large center hall with permanent seating that could double as a sports and entertainment complex.

Two decades later it was apparent that time had passed the District's convention center by: it was so small by contemporary standards that it could no longer accommodate the major conventions, a disaster in a town dependent upon visitor dollars. The number of conventions had fallen by half in recent years, as had convention delegate hotel stays (*Washington Post*, "Washington Business" section, January 9, 1995, 13). Naturally, many assumed the District was shortsighted in not anticipating the growth of conventions.

At any rate, in 1994 the District planned a larger center, attempting to beat other jurisdictions, such as nearby Alexandria, to the opportunity. Financing the planning and construction of the larger center, however, required the establishment of a fund, which in turn required congressional approval. The District's business and political leaders were unified in their desire to spring into action. However, while Congress debated whether to give the nod, the District had to wait and fend off interlopers in what it considered its convention business. The president of the Hotel Association of Washington, Emily Vetter, told this writer (October 4, 1994), "It's ludicrous that money that is being taxed and collected from our own people and for a specific purpose has to wait for clowns from who knows where to tell us how to use it."

Meanwhile, also in 1994, Abe Pollin, the owner of the suburban arena who helped pull the strings to downsize the District's convention center in the first place, redeemed himself in the eyes of all, saying, "I believe in the future of the nation's capital. It deserves to be enlivened" (*Washington Post*, January 1, 1995, D4). Pollin decided to locate his own new arena in downtown D.C., near the proposed new convention center. However, there was one problem: the arena, as proposed, would be publicly financed and therefore subject to congressional approval. District political leaders and the business community were willing to take some risks as necessary to secure a better economic future. However, seventeen Republican U.S. senators thought otherwise. After reviewing the District's fragile financial condition, the senators publicly opposed the new downtown arena (*Washington Post*, December 17, 1994, F5). In this case, the senators' attention proved more advantageous than interventionist. The owner of the professional basketball and hockey franchises, Abe Pollin, who proposed the new arena, read the congressional cards and decided to finance the project himself. Would the District have had the leverage on its own to swing the better deal? Probably not.

While Pollin was seeking the bright lights of downtown, another pro sports owner, Jack Kent Cooke, was hoping to get out of Dodge. Cooke, owner of Washington's beloved Redskins, first tried Alexandria, Virginia, but was rebuffed by the citizenry there and then fell back in love with the D.C. site that, from a TV blimp, exquisitely aligned with the Capitol, the Washington Monument, and the Lincoln Memorial. However, Cooke became frustrated by Washington red tape and pulled up stakes for Prince George's County in suburban Maryland, where his team would "fight for old P.G."

The District's local government was charged with the fumble. However, the new stadium would sit on federal land, and Congress, exercising appropriate oversight, could not give its approval within a time frame that suited Cooke. If Congress had been a true state surrogate, however, it would have acted expeditiously to help the District with a critical economic development project that held such symbolic value in rallying community spirit. The state of Maryland serves as a nearby example of an entity dedicated to Baltimore's economic revitalization, committing to finance new baseball and football stadia. Congress does not see its role as D.C.'s booster in the same way that Maryland unabashedly does as Baltimore's. The District, consequently, had no choice but to fight on its own to try to keep the football team, without a true ally promoting its interests.

The District also from time to time has attempted to lure a major league baseball franchise to its District-owned stadium, which was built for baseball. The District has consistently struck out in its efforts while Congress watched silently in the grandstand. This is not to say that Congress had any obligation to pull strings for a D.C. franchise.[1] Congress does not serve as a surrogate state, as is sometimes assumed, vigilantly looking out for its center city's interests. Representative Tom Davis, chair of the House District Subcommittee, vigorously supported the downtown D.C. arena and convention center, but could not be expected to fight for a major league franchise, since he has worked for several years to secure a team for Northern Virginia (*Washington Post*, November 16, 1995, B7).

Not having a state booster for the central city has other effects as well, apart from sports. Empowerment zones, also called enterprise zones, are widely supported by conservatives, since unlike many federal grants, they help a community help itself through attraction of private sector opportunities. While six cities submitted superior grant proposals that fetched $100 million in aid, and several second tier applications raked in $25 million each, the District received just $3 million of the $3.5 billion empowerment zone pie sliced in late 1994. Naturally, a member of Congress has as his or her first duty to advocate grants for the home district. D.C. business writer Rudolph Pyatt (*Washington Post*, December 26, 1994) noted:

> If ever there was an opportunity for the federal government to help underwrite an economic renewal demonstration project in the nation's capital, this was it. But then, why should anyone be surprised by the outcome? The District lacks the clout and votes to be found in other big cities.

Pyatt (ibid.) reported that federal officials gave the District high marks for its grant proposal. The point remains that the District has lacked a higher government entity (a state or the federal government as a state surrogate) that watches out for its interests and provides it with opportunities as well as discipline. The District's federally imposed financial control board, however, explicitly shifted responsibility for the District's well-being to federal appointees, who could receive greater respect for proposed enterprise zones grant funding than that accorded to District officials.

It is not just the big ticket items on which the District lacks the alliance of friendly oversight. As an example of the smallest of details, Congress has

1. Critics of the District's efforts note that D.C. has failed twice in its ability to support a franchise. However, from 1946 to 1971 (the last year of a D.C. team), the team lost an average of 91 games in a 154 game season, 34 games off the pace. The team's best results during the span were two fourth place finishes: in 1946, when it had a losing record and was 28 games short of a pennant, and in 1969 when it was 23 games out, but nonetheless sported a 68 percent boost in attendance that year.

continually ignored the District's request to improve the District's court system through an increase in the ceiling, from two thousand to five thousand dollars, under which citizens could take disputes to small claims court. The congressional attitude seems to be, "Here are the rules—like them or not, play with them." Because the District lacks authority to take this trivial action on its own, one writer was prompted to wonder, "What *were* the founders smoking?" (Twomey 1993, 12, emphasis his).

THE D.C. BUDGETS: IS CONGRESS THE WORLD'S LARGEST CITY COUNCIL?

The District's budgets are the vehicles through which congressional wishes have been implemented. One analyst of the District (Harris 1989, 68) said, "Although there was little or no indication that the [District's] budget would be an instrument for regular intervention in D.C. affairs, leverage tends to be used when it is available." A congressional staffer explained to this writer that Congress has no particular desire to exercise power over D.C. budgets; rather, the members "don't want to see the District fall apart on their watch." Of course, once the members become involved, they act in far-reaching, political, and unpredictable ways. Congress has overridden the budgetary actions of the elected council and mayor in recent years by, for example, increasing the number of uniformed police officers to a specified level, retaining a fire department engine company located near Capitol Hill, and placing a ceiling on the number of District government employees (ibid., 74).

In fiscal year 1994 and subsequent budgets, Congress rejected the District's revision to its health insurance program, which would have allowed unmarried city workers to designate a domestic partner and obtain insurance for that person. Congressional critics thought this measure would legally recognize homosexual relationships (*Washington Post*, July 28, 1993, A1, A9). For five years (1989–1993) Congress banned the District's use of its own funds to provide abortions to low-income women (*Washington Post*, October 28, 1993, A1) and resumed the prohibition for fiscal 1996. And, during a budget debate, a member of Congress threatened to remove his support for the District and its future budgets because the District failed to respond to his requests for a pothole repair, leading the *Washington Post* (July 8, 1993, A16) to editorialize that "the fate of local democracy in the District should not depend on kowtowing to a lone congressman's pothole tantrum."

The fiscal year 1995 and 1996 budgets demonstrated the boundless congressional authority over D.C. Congress knew at an early stage that these budgets were more precarious than usual. The chairs of two House committees that controlled the District asked the U.S. General Accounting Office (GAO) to investigate concerns expressed by their colleagues in Congress that, in the words of Representative Julian Dixon, D.C. officials "don't have the discipline to put their house in order" (*Washington Post*, March 27, 1994, B1). The lawmakers thought the District could run short of cash to pay its bills at some point during the fiscal year, forcing the District to seek a federal bailout—that is, a loan from the U.S. Treasury (*Washington Post*, March 30, 1994, A1, A4). The GAO (1994, 13–22) detailed a precipitous $200 million decline in the District's cash position since 1991 and said that the District could indeed be forced to borrow from the U.S. Treasury by fiscal 1995 unless it implemented policy changes (ibid, 3). One of the congressional leaders who requested the GAO study, Representative Pete Stark (D–Ca.), indicated that "drastic changes" were needed to stave off bankruptcy, and Congress would have to make those changes "because the District government, as a unit, refuses to make the tough decisions to be fiscally responsible" (*Washington Post*, June 23, 1994, B1).

Predictably, D.C. leaders urged Congress to stay out of D.C. affairs, promising actions that would yield fiscal integrity. However, Representative Thomas Bliley (R–Va.) spoke for the majority when he said, "I think they are simply going to have to make the changes" that Congress would soon be initiating (*Washington Post*, June 30, 1994, B4). Congress then proceeded to mandate $140 million in unspecified budget cuts and required the District to present it with a detailed plan to achieve the reductions. In the process, Congress further provided that for each dollar the District fell short of achieving the $140 million in congressionally mandated spending cuts, the 1996 federal payment would be cut by another dollar (*Washington Post*, August 9, 1994, B1).

It soon became apparent that Congress was on target in mandating the cuts. The estimated size of the District's deficit mounted weekly. Representative Bliley warned of a potential $1 billion budget gap by the turn of the century and reminded D.C. residents (*Washington Post*, November 23, 1994, A19): "Congress has only *delegated* its constitutionally mandated authority. The responsibility for the nation's capital remains with Congress. As such, Congress can *re-delegate* certain powers [to itself] and still remain faithful to the concept of self-government" (emphasis his).

The District's 1994 and 1995 budgets were election year budgets. Then-Mayor Kelly and other political incumbents hid the abysmal fiscal news from an electorate that was already alarmed by runaway crime, poor public schools, government waste, deteriorating services, and what have come to be known as the usual D.C. follies. One can only guess whether the District, in the postelection aftermath, on its own initiative and without congressional intervention, would have had the courage to confront the depths of its financial crisis. Nonetheless, as much as stern congressional actions are detested by local leaders, these budgets produced a clear example to Congress of how external oversight was warranted. By the time the new Barry administration assumed office in 1995, the District faced the prospect of quintupling the $140 million in budget reductions mandated by Congress. The chair of the House Subcommittee of D.C. Appropriations, Representative James T. Walsh (R–N.Y.), made it clear that if the District failed to solve its financial shortfall, a congressionally appointed financial control board would manage the District's finances (*Washington Times*, December 15, 1994, A1, A13). Congress seemed as much concerned about D.C. officials' "deceit" in covering up the looming deficit as it was over the deficit itself and the junk bond ratings.

FINANCIAL CONTROL BOARD

A financial control board was implemented in the spring of 1995. An author of the bill that created the board, Representative Tom Davis (R–Va.) said, "Washington, D.C. is coming apart at the seams." Noting that the District "has more than adequate revenue," Davis added: "It tries to fund everything it wants instead of the things it needs" (*Washington Post*, April 4, 1995, A1, A16). The legislation noted that the District failed to provide adequately for education, health care, crime prevention, trash collection, drug abuse treatment and prevention, and training of government personnel.

The board's mandate was to review all D.C. budgets and other financial actions, overturn those it felt necessary, replace D.C. actions with spending plans of their own, and eliminate red ink before the new millennium. The board can review labor and other contracts and order staffing and organizational changes in the D.C. government (*Washington Post*, April 18, 1995, A1, A10; July 15, 1995, A14). The U.S. Treasury, at the board's behest, can now loan funds to the District to cover cash shortfalls—hence, the term "bailout" can be applied.

Although board chair Andrew Brimmer said, "We do not plan to replace elected officials in any way" (*Washington Post*, July 14, 1995, C5), the board felt compelled to do just that. In its first major action, the board capped the payroll at 35,771 positions, or nearly 10,000 fewer than were provided for in the original 1996 budget (D.C. Financial Responsibility and Management Assistance Authority 1995). Mayor Marion Barry labeled the board's action "unscientific," adding, "Everybody says we have a government that is too big and too inefficient and too ineffective. If you tell a lie long enough like that, it becomes the truth" (*Washington Post*, July 29, 1995, A10). However, fighting concerns that he was becoming irrelevant, Barry reversed himself by issuing a "transformation plan" that would reduce D.C. workers to 30,000 by the year 2000 (*Washington Post*, February 15, 1996, A1).

The board can be viewed as another self-government setback, yet another indication that D.C. people are incapable of electing responsible leaders. Alternatively, the financial crisis and control board can be viewed as an inevitable outgrowth of a fatally flawed state-county-local government design, with dwindling resources to cope by itself with the overwhelming urban challenges.

The board's origins and purposes virtually preclude board members from winning D.C. residents' favor. Nonetheless, during the 1996 budget process, federally appointed board members advocated residents' needs to a greater degree than did the District's congressional overseers. For example, Congress did not immediately accept the control board's recommended budget level, trimming an additional $256 million. The control board, however, was instrumental in gaining congressional restoration of $120 million of those cuts. Thus, the control board became an intermediary between the nation's and the District's elected representatives.

Congress agreed on the District's 1996 budget level at the beginning of the fiscal year and imposed the expected "moral" restrictions against abortions in D.C. government medical facilities and against the District's domestic partner law. The budget was delayed for months, however, until Congress could debate (and then delete) an experimental scholarship program for low-income D.C. students that would enable students to attend private (including religious) schools or suburban public schools. Some D.C. residents thought the plan would help their children escape economically segregated and poorly performing D.C. schools. Others thought the plan would subvert D.C. public schools and their efforts toward improvement. However, this matter was not for local residents and their elected representatives to decide.

Without a budget, several financial reforms were delayed for months and a D.C. government shutdown at one point cost the District millions in lost productivity. A nation's legislative process is inherently chaotic, and subjecting a local government to this process imposes a special burden beyond that experienced by any state. By the time this budget was adopted, the hodgepodge of actors had included, among others, House and Senate appropriations committees, the Speaker of the House, a control board, the Mayor, and the D.C. Council, with all of these cooks attempting to brew financial stability. The disastrous mid-1990s budgets were exacerbated by a crashing urban economy and a tax base riddled with exemptions for not only non-

TABLE 2.1 Budget Surpluses (or Deficits), D.C. and U.S. Governments (D.C. in millions, U.S. in billions of dollars), Fiscal Years 1981–1995

	D.C.	*% of Outlays*	*U.S.*	*% of Outlays*
1981	68.3	0.5	(79.0)	(11.6)
1982	13.1	0.1	(128.0)	(17.2)
1983	12.9	0.1	(207.8)	(25.7)
1984	17.5	1.0	(185.4)	(21.8)
1985	24.9	1.2	(212.3)	(22.4)
1986	20.1	0.1	(221.2)	(22.3)
1987	20.1	0.1	(149.8)	(14.8)
1988	(14.3)	(0.1)	(155.2)	(14.9)
1989	5.5	–	(152.5)	(13.3)
1990	(118.2)	(4.0)	(221.4)	(17.7)
1991	333.2	11.0	(269.5)	(20.4)
1992	2.0	–	(290.4)	(21.0)
1993	7.8	–	(254.7)	(18.1)
1994	(335.4)	(9.8)	(203.2)	(13.9)
1995	(54.4)	(1.7)	(163.8)	(10.8)

Sources: D.C. data computed from Coopers & Lybrand data of January 31, 1995; U.S. data computed from U.S. Census Bureau (1994, 330, 332); 1994 and 1995 U.S. data from Congressional Budget Office, by phone, 4/17/95 and 2/12/96.

profit organizations (many of which are located in D.C. to lobby Congress) and the federal government but also for every government in the world that has property and employees in the nation's capital.

THE DISTRICT'S FINANCIAL FAILINGS IN PERSPECTIVE

Congressional criticisms of the District's financial actions are almost always on target, although it is helpful to wink at Congress' own fiscal record when heeding their admonishments. In 1980 the District initiated a thorough review of its finances and developed a comprehensive financial plan designed to produce balanced budgets. Consequently, from fiscal years 1981 to 1995, independent audits indicate that the District achieved balanced budgets in all years except 1988, 1990, 1994, and 1995 (see table 2.1). In contrast, the federal government failed to produce a balanced budget every year during the same span (as it had in the previous decade as well), averaging $200 billion in annual deficits over that period.

The District in this 1981–1995 span had an 11–4 record of balanced-to-unbalanced budgets, while the federal government went 0–15. In football, it would be clear which team had the better record. However, in politics, what counts is who is higher on the food chain. The District is mere plankton in the political sea.

Members of Congress and their staffs grumble that the D.C. surpluses exist on paper only and that they should more properly be viewed as deficits by adjusting for deficiencies in accounting treatment. John W. Hill, Jr., director of Audit Support and Analysis for the U.S. Government Accounting office (GAO), who went on to head the D.C. financial control board's staff, confirmed such suspicions in a conversation (May 17, 1995) with this writer. Starting in 1990, the District made loans to D.C. General Hospital beyond the beleaguered hospital's subsidy and beyond its ability to repay. These loans, amounting to $85 million, cumulatively, from 1990 to 1994, should have been treated as part of a larger subsidy. The surpluses of 1992 and 1993 would have been transformed into deficits of $11 million and $9.2 million, respectively. The deficits are rather small (well under a tenth of one percent of total D.C. expenditures), but nonetheless, this adjustment would convert the 11–4 playoff-bound D.C. government financial players to a team with a more modest 9–6 record.

Hill (ibid.) also questioned the District's large 1991 surplus of $333.2 million. First, $18 million can be traced to the same questionable D.C. General accounting practice. More importantly, the District received a loan of $331 million in 1991 to a fund other than its general fund, transferred the loan proceeds into the general fund, and only recorded debt service (annual payments on a loan) as expenditures. Hill acknowledged that this device conformed to Generally Accepted Accounting Principles (GAAP) for municipalities and thus can still be technically considered a surplus (as opposed to another under-one-tenth-of-one-percent deficit). If Hill had his way, no fiscal year in the 1990s would be considered a surplus year for D.C.

When the District's deficit reached 10 percent of its outlays in 1994, federal intervention became mandatory. However, as seen in table 2.1, federal deficits were in double digits as a percentage of federal expenditures every year during this span, and in several years the federal deficit amounted to over 20 percent of outlays.

In no year in the entire fifteen year span was the District's deficit larger, proportionally, than the federal government's deficit. The federal government awarded cost-of-living increases to its employees every year during the accumulation of its deficits, while D.C. government employees experienced wage freezes or pay reductions via furloughs during nearly all recent years. Congress in 1995 boasted that it would balance federal budgets in seven years, but it rescinded local control from the District when the District requested a much shorter period of time to balance its budgets. While the D.C. government is often called the worst government in America, it may not even be the more financially reckless government in its own town, nor even the more inefficient.

The District's 1994 and 1995 election year deficits were undoubtedly driven by expediency, since massive layoffs of employees would surely have lost key constituency groups. Moreover, during the Barry years, beginning in 1979, new agencies and thousands of new hirees fueled governmental dependency on a reasonably healthy economy for the necessary tax revenues. When the D.C. economy faltered, the D.C. government toppled. Over a similar period, the federal government institutionalized its deficits, driven by the expedient desire to achieve popular tax cuts without the associated expenditure discipline. During this time, no one suggested that the American people were incapable of governing themselves or that some unelected board was needed to give Congress a guiding hand. Not even the most fanatical of deficit hawks favored suspending Americans' democratic rights because their elected representatives quintupled the federal debt since the start of the Reagan years.

The federal government, however, is not bound (as yet) by a constitutional requirement to balance its budget; the District, like many states, must by law live within its means. A random selection of people from any state's phone book, including the District's, could have restrained the accretion of the federal debt in recent times if such a group had the requisite oversight authority. By the same token, it is equally clear that the District would have ground to a halt without congressional actions, including the granting of borrowing authority from the U.S. Treasury, during the mid-1990s.

VOTING REPRESENTATION, OR LACK THEREOF

The District's most distinctive political characteristic is the lack of representation of its residents in the national legislative body, the U.S. Congress, that controls it. The District of Columbia Election Act of 1970, P.L. 91–405, created a delegate to the House of Representatives from the District who has a "right of debate, but not of voting." With this act, the District was granted the same type of nonvoting representation as held by Puerto Rico, Guam, American Samoa, and the Virgin Islands. In 1978, Congress approved a constitutional amendment that would have given the District full voting representation in both houses of Congress; however, this amendment was ratified by only sixteen of the required thirty-eight states within the seven year time limit (Seidman 1990, 375, n.10).

According to the District's delegate to Congress, Eleanor Holmes Norton (*Washington Post*, January 4, 1993, A21):

> We [the District] are lowest in America's democratic hierarchy. We are lower than the fifty states and four "possessions." Unlike the other four territories, whose residents pay no federal income taxes, our laws and our locally raised budget are supervised and changed by Congress at will.

This inconsistency provokes quirky behavior. For example, this writer arranged a press conference in 1989 for the mayor, Jesse Jackson, and other political and labor leaders to demand an end to federal taxation of D.C. citizens until such time as the District achieved statehood. This central theme of the press conference was softened at the last minute by Jackson, because it was his belief that the media and members of Congress might not catch the ironic ploy. Jackson feared that Congress could misconstrue the message as a willingness among D.C. leaders to accept lack of congressional voting representation if the price was right, thereby jeopardizing the District's drive to statehood.

THE SAGA OF THE VOTE THAT DID NOT COUNT

A modest improvement in the District's status was gained in early 1993, when the delegates of the District and four territories received authority to vote in the House Committee of the Whole. Virtually all votes in the House take place in the Committee of the Whole, which has a lower quorum requirement than is the case with votes taken on the floor (*Washington Post*, January 6, 1993, A1, A11).

Under that procedure, any time the delegates' votes played a decisive role in the margin of victory of legislation, a second vote was held and the delegates were excluded from voting. This measure portrayed Congress' perplexity about the District's and the territories' political status. As Representative James Moran of nearby Virginia observed, "Any time their votes count, they don't count." The voting privilege was similar to receiving a gift basket of lottery tickets, with the condition that those tickets that turn out to be winners must be handed back to the gift giver. House Republicans filed a suit in federal court challenging the District's and territories' newly won authority. However, a federal judge rejected the challenge on the grounds that the delegates' votes were "meaningless," since the vote could not "affect the ultimate results" (*Washington Post*, March 9, 1993, A1, A7). These voting privileges gave the District the same power in Congress as populous Puerto Rico

(3,522,037 people in 1990), but also the same power as American Samoa (46,773), Guam (133,152), and the Virgin Islands (101,809) (U.S. Census Bureau 1991, press releases 91–242, 263, 275, 276).

Norton was informed in an interview with this writer (1993) that her hard-won reform to have delegates of D.C. and the four territories vote in the House Committee of the Whole had provoked laughter in focus groups, especially when it was pointed out to the panelists that the delegates' votes would be tossed out if they influenced a vote's outcome. The temperature in her office dropped 20 degrees, and she stated that the focus group moderator must not have described the procedure properly. Norton indicated that in any given session only two or three Committee of the Whole votes are decided by five votes or less, "so my vote counts as much as Jim Moran's." Upon reflection, anyone who has had to sit in one's office while her or his colleagues marched out to vote would be similarly incensed by deprecation of a reform that produced any improved participation.

The Republicans terminated the largely symbolic reform on their first day of congressional control, erasing the District's and territories' delegates from the official House roster. Speaking against the erasure, D.C. Delegate Norton said to her erstwhile colleagues (*Washington Post*, January 12, 1995, D.C. 2):

> Suppose your constituents paid $1.6 billion annually to the Treasury of the United States. Suppose your constituents were third per capita in federal taxes in the United States of America. Suppose your constituents paid more taxes than each of six states. How would you feel if you watched other members vote on your taxes . . . ?

TRADITION OF SUBJUGATION

That Delegate Norton fought voraciously to retain this token vote speaks to the desperation of D.C. people to be included as partners with their fellow Americans in the federal system. This modest and ephemeral step forward was considered helpful only when viewed in the context of many decades of political control by the District's congressional overseers. For example, from 1948 to 1972, Representative John McMillan (from Florence, S.C., population 25,000), chaired the powerful House committee that oversaw policies affecting daily lives of Washingtonians and "ruled with courtly indifference to the demands and concerns of the city's residents" (Smith 1974, 142). Smith (1974, 142–43) recounted McMillan's numerous attempts to limit the District's self-government during that span. While McMillan has a well-earned villainous reputation in the District's history, his 1972 statement remains prescient: "The only way you [the District] are going to get pure, unadulterated representation is by ceding the city back to Maryland or through statehood" (Smith 1974, 272).

As a response—some would say overreaction—to historic mistreatment, in 1987, 1991, and again in 1993, the District applied to Congress for admission to the Union as a state. By this time, most D.C. leaders seemed willing to settle for nothing less than full political equality for D.C. citizens, and statehood was perceived by many to be the only practical way of attaining this goal. The House District Committee favorably reported the statehood admission bill in 1987, but the measure failed to proceed further in Congress. The national Democratic party endorsed statehood for the District in its 1984 and 1988 platforms (Brown, 1991, 1) as well as in 1992.

In 1989 President Bush expressed considerable interest in supporting statehood for Puerto Rico, but he opposed statehood for the District (Schrag 1990, 317, n.42). With the nation's executive branch in control of the Republican party from 1981 to 1992, the District's drive toward statehood did not gather much national momentum. Nonetheless, the statehood movement experienced revitalization locally in those years. By a 60–to–40 percent margin, District residents voted in 1980 for an initiative to call a constitutional convention (Schrag 1985, 3) and, at the same time, elected delegates to the convention. Then in 1982, by a 53–to–47 percent margin, the District ratified the constitution produced by the convention. The constitution established the "free and sovereign state of New Columbia"[2] (Schrag 1990, 351, n.195; Schrag 1985, 259). Under New Columbia's constitution, the current D.C. government agencies, which already provide state services, would simply become state agencies without an added layer of bureaucracy. The District's 13-member legislative body would be replaced by a 25-member state legislature called the House of Delegates. State authority to appoint judges and prosecute crimes would replace federal authority in these regards. Under proposed 1993 D.C. statehood legislation in Congress (H.R. 51), a 13-member

2. "New Columbia" is the name chosen in the District's constitutional convention. There is no known way to abbreviate it for mail delivery, without duplicating an existing state's abbreviation. Smith (1993) observed that the new name may create some initial confusion, as some may try to draw a connection with "old" Columbias (e.g., in South America, South Carolina), with which the District has little historic or cultural association. Smith suggested the name "Potomac," which has roots in the area's indigenous population and is the name of a D.C.'s largest river. The Maryland suburbs, however, already have an affluent town named Potomac. As an option to Smith's suggestion, the euphonious name for D.C.'s other river is Anacostia, a name which, if ultimately preferred to New Columbia, would signify a commitment to improving the fortunes of the low-and-moderate-income residents who live near the banks of that river.

Statehood Transition Commission, to be appointed by the president, Congress, the mayor, and the D.C. legislative body, would have guided D.C.'s transition to statehood during the first two years.

The local legislative body in 1990 voted to proceed with the election of unpaid "shadow representatives" (one "shadow" representative and two "shadow" senators) to lobby extensively for statehood (Laney 1991). The shadow delegation plan was first used by Tennessee in 1796 to gain admittance to the Union and is therefore designated the Tennessee Plan. Prior to the District's action, seven other political entities used the Tennessee Plan in their statehood drives, all with success (Laney 1991, 6; Bowkett 1989, 78–79; Jackson 1990, 308).

A missing piece in the District's statehood effort in recent years has been a lack of demonstrable local interest in the issue among much of the citizenry. One analyst wrote that mass demonstrations, with significant leadership and participation by the District's student and church communities, would likely be necessary to heighten the nation's interest in this issue (Raskin 1990, 438). D.C. Mayor Sharon Pratt Kelly initiated a number of statehood rallies, demonstrations, and seminars preceding the House vote on this issue. However, Kelly's runaway budget deficits gave Congress impetus to abrogate much of the existing D.C. self-government authority, leaving statehood as an inconceivable fantasy for an extended time. Additionally, the 104th Republican-led Congress relegated the House District Committee to subcommittee status, ending a history of a body that gave and retracted favor, but which also served as a forum in recent years for considering structural improvement—a formula-based federal payment, voting rights in Congress, and statehood.

THE DISTRICT'S SOCIAL AND ECONOMIC STATUS

The District is renowned for its physical beauty, its monuments, stately federal buildings, trees, and dramatic vistas. D.C. is the gateway to the southern sunbelt, and its climate is relatively moderate. Its economy is aided by the stability and strength of the federal presence, a base industry with greater permanence than any steel mill or auto plant. Anguished D.C. officials often charge the federal government with lack of support, but they are first to insist that a federal agency stay home and not yield to the low-rent temptations offered by suburban suitors.

The cultural and historical attractions of the nation's capital add to the District's employment base, and tourism seems just as stable as the federal monuments that support it. The District's tourist trade benefits from free "advertising" from dramatic national events in the nightly news. The District is blessed with several highly regarded universities and possesses a labor force which is rather skilled for an urban center.

The District is the heart of a thriving and affluent metropolitan region of 3.9 million people that is the eighth largest in America (U.S. Bureau of the Census 1992, 34). The Washington metropolitan region ranked first in the 1990 Census in its per capita income, its low unemployment rate, its proportion of jobs in professional, managerial, and technical areas, and its percentage of highly educated residents. The District itself ranked highly in many categories. The city was fifth among the twenty-five largest cities in household income, third in proportion of residents completing college, and first in employment in professional, managerial, and technical jobs. It had the greatest decline in poverty among these cities in the 1980s (McKinsey & Co. 1994, 2, Exh. 1).

The District is also like other troubled urban centers up and down the eastern seaboard and in the Midwest. Indeed, the District is often said to be among the "worst" places in America for its homicide, school dropout, teen pregnancy and illegitimacy, abortion, infant mortality, and other rates. Edmonds and Keating (1995) documented the "worst" data, placing D.C. last among states in total crime rate and at or near the bottom in a host of socioeconomic categories. The District spent more than any state per pupil in schools, but its students performed unimpressively in scholastic achievement. The District also had the highest per capita government debt among several U.S. cities listed.

Overall, federal per capita spending on D.C. was $36,536 in 1994, sixth highest among all counties and localities in the U.S. (*Washington Post*, April 18, 1995, A15); yet the District's socioeconomic conditions continue to plummet at a startling pace. For example, the District's median household income at $27,304 in 1993 was not far from the national average of $31,241; however, the District's income plunged by 12 percent in real dollars in just one year, compared to a 1 percent decline nationally. Moreover, the District's poverty rate of 26.4 percent in 1993 jumped up over six percentage points in just one year (U.S. Bureau of the Census 1994, news release CB94–159, Oct. 6), while the national rate increased a fraction of a percent. The District's financial crisis, attributed to D.C. government mismanagement, has overshadowed a more significant urban crisis.

A key to understanding America's unique city-county-state of Washington, D.C. is to ask: What would any entity look like if it were urban border-to-border, had state responsibilities, and had only the resources of a city to draw upon? D.C. is sometimes asked to emulate Philadelphia's government

(*Washington Post*, March 10, 1994, A1, A25), and its northern neighbor has much to instruct. However, what would the finances of a "state of Philadelphia" look like if it had no state of Pennsylvania to redistribute resources to it from affluent areas of the state, if Philadelphia were prohibited from taxing nonresident income (and thus lost its nonresident tax), if Philadelphia had state welfare and Medicaid funding, state auto tag licensing, state environmental, utility, and professional services regulation, state social services, a county hospital, state prisons, a state university, and the like to administer? Add to the "state of Philadelphia" picture a situation where more than half the "state's" land is tax exempt but where the entity creating the tax exemptions, the federal government, compensates the state for only a fraction of the value of the exemptions. Is this a formula for success?

The District's "worst" conditions are often traced by analysts to the District's local government, thought by many to be bloated, inept, corrupt, or all three. The *Economist* (February 25, 1995, 24) offered this hyperbolic example:

> Taxes are sky-high, but city services stink. The rubbish is rarely picked up. The roads are full of craters. City employees, of whom there are more per head than anywhere else in the country, are uniformly indolent.
>
> Many police officers are as crooked as the criminals they supposedly pursue—criminals who make the city the violence capital of America. And then there is Marion Barry: the mayor who oversaw the city's decline in the 1980s while indulging a fabulous cocaine habit for which he went to jail, only to be re-elected last November.

The D.C. government has always been in need of management improvement. In the past, District bashing was often of the you-just-can't-get-good-help-anymore variety, accompanied by a moan of disgust whenever a new pothole was discovered. D.C. government employees often referred to the steady stream of rebukes as reflective of a "Ward 3 mentality," named after residents of the District's most affluent, largely white political ward. The people who seemed most angered by D.C. government services were often the same ones who had the greatest wealth and therefore the least reason to complain.

Today, however, it is not just outside critics or Ward 3 residents who have serious complaints about the D.C. government. A malaise pervades. A *Washington Post* poll (March 13, 1994, A18) indicated that 57 percent of D.C. residents believed that corruption was a big problem in their government, although "only" 37 percent of Marylanders and 32 percent of Virginians felt that way about their governments. Moreover, 70 percent of D.C. residents polled thought their government was "inefficient," compared to 45 percent in Maryland and 31 percent in Virginia.

The perceptions of corruption and inefficiency are derived from a barrage of news accounts. During 1992 and 1993, over one hundred police officers were indicted on a variety of criminal charges (Jaffe and Sherwood 1994, 310). Meanwhile, crime was ranked the top problem in D.C. by 69 percent of its residents—probably because 82 percent of D.C. residents said there was a violent crime incident in their neighborhoods in the last five years (*Washington Post*, March 13, 1994, A18).

As another example of D.C. corruption, the FBI uncovered a D.C. housing agency scheme where, between 1990 and 1993, nearly everyone who received a rent subsidy had to bribe agency staff to obtain the voucher (*Washington Post*, April 14, 1994, A1, A18). D.C. and federal housing officials also uncovered overpayments of up to $500,000 per year over several years in federal rent subsidies to D.C. landlords for tenants who died or moved away (*Washington Post*, September 29, 1994, C1). Moreover, over a period of six years, the District's public housing agency, "with much of its housing stock falling apart and thousands of families waiting for a place to live," failed to spend $143.5 million in federal funds to modernize the public housing units, according to ACORN, a community housing activists group (*Washington Post*, August 17, 1994). The District was able to spend only 5 percent of its federal modernization funds since 1989, ACORN charged, the lowest among twenty-nine jurisdictions studied. Meanwhile the public housing agency was able to spend $1.3 million over the past few years to renovate and furnish its own agency offices (*Washington Post*, June 17, 1994). The U.S. Department of Housing and Urban Development rated the District last in performance among all public housing agencies in America, and the D.C. public housing agency seems destined for an extended period of oversight by the courts.

Much the same story could be told about the District's overwhelmed foster care program and its overcrowded prisons, both of which have also been subject to court-ordered oversight (*Washington Post*, August 19, 1994, A1, A35; September 17, 1994, A1, A6; January 12, 1995, B2). The D.C. Department of Corrections also was handed a court-appointed official to administer sexual harassment complaints after fourteen years of agency noncompliance with court orders. Moreover, a local judge made a surprise visit to a receiving home for juvenile arrestees and found not only overcrowded conditions but children who said they were either going unfed or given a steady diet of bologna sandwiches (*Washington Post*, August 18, 1995, B1, B6). D.C. managers are often portrayed as antichildren, ornery, unfeeling bureaucrats interested only in combatting the efforts of caring community leaders to provide humane treatment (e.g., *Washington Post*, August 15, 1995, A16).

Agency employees, meanwhile, are frustrated by a lack of funds. Added millions, they say, are needed to begin to replicate the comprehensive services delivered in wealthier jurisdictions. The only answers they hear to the overwhelming urban conditions are "spend less" and "fire employees." The rampant mismanagement or lack of financial support in several key D.C. agencies has overshadowed the efforts of thousands of diligent, dedicated, and honest D.C. government employees over the years.

The District's structural socioeconomic problems that underlie its "worst" statistics are often lost in the conflict over whom to bless and whom to blame. The critics of the government and the elected leaders are usually quite accurate, but they mask the overriding social phenomena. Columnist Mary McGrory (*Washington Post*, March 26, 1995, C1, C5) wrote:

> Ineptitude seems to be an incurable disease in the District government. . . . The District seems headed back to the colonial status of pre-home-rule days. It's just what they deserve. The children have to be protected from those officially charged with their welfare.

It is fine to rail against an inept D.C. government, but other forces, requiring everything from greater personal responsibility by urban residents to regional resource redistribution to workable federal policies, could also be cited to improve the urban conditions. Columnist Bill Rice (*Washington Post*, July 18, 1993, C1) provided another example:

> Despite unprecedented money, power, and control—authority bestowed on her by an optimistic Congress and Council—[Mayor Kelly] has proved only marginally effective in taking on the needs of D.C. residents.

All three mayors in D.C.'s limited home rule era have been judged ineffective, and a large body of evidence is offered to support the judgment. Nonetheless, one has to wonder what power or level of control is bestowed upon a D.C. mayor. A demographic analysis would probably yield a finding that the high rates of social pathology can be traced primarily to heavy concentrations of at-risk populations and not just to a bumbling, fumbling government.

CHILD AND FAMILY WELL-BEING

A brief comparison of D.C. and U.S. data on at-risk populations reveals one source of the District's economic and social difficulties. Children from at-risk households face greater odds wherever they are found; D.C. simply has a much higher proportion of such households. In the United States, 78.1 percent of all families in 1991 consisted of married-couple households of all races, and these "normal" households had a poverty rate of 6.0 percent. Nationally, 17.4 percent of families were female-based households (no spouse present), and the poverty rate for those households was 35.6 percent. The poverty rate for the U.S. black female-headed households was 51.2 percent. The poverty rate in the United States for children under eighteen years old living in female-headed households was an astounding 68.2 percent (U.S. Bureau of the Census 1992b, 1, 14). Across America, 62.3 percent of children of all races living in female-headed households in central cities were living in poverty (ibid., 40).

The socioeconomic status of the District is a distorted reflection of these national conditions. Using national statistics as a guide, the District has a disproportionate number of families susceptible to poverty. In 1990, 51.7 percent of all families (not counting the large numbers of households in the District consisting of individuals or unrelated people) were composed of married couples. The remaining 48.3 percent of D.C. households consisted of single-parent-headed households (D.C. Office of Policy and Program Evaluation 1991, 190). Only 34.3 percent of all D.C. children in 1990 lived in married households with both of their biological parents, while 33.8 percent of D.C. children lived in female-headed households, and another 28.2 percent of D.C. children lived in households headed by others than their biological parents, or in institutions (Population Reference Bureau 1992, 23). In contrast, 71.2 percent of all children nationally lived in married-couple households with their biological parents (ibid.).

In the District, the number of children living in "subfamilies" (with at least one parent in a relative's household) increased 128.3 percent during the 1980s (ibid., 20, 24), while the number of D.C. children living in single parent subfamilies increased 148.2 percent. The number of married couple families living with their biological children declined 25.3 percent in the District during the 1980s, while D.C. black families of this type declined by 43.2 percent. Much of this decline was due to migration of stable families—primarily to the suburbs—while a large part was also due to continued family disintegration. In the United States, meanwhile, the number of married couples living with their biological children declined by 2.2 percent (ibid., 35).

In the United States, the income of married-couple families living with their biological children grew by 11.2 percent during the 1980s—after adjusting for inflation—to $48,880. Meanwhile, the income of the female-headed families with children declined by 1.4 percent—also after adjusting for inflation—to $16,568 (ibid., 49).

Married-couple families in D.C. are generally financially viable, but there are just not enough of them to produce societal well-being. In the District, the average income of a married couple (all races) living with their own children in 1990 was a healthy $76,641, a figure that grew 37.8 percent during the 1980s (no adjustment for inflation). Meanwhile, the income of the female-headed households with children was just $20,900, a growth of only 7.1 percent. While only 7.9 percent of the District children living in married-couple families lived in poverty in 1990, 40.2 percent of the District's children in female-headed households lived in poverty. Significantly, the number of D.C. children living in a female-headed household outnumbered children living in married couple households by a six-to-one margin in 1990 (ibid., 51).

In the District, 25.5 percent of all children, no matter what race or family status, lived in poverty, compared to 18.3 percent for the nation as a whole (ibid., 56, 63). However, if one were to adjust for (1) population of the central city (since cities of high population levels, such as the District, are likely to have higher poverty rates); (2) race of population (since race can serve as a proxy for residual effects of longstanding job and housing discrimination); and (3) geographic size of the city (the District has only sixty-nine square miles and is thus not as able to contain within its boundaries families of all races living in outlying areas with a preponderance of stable, affluent, suburban-like characteristics, as are cities of greater land areas), the District may find itself in no worse sociological shape than many other central cities. These adjustments are seldom made, and thus the District finds itself ranked last in many measures of urban distress.

URBAN DISTRESS

The District, unlike the fifty states, is a 100 percent urban area with a disproportionately large share of at-risk families, as discussed above. Moreover, unlike other major American cities, D.C. does not have access to the resources of its affluent suburbs, whether through taxation of nonresident income or through redistribution of suburban-urban resource disparities via a state government. These characteristics place the District and its people at a distinct economic disadvantage relative to the fifty states under the current political structure.

Stereotypes aside, the vast majority of D.C.'s young people are caring, honest people, dedicated to doing the best for themselves and others. Yet the data demonstrate that the nation's maladies pervade the District more than in any of the states. The Annie E. Casey Foundation (1994, 49) ranked the fifty states and the District on a variety of factors indicative of child well-being, and the District ranked last in the Center's national composite. The District ranked last among all fifty-one jurisdictions in its percentage of low birth weight babies, last in infant mortality rate, last in child death rate (ages one to fourteen), last in teen violent death rate, last in percentage of all births that were to single teens, last in its juvenile violent crime arrest rate, last in its percentage of students graduating from high schools on time, forty-ninth in its percentage of children living in poverty, and last in its percentage of children living in single-parent families. Moreover, most child well-being indicators have been sinking rapidly in D.C. Over just a six-year period from 1985 to 1991, the D.C. teen violent death rate increased sixfold, and by 1991 D.C. teens were dying from violence at four times the national rate. The foundation also reported that by 1991 D.C. teens were nearly twice as likely to be idle (not in school or in the labor force) as they were in 1985, and by 1991 they were idle at more than triple the rate of teens nationally. Only about half of D.C. youths were graduating from high school on time by 1991, while the U.S. rate was 69 percent (ibid.). The infant mortality rate had been improving from twenty-two per one thousand live births in 1989 to less than seventeen in 1993, but drug dependency and poor prenatal care increased the rate to 18.2 in 1994 (*Washington Post*, December 21, 1995, A1).

The District had the distinction of being the "murder capital of the nation" among the largest cities from the late 1980s through 1993 (*Washington Post*, December 31, 1994, A1). The District has been so dubbed since *Newsweek* did so in 1941 (Jaffe and Sherwood, 1994, 26).

A glaring example of D.C.'s social realities is its incarceration level. The number of prisoners from the District increased by 82 percent from 1982 to 1992 (D.C. Office of Policy and Program Evaluation 1993, 331; 1987, 230). This pattern mirrors national trends in this regard. However, Jaffe and Sherwood (1994, 14) point out that the District "jails more black men than it graduates from high school every year," which has to be considered a national as well as a D.C. tragedy.[3] As another example among many that

3. The authors' statement, while entirely accurate, needs some explanation. In 1992, 3,385 D.C. students graduated from public high schools and another 768 earned a high school equivalency degree (D.C. Office of Policy and Evaluation 1993, 264, 267). In 1992, the number of sentenced prisoners declined by 479 from the previous year, while the number of unsentenced detainees declined by 13 (*ibid.*, 324, 331). However, many more at any given time were imprisoned than were graduated in one year.

could be cited, the District's per capita expenditures for welfare were exceeded only by those of California (U.S. Department of Commerce 1991).

To some, the District's bleak socioeconomic statistics point to a lack of readiness for self-government. To others, the data provide a clear indication that a new political structure is urgently needed. It is not surprising that the D.C. government is assigned blame for the growth in such horrible statistics, for otherwise the nation as a whole as well as individuals in the region would have to shoulder greater responsibility for the problems and their solutions.

THE DISTRICT'S SHARE OF SOCIOECONOMIC BURDENS IN ITS REGION

The District is a unique jurisdiction. No other city in America has the District's state functions of welfare and Medicaid responsibility, maintenance of a state court, prison, and parole system, a state-level university, a state-level employment service and job training administration, disability compensation, state occupational safety and health enforcement, state licensing and utility and banking regulation, motor vehicle registration, and the like, in addition to such county functions as a county hospital, nursing homes, community mental health facilities, alcohol and drug abuse services, and public libraries, along with the usual city services such as police, fire, public works, traffic control, and recreation. Moreover, none of the fifty states lacks the authority to tax nonresidents who earn income within the state's borders, and forty-five currently require withholding on income earned within the state's borders (McKinsey & Co., 1994, Exh. 11). None of the states lacks the authority to draw resources from affluent suburbs surrounding hard-pressed urban centers within the state's boarders and redirect those resources to meet urban needs. For example, neighboring Maryland provided $2.4 billion in state aid to its local governments in 1989, while the District's other neighbor, Virginia, provided $2.7 billion (U.S. Bureau of the Census 1992c, 295). The District is also unique among state-type governments in that it does not have full autonomy over its own budgets and laws because Congress reserves that authority for itself. Finally, the District is unique because its citizens do not have voting representation in the U.S. Congress, unlike U.S. citizens in the fifty states. District citizens therefore cannot influence federal efforts to improve urban America, including their own jurisdiction, through their elected representatives.

These unique responsibilities and restrictions would likely be manageable (aside from the psychological wounds inflicted upon District citizenry by exclusion from the nation's democratic processes) were it not for the heavy share of socioeconomic burdens that the District shoulders in its region. The District manages most of the social problems of the region without sharing in the region's resources.

A study prepared by this writer (Meyers 1990) for the D.C. Commission on Budget and Financial Priorities (known as the Rivlin Commission) surveyed area budget officers regarding government services in the District and in the major nearby counties of the Washington, D.C. region. To assure full comparability, budget officers were asked to include all levels of nonfederal funding (state, county, and local) in their calculations.

The District had a little over a fifth (20.8 percent) of the population of the six major jurisdictions in the region, yet the District provided a greatly disproportionate share of expenditures for the surveyed services (see table 2.2).

For example, the District had 74.4 percent of the region's public housing units. Most of these units were constructed under federal rule, prior to the District's current limited home rule era. Some of these units are the oldest in the United States. Historically, suburban jurisdictions assiduously avoided constructing such units as part of a pattern of zoning and discriminatory real estate transactions (Brazer 1957, 92). While the District is notorious for its inefficient public housing programs, some of the problems of the public housing agency likely can be traced to the District's heavy share of public housing.

The District had 76.9 percent of the region's homeless beds. Perhaps half the homeless are transients from other areas (U.S. Conference of Mayors 1984, 5). Thus the homeless become the responsibility of cities, which are expected to meet the need. Supply of homeless beds often creates its own demand. Were more suburban jurisdictions to build homeless shelters and subsidized housing units, they would likely encounter little difficulty in attracting the clientele. Suburbs often view such construction as a proper function of cities, where street people, after all, are seemingly omnipresent. Instead of accepting a fair share of the burden, a suburb will often win plaudits with a small, innovative homeless shelter that serves as a model of efficiency which the overwhelmed city is exhorted to emulate.

Aid to Families with Dependent Children (AFDC or "welfare") is another example of the District doing much more than its fair share in its region. As a result of exclusionary zoning and real estate practices in the suburbs that are only in recent years being lifted (Brazer 1957, 92; Grier 1993), lower income people have been contained disproportionately in the District and other central cities. The District, with 20.8 percent of the region's population, had 60.5 percent of the AFDC caseload and 58.1 percent of the Medicaid

Table 2.2 Washington D.C.'s Share of Selected Services and Expenditures in Six Area Jurisdictions, FY 1988

Population	20.8%
AFDC Caseload	60.5%
AFDC Expenditures	60.7%
Medicaid Expenditures	65.7%
Medicaid Caseload	58.1%
Senior Citizens Expenditures	55.6%
Job and Training Expenditures	95.4%
Housing Assistance	72.1%
Public Housing Units	74.4%
Homeless Beds	76.9%
Homeless Expenditures	61.4%
Child Care Expenditures	61.4%
Contracts to Minority Firms	75.8%
Substance Abuse Expenditures	67.7%
Incarcerated Population	54.5%
Corrections Expenditures	65.5%
Police Personnel	47.1%
Police Expenditures	46.1%

The six jurisdictions include the District, Alexandria, Arlington County, Fairfax County, Montgomery County, and Prince George's County.

Source: Computed from data supplied in telephone survey, D.C. Office of Policy, March 1988.

caseload (Medicaid, or public health insurance for qualifying low-income people, uses similar eligibility standards as AFDC). AFDC and Medicaid are funded fifty-fifty by states and the federal government. Therefore, in the fifty states, the disproportionate distribution of AFDC and Medicaid caseloads in cities is somewhat less of a financial problem than it is in D.C. The states fund the programs from resources collected in rural, suburban, and urban areas, while the District does not have this resource distribution option. The costs of most other services in the District are also likely higher because of the disproportionate numbers of people who, in addition to receiving AFDC and Medicaid, are more dependent than others on a variety of government services.

The District made 65.6 percent of the region's corrections expenditures (over three times its "fair share" in the region). A *Washington Post* editorial (April 11, 1994, A18) wrote of the "sorry spectacle" of youth detention facilities, where the District has "ignored" a 1986 court order fining the District one thousand dollars per day for its "horrible" overcrowded conditions. Youth detention conditions are deplorable, yet how much of them are due to incompetence and indifference and how much to the District's disproportionate burden in the region?

As seen in table 2.3, the same situation prevails for a variety of other services as well: employment and training, senior citizen care, subsidized child care, drug treatment, and police services. The District is attempting to provide double or triple its proportional share of services with a tax base that is increasingly shifting to the suburbs. Table 2.3 (Meyers 1990, 12) summarizes the per capita expenditures in the District, compared to other local jurisdictions, that are needed to contend with the disproportionate levels of social and economic problems. Again, the data were made comparable by combining city, county, and state funding in each of the jurisdictions.

Suburban jurisdictions are never going to thank the District for its handling of most of the region's social problems. Amid all the howling over the District's ineptitude, they could at least acknowledge the extraordinary burdens. However, the data can be read another way. Representative Tom Davis (1995) told this writer that "the District policies created the demographics." D.C.'s politicians have "not appealed to the professionals" who move out "because they get better value for their tax dollars, better public safety, better education in other jurisdictions." Instead, local policies have made D.C. a magnet for the poor and have built AFDC caseloads, attracting people because of the easy benefits. Indeed average 1994 welfare payments in D.C. were 7 percent higher than they were in Virginia counties and 13 percent more than in Maryland counties (*Washington Post*, June 29, 1995, DC 3). Davis urged the District to develop a "demographics strategy." For example, Davis would sell off public housing units for a dollar each to entrepreneurs who would improve the units before renting them out. In contrast to such creative approaches, Davis said that the city has "stupid rules that say if you tear down a house, you have to put up another," thus thwarting reinvestment.

Davis (1995) also said that good schools are essential to keep the middle class, but D.C.'s schools have failed: "[N]ine thousand bucks a student and they are getting zip for it." Davis said that he was not an advocate of school vouchers, but almost any new strategy is better than the present one.

Davis's point of view holds that the District should not get an "A" for attempting to serve the region's poor, but an "F" for failing to discourage the poor from locating or remaining in D.C. Davis's Fairfax County is a role model for attracting and retaining wealth and has also been a beneficiary of federal pre-home rule zoning policies. These policies attracted thousands of

TABLE 2.3 State/Local Per Capita Expenditures, FY88 (Federal funding not included)

	District of Columbia	Alexandria	Arlington	Fairfax	Montgomery	Prince George's	Region
AFDC	$ 126.51	$ 33.96	$ 16.63	$ 10.31	$ 18.51	$ 35.72	$ 43.31
Medicaid	576.29	77.88	64.04	31.19	91.39	123.01	182.45
Senior Citizen Services	18.37	4.65	2.25	2.56	5.56	3.84	6.87
Job & Training Programs	52.12	–	1.12	1.87	–	–	11.37
Housing Assistance	41.08	3.29	4.33	9.98	0.91	0.95	11.76
Public Housing Operating Assistance	11.10	–	–	–	1.52	0.63	2.79
Homelessness	12.55	1.29	2.23	4.00	0.99	1.09	4.25
Child Care	28.28	7.66	9.58	4.36	2.88	10.62	
Substance Abuse Services	40.59	6.92	8.85	4.12	9.03	1.64	11.85
Corrections	243.87	87.38	79.08	37.52	16.65	27.22	77.42
Police	287.64	160.46	127.32	65.93	88.57	91.75	129.72
TOTALS	$ 1,438.40	$ 383.49	$ 313.81	$ 176.79	$ 237.49	$ 288.73	$492.41

Source: Office of Policy, telephone survey, February 1988.

low-rent housing units in the District's private market and built twelve thousand public housing units as well.

In assisting the District's disadvantaged, charitable contributions do not help as much as they used to. Maudine Cooper, head of the Washington Urban League, told this writer (January 6, 1995): "We're just fattening frogs for snakes." The League targets inner city residents in job training, stay-in-school, and college scholarship programs. As soon as a young person is transformed into a productive citizen through intensive help from the League or another nonprofit agency, the "frog" moves to Prince George's County or other suburb, feeding those economies. The cycle is venomous to D.C.'s economy.

TAX BURDENS

The District's weak tax base, high tax rates, and extensive dependent populations are sometimes cited as not meeting Congress' criterion of self-sufficiency for admission into the Union or for political autonomy in any form.

Tax burdens on D.C. residents and corporations are relatively heavy because of (1) the amount of tax exempt land in the District; (2) the unique congressional restriction against taxation of nonresidents earning income within the District's borders; (3) the extent of poverty-related conditions in the District; (4) the lack of a state government to redistribute income from relatively affluent suburbs to urban centers; (5) a regional tax base whose strength is primarily found in the suburbs; (6) reduced federal funding of several major urban-oriented programs in recent years; and (7) a large city-county-state workforce, often referred to as a "bloated bureaucracy." The D.C. government has attempted to accept responsibility for a wide array of socioeconomic problems, and it has been employer of last resort for D.C. residents.

The D.C. Department of Finance and Revenue (1992, 44) compared the tax burdens of D.C. residents at various income levels with those of residents of the fifty states (using residential tax burdens in the largest city in each state for the purpose of comparison). As table 2.4 shows, D.C. tax burdens are on average considerably higher than those in the fifty states, though rather competitive in its metro area with burdens in other jurisdictions (McKinsey & Co. 1994, Exh. 16).

D.C.'s revenues did not grow at all in real dollars between 1988 and 1993, and income and sales tax revenues lost considerable ground to inflation during that time (ibid., Exh. 6). Local supply-siders often advocate D.C. tax rate reductions as a means to restore economic vitality; however, the tax

TABLE 2.4 Tax Burdens of Residents of D.C. and the States, Various Income Levels, 1992 (Family of Four)

Annual Income	*Average Tax D.C.*	*Average Tax All States*	*Difference*
$25,000	$2,358	$2,182	8.1%
$50,000	$5,159	$4,556	13.2%
$75,000	$8,521	$7,466	14.1%
$100,000	$11,670	$9,971	17.0%

department is aware of the elasticity calculations. Tax rate reductions compute into larger deficits, at least for a period of several years—a situation neither the District nor Congress will tolerate. Some structural reform is needed to restore a healthy D.C. economy.

Of all factors contributing to high D.C. tax rates, the District's lack of nonresident income taxing authority could be the most significant. All fifty states and such major cities as Philadelphia, Pittsburgh, Detroit, St. Louis, Cincinnati, Columbus, Dayton, Cleveland, Kansas City, Louisville, and New York City, along with forty other cities with populations over fifty thousand, have this rather standard taxing authority (Meyers 1990, 6). As indicated in table 2.5, the value of this tax authority in fiscal year 1993 was $1.36 billion at full rates. If implemented, the tax rate would be set at far less than the full income tax rate that D.C. residents pay. Nonetheless, even a 2 percent nonresident tax would net the District $370 million a year (D.C. Department of Finance and Revenue, by phone, April 21, 1995). As D.C. Delegate Eleanor Holmes Norton said, "The reason we are so highly taxed is they [District officials] cannot tax those who in fairness owe taxes" to the District (*Washington Times*, March 31, 1992, A6). The District, with 437,000 daily suburban commuters, led the nation in 1990 in the percentage of income earned in the city by nonresidents—67 percent; St. Louis was a distant second at 54 percent (McKinsey & Co. 1994, Exh. 10).

The District's tax rates are also high to compensate for a weak tax base inside the District's borders. The District has three times the number of tax filers earning below $15,000 than it does filers earning over $100,000. None of the D.C. suburbs has anywhere close to such an imbalance, and some D.C. suburbs have two and three times the number of $100,000 filers as filers under $15,000 (Dearborn 1992, 16).

As with most major urban centers, income disparities by race account for a large share of the overall urban-suburban income gap. According to Grier (1993), it has only been since the 1970s—and primarily since 1980—

TABLE 2.5 Tax Revenues Foregone Because of Federal Presence and Policies, FY 93 ($ Millions)

Revenues lost because of federally mandated exemptions from District property taxes:	
Federal real estate	448.1
Other exemptions (foreign governments and special acts of Congress)	76.3
Federal and other personal property	54.8
Subtotal	579.2
Revenue lost due to federal restrictions on District taxing authority:	
Nonresident individual income tax	1,356.3
Presidential appointees and Congressional employees	9.4
Subtotal	1,365.7
Nonproperty tax revenues lost from diplomatic exemptions	24.3
Revenues lost because of Federal restrictions on taxation of the military	30.0
Total tax revenue forgone	1,999.2

Source: D.C. Office of the Budget, *Budget Fiscal Year 1994*, p. 89.

that blacks have gained access to suburban residential neighborhoods in the Washington metropolitan area. In the decade of the 1980s, D.C.'s black population declined by 11 percent, while the population of other all races increased (Office of Policy and Program Evaluation 1991, 79).

This relatively recent trend barely begins to counteract the effects of decades of racial segregation in housing, employment, and schools (Smith 1974, 55–94, 111–34, 168–302). The District has large minority populations; 65.8 percent of the District's population was black in 1990, and the Hispanic population was officially 5.4 percent (D.C. Office of Policy and Program Evaluation 1991, 79). Much of the American population shares the belief that conditions in America are improving significantly for minority families (Schuman, Steeh, and Bobo 1985; Kluegel and Smith 1986). While this belief is accurate for millions of success stories, it is far from the norm. The ratio of black-to-white median family income in the United States in 1993 (59.3 percent) was not much better than it was a quarter century ago (58.1 percent in

1967) (U.S. Bureau of the Census 1995, table D–1). Many Americans assume much more racial progress than the facts substantiate.

The Washington, D.C. region not only has greater proportions of high income earners than does the nation as a whole, it also has a disproportionately large number of black families with high incomes. Unfortunately for the District, the suburbs house many of these families. The 1990 Census (U.S. Bureau of the Census 1991) found that, after a decade or more of black outmigration, the remaining black D.C. residents comprised only 38.8 percent of blacks living in the Washington, D.C. metropolitan area. Many of the blacks who migrated to the suburbs were affluent relative to those who chose or felt economically restrained to remain in the District. The median household income of black D.C. households was $24,618, compared to $44,218 for black Maryland households and $37,623 for black Virginia households (computed from U.S. Census 1991). This phenomenon further explains the District's weak tax base.

Nor can the District's large commercial segment compensate for weaknesses in other components of the District's tax base. Private sector jobs constituted 59.6 percent of all jobs in the District in 1990, compared to 54.2 percent ten years earlier (D.C. Office of Policy and Program Evaluation 1991, 171). However, the District's corporate income tax rate already is higher than that of forty-six states (D.C. Department of Finance of Revenue 1992, 58). It is unrealistic to expect much more tax revenue from the commercial segment. D.C. businesses assign D.C. business taxes a negative 4.2 on a scale of 5, constituting the biggest reason why D.C. businesses are considering moving out (*Washington Post*, Dec. 7, 1994, F1).

While some commercial segments remain strong, others are declining. For example, D.C. was once the region's center for retail sales. However, because of the outflow of middle-class families, high parking costs, the loss of several large clothing, appliance, and department stores, and the continued growth of massive suburban shopping malls, retail sales declined 5 percent between 1989 and 1992 while gaining anywhere from 4 to 22 percent in suburban jurisdictions (*Washington Post*, May 22, 1994, A1, A4). Consequently, the District's sales tax revenues have been declining dramatically, from a high of $466.6 million in fiscal 1990 to $410.1 million in fiscal 1993 (D.C. Department of Finance and Revenue, by phone, August, 1994). Purchases by diplomatic and military customers, exempt from the sales tax, cost the District $70 million a year (McKinsey & Co. 1994, 7).

Another contributing factor to the District's weak tax base, and consequently to high tax rates, is the extent of tax exempt land in the District. The District contains only 29,687 acres of land, excluding public rights-of-way, and 57.1 percent is tax exempt. The federal government owns 41.5 percent of the District's total land area, comprising almost three-fourths of the tax exempt land (D.C. Office of Policy and Program Evaluation 1991, 93). If one includes streets and highways, then the percentage of D.C.'s land that is tax exempt increases to 62.2 percent (computed from ibid.).

The value of all federal tax exemptions for fiscal 1993, as computed by the D.C. government, is nearly $2 billion (see table 2.4). The federal and foreign governments together account for about half of all the tax exempt properties in the District but, because of their prime locations, comprise over 70 percent of the value of all the D.C. tax exemptions (D.C. Department of Finance and Revenue 1995, 1, 10). D.C.'s extent of property tax exemptions was highest among several cities studied (ibid. 9, 10). The District is unable to tax 43 percent of all its real property value, a figure that compares unfavorably to Boston's 33 percent, Philadelphia's 33 percent, New York City's 17 percent, and Atlanta's 8 percent, and is also much higher than Maryland's 14 percent and Virginia's 15 percent. The federal government also made $3,957.1 million in purchases in the District in 1993, purchases that are exempt from the sales tax (ibid., 24, citing Greater Washington Research Center data).

As if all those tax exemptions were not enough, Congress specifically provides $14.4 million in annual D.C. property tax exemptions to twenty-eight national organizations that would not otherwise qualify for the exemption under D.C. law (D.C. Department of Finance and Revenue, by fax, January 6, 1995). Organizations such as the Daughters of the American Revolution, the National Society of Colonial Dames, the National Education Association, the Army Distaff Foundation, Gallaudet College, and the National Geographic Society are treasured by many Americans, but D.C. taxpayers are congressionally mandated to love them much more than all other Americans do, generously subsidizing their activities by forgoing big chunks of dwindling local resources.

Most Americans also applaud the fine work of Fannie Mae (the Federal National Mortgage Association), established by Congress after the Great Depression to make mortgages widely available, especially to moderate-income families. However, D.C. residents are required to thank Fannie Mae more than other Americans, since Congress exempted the privately held corporation from corporate income taxes across America. The District's disproportionate subsidy to Fannie Mae stems from the fact that 70 percent of the company's payroll and 17 percent of its property (two components of the income tax) are based in D.C. (D.C. Department of Finance and Revenue 1995, 20). D.C. residents thus subsidize a corporation that makes loans all across America, with 86.7 percent of those loans made to white, non-Hispanics (D.C. is composed of nearly three quarters minority). Also, 85 percent of Fannie Mae's employees are suburbanites and therefore congressionally exempted from D.C. personal income tax liability. Fannie Mae's D.C. corporate tax exemption was valued at $300 million for 1994, enough to close much of the D.C. fiscal gap (*Washington Post*, January 15, 1995, A1, A20).

The District received a federal payment of $625 million in fiscal year 1993 to help compensate it for federal tax restrictions. Thus the federal payment amounted to less than a third of the $2 billion value of federal tax exemptions, at least according to the District's calculations. The federal payment also amounted to about 41 percent of the value of nonresident income taxation that the District could have received had there been no federal restriction against such taxation (see table 2.5) and had nonresident income been taxed at the same rate as D.C. residents' income.

Also affecting the District's ability to moderate its tax rates has been a shift in recent years in federal spending for urban areas. Using inflation-adjusted dollars, the National League of Cities calculated federal spending on housing, employment, mass transit, urban development, and general revenue sharing programs as declining by 54 percent between 1980 and 1992 in real dollars (*Washington Post*, July 9, 1992, A21). Much of these expenditures went directly to state and local governments. Moreover, welfare and Medicaid reforms (i.e., reduced federal funding) are around the corner.

The District's "bloated bureaucracy" contributes mightily to high D.C. tax rates. The District's defenders and foes alike generally regard the forty-five thousand D.C. government employees (McKinsey & Co. 1994, 4) for a jurisdiction of fewer than six hundred thousand as a preposterous number—with the exception of Mayor Barry, who at one time regarded the D.C. bloat as a "myth" (*Washington Post*, March 9, 1995, A1; July 29, 1995, A10). Whether one compares the D.C. government workforce with other city or state government workforces, the District government's rate of employees per capita can be found at the very top.

D.C.'s elected leaders are always the losers in the blame game when the District's payroll numbers are examined. However, seldom mentioned is the fact that the D.C. government had several thousand more employees in 1974, its last year under direct federal government control, than it has had in recent years under its own elected government. In 1974, the District had 48,291 employees and 50,081 full-time equivalent (counting part-time) employees (U.S. Bureau of the Census 1975, table 8). Newspaper accounts notwithstanding, D.C. elected leaders did not invent all the bloat.

Because the District is a unique city-county-state form of government, it is difficult to compare its workforce size with that of other governments. In 1982 the U.S. Census Bureau compared the number of employees in the D.C.

TABLE 2.6 Government Workforce Size, Selected Cities, October 1980 (full-time equivalent employment per 10,000 population)

Newark	903.3
Baltimore	784.4
Atlanta	706.3
St. Louis	684.7
Washington, D.C.	650.8
Cleveland	593.4
Detroit	535.6
Philadelphia	438.1

government workforce with employment levels found in seven similar cities and added into the other cities' workforce data the county and state employment for the variety of services performed by those other levels of government in those cities. Such a step was taken to place all eight cities on a comparable basis, since the D.C. workforce has county and state functions in addition to municipal functions. The results of the Census tabulations are provided in table 2.6.

The D.C. government has grown since the U.S. Census tabulations. From 1992 until 1994, the District government workforce grew 15.2 percent (computed from Office of Policy and Program Evaluation 1987, 78; McKinsey & Co. 1994, 4). If one were to subtract the 3,074 employees transferred from the federal to the D.C. workforce when St. Elizabeth's Hospital was transferred to the District's responsibility in 1987, then the net growth would be 2,868 employees, or 7.3 percent. Over a similar but smaller span of years, the number of state and local governments across the United States grew 19.3 percent (U.S. Bureau of the Census 1994b, 319). Thus, while no one disputes the District's bloat, its workforce level in 1980 was in line with those of comparable cities, adjusting for state and county responsibilities, and its growth since those days has been much less than the national average.

The District was not able to reduce sharply its bloated bureaucracy in recent years because of overly rigid personnel rules, strong labor unions, the clout of employees at the voting booths, and because of a concern over the injurious effects of massive layoffs to the District's fragile economy and communities. The District is in the midst of what inevitably will be an extended period of government downsizing. The D.C. Commission on Budget and Financial Priorities (1990, 2–18 to 2–20) targeted reductions in the D.C.

government workforce from 48,000 to 42,000, and the federally appointed financial control board in the summer of 1995 reduced the level to under 36,000 jobs. Then in 1996 Mayor Barry proposed a level of 30,000 by the year 2000, saying, "If I had this vision early on in the '80s, we would be in much better shape" (*Washington Post*, March 4, 1996, B1).

CONCLUSION: D.C.'S STRUCTURAL PROBLEMS ABOUND

A *Washington Post* editorial (February 5, 1995, C6) reminded: "The Home Rule Charter didn't plunge the District into this financial crisis." Rather, it said, it was the government's failure to trim its budgets and its workforce that caused the crisis.

Nonetheless, America's continuing urban crisis also has a major role to play in the District's financial drama. Urbanologist David Rusk classified U.S. cities into five categories from "zero-elasticity" through middle ranges to "hyper-elasticity" cities. Low-elasticity cities have frozen city limits and are surrounded by growing suburbs. All thirty of Rusk's zero-elasticity cities, including D.C., have lost population, most notably their middle class, and have large and increasing concentrations of racially segregated, poverty-ridden populations. Unless all of these jurisdictions are guilty of mismanagement, some larger national phenomena are at work. Because the income gap between city and suburbs is rising among these cities, the urban government "is squeezed between rising service needs and eroding incomes" (Rusk 1993, 47). These cities are most reliant upon state and federal assistance. Of 145 major cities classified, the District was ranked the sixth worst in elasticity (ibid., Appendix A–1).

Rusk wrote that "[i]nelastic cities, in the battle over middle-class America, have lost to their suburbs" (ibid., 122). Such cities have thousands of success stories in which their citizens, minority and otherwise, are able to escape poverty. However, such individual successes do not translate into community success. The successful move away and, consequently, "city budgets are unable to meet rising social needs" (ibid., 121). Rusk warns that while suburban growth initially comes at the expense of deteriorating cities, suburbs of dying cities may also wither: "Limbs cannot survive without the heart" (ibid., 89). America's cities are in precarious health, but the urban victims usually receive the blame.

Rusk prescribes state action (ibid., 124). States should facilitate annexation laws to enable central cities to expand, enact "fair share" housing laws so that all jurisdictions in a region share affordable housing burdens, and legislate tax-sharing arrangements or assure that state aid to central cities acts as a revenue-equalizing mechanism (ibid.). The District, because of its unique structure, cannot partake in any of Rusk's suggested remedies.

The District, therefore, must first help itself. The District from 1988 to 1993 essentially held real expenditures flat and achieved significant real-dollar reductions in several discretionary areas, offsetting large increases in Medicaid, pensions, and debt service (ibid., Exh. 3). Nonetheless, to win broader support, the District must do much better, as the disastrous deficits of the mid-1990s demonstrate.

With continually deeper reductions, produced by the D.C. executive and legislative branches in cooperation with the financial control board, the District may gain some long-sought recognition by Congress that the District cannot solve its financial problems without structural reform. In a report to D.C. business leaders, McKinsey & Co. (1994, 2) estimated that only one-third of the District's problems results from its bloated expenditures, while two-thirds are due to structural revenue deficiencies. The report notes (ibid., 5): "All American cities are facing dwindling populations and revenues. The District is no different. But the impact of population loss hits the District's finances much harder than it hits other cities' finances." When a middle-class family moves away from the District, "the tax loss is complete." In other cities, the loss of middle-class population is cushioned by intergovernmental transfers—that is, by compensatory state funds recycled into cities and by nonresident income taxes (ibid., 7). Including the federal payment and other federal funding, the District receives 32 percent of its revenues from external sources, while U.S. cities on average receive 74 percent from federal and state entities (ibid., exhibit 7). The District is three times more reliant on its own local (sales, income, property tax) revenue sources than is the average U.S. city.

The District's woes have produced greater scrutiny of the District's financial actions than ever before—from Congress, Wall Street, the business community, and the media—and the potential for greater understanding as well. The stage seems set for the next act: the financial control board, D.C. elected leaders, and Congress immolate the D.C. governmental bloat while Congress, either in partnership with D.C. or (more typically) unilaterally, shapes a new D.C. financial and political structure that provides for stability and self-sufficiency.

3

Ten Policy Options for the Nation's Capital

> *"Part of the city's problems is that the previous Democratic Congress would not interfere when they should have. That's where the fiscal mess came from. They were afraid to touch the city. If Congress had worked with the city a little better, we would not have had the train wreck that we have right now."*
>
> Representative Tom Davis (R–Va.), Chair, House Subcommittee on the District of Columbia (1995)

Opening chapters discussed the District's current status, including its financial crisis and external controls that further limit the District's self-government authority. This chapter discusses the District's future political options.

The mission of the District government over the next several years, in cooperation with the financial control board, is to restore financial solvency and produce balanced budgets. During this period, Congress, the President, D.C. leaders, and the control board are examining the District's financial and political structure so that a form of government can be designed to keep the District from reverting to a state of financial crisis. This chapter outlines the political options open to policymakers once D.C. emerges from its financial crisis. Later chapters tap the thinking of focus group panelists around the nation and of national and D.C. leaders.

"PRO" AND "CON" VIEWS ON D.C. SELF-GOVERNMENT AND VOTING RIGHTS

Following are arguments in favor of full political autonomy and voting rights for the District once financial solvency is established:

TABLE 3.1 Population (1995) and Voting Age Populations (1994) of Lowest-Populated States, in Thousands

Rank	*State*	*Population*	*Voting Age Population*
51	Wyoming	480	343
50	District of Columbia	554	452
49	Vermont	585	429
48	Alaska	604	429
47	North Dakota	641	467
46	Delaware	717	534
45	South Dakota	729	522

Sources: Population data from U.S. Bureau of Census, News Release CB96–10, Jan. 26, 1996; Voting age data from U.S. Bureau of Census, 1994b, 289, using projected data.

"Pro"

1. *The District's population is not large, but it is sufficient to assure that District citizens have equal political standing with other Americans.* A 1996 U.S. Census Bureau news release (CB96–10) cited D.C. as America's fastest loser in population among the states. D.C.'s births exceeded deaths by a wide margin, but out-migrations produced the decline. As of 1995, D.C. exceeded only Wyoming in population, with Vermont and Alaska passing D.C. in recent years. Voting-age population is perhaps more relevant, since taxation and congressional representation are intertwined with debates over D.C.'s political status. D.C.'s voting-age population exceeds that of Wyoming, Vermont, and Alaska, and is close to that of North Dakota (see table 3.1).

The District's population is also close to Hawaii's 633,000 and two and one-half times Alaska's 226,000 in the 1960 census, a year after those states were admitted to the Union (U.S. Bureau of the Census, 1991, 20). It may be argued that simply because a person is a resident of a low-population state, that residency should not preclude her or him from representation in Congress and from self-government. Other residents of low-population states have full democratic rights, so why should not D.C. residents?

In hearings into D.C. statehood and policy alternatives, Raskin (1994) advised the committee chair, Senator John Glenn, that when Glenn's state of Ohio was admitted into the Union in l803, its population was 41,915—which not only was "dead last" among the then-existing states but was also below the 60,000 threshold established by Congress in the Northwest Ordinance for admittance. Jesse Jackson (1994) added that when he ran for the unpaid lobbyist position of "shadow" senator in 1992, he received fifty thousand more votes in D.C. than Alan Simpson received in Wyoming as a "real" senator and just two thousand fewer than received by Delaware's Senator Joseph Biden.

Moreover, urban centers contain disproportionate numbers of low-income people who are significantly undercounted. Urban people are transient, they double up with other families, they live informally with others in subsidized housing, and sometimes do not complete census forms or participate in the surveys because of an often mutual distrust between urban residents and government survey-takers. Cities also contain unknown numbers of undocumented immigrants who sometimes do not report their residency until they are securely on the road to worker status and citizenship. The official estimate of undercount in the District's 1990 population is 21,000 (U.S. Census Bureau 1992, press release 92–275). If the undercount were to be added to the District's 1995 population, one would arrive at a level of 575,000; however, many urban demographers would argue for a much higher, though undeterminable, level (Grier 1993).

The Washington metropolitan area's leading demographer, George Grier (1993), was startled by population losses in the District in recent years. Grier cited double-digit vacancy rates in some D.C. census tracts. Grier also emphasized the difficulty of accurately counting the District's population, stating that the numbers of the undercounted were substantial but unknown. He noted that the federal government's policy has been to keep the urban population counts as low as possible to reduce population-based federal grants. Nonetheless, Grier (ibid.) pointed out that the District's population in 1950 was 802,178, "so I don't think there is any question that D.C could hold that many and more" in decades to come.

The District's population has decreased since 1950 as family size has decreased and as new, smaller households have replaced larger households moving to the suburbs. Around 1980, black families in large numbers gained greater access to suburban housing, and these families are not being replaced by new families moving into the District (ibid.). Concern over safety has accelerated in some of the District's census tracts, especially in those affected most by the crime and drug epidemics (ibid.). Grier (1994) analyzed 1985 to 1990 Census data and found that households moving out were more than twice as likely to be married-couple families and more than twice as likely to have children as those moving into the District. The household size of those moving out was 2.3, while the size of households moving in was under 2. The vast majority of those moving out were the middle class, and nearly half of those moving out were blacks and other minorities. The District is still attracting white, middle-class, professional, single people, but is experiencing considerable difficulty in portraying itself as a place where families move in, establish community roots, place their children in the public schools, and stay for the long haul.

With a new financial structure, better crime control, dramatically improved schools, lower taxes, and new industry, it is conceivable that the District's population could begin a long climb back to its former population levels and higher. Another national capital, Paris, also has a small land area—just forty square miles, considerably fewer than the District's sixty-nine—and Paris's population is over 2.1 million. Paris has a population density more than six times greater than that of Washington, D.C. The District's population size cannot be expected to mirror that of Paris for many years to come, but who can predict economic and social transformations? One psychological phenomenon of any cycle (e.g., a business cycle, the stock market, the housing market) is that one tends to extrapolate the future from the present, with no way of knowing the shifts and swings that could produce a radically different future.

The U.S. Census Bureau does not project Paris-like growth for D.C. In fact, it projects a dip to 537,000 by the year 2000 and an increase to 636,000 by the year 2020. The projected 10.2 percent growth between 1990 and 2020 would make D.C. the forty-third fastest growing among the states. However, Wyoming (658,000 by the year 2020), Vermont (also 658,000), North Dakota (719,000), and Alaska (866,000) would all exceed D.C.'s population levels by that time according to these projections, thus placing D.C.'s population last among the state population levels (U.S. Bureau of the Census 1994a, 1).

2. *No American should be taxed without representation in Congress.* Currently the District has "taxation without representation," a rallying cry that helped achieve American independence. Table 3.2 captures the District's gripe with Congress over their lack of voting rights. District residents paid $1.5 billion in federal individual income taxes in 1991, more than that of eight states. On a per capita basis, the District ranked third highest in the nation in the payment of federal individual income taxes, exceeded only by Connecticut and New Jersey.

There may be some misconception that the District is supported by the federal government. For example, President Bush was quoted as saying that the District "should remain a Federal city" because "its funds come almost exclusively from the Federal Government" (Schrag 1990, 317, n.42). In contrast, the U.S. Census Bureau (1991, 286) data indicate that the District (a state-type taxing jurisdiction) ranked second among all states, next to Alaska, in the amount of taxes per capita raised from its own resources. In absolute dollars, the District ranked ahead of eighteen states in the collection of state

TABLE 3.2 Federal Individual Income Tax Payments, 1991

Rank	State	Taxes Paid (Millions of $)	Per Capita ($)
51	Wyoming	835	1,816
50	Vermont	903	1,593
49	North Dakota	911	1,435
48	South Dakota	1,016	1,446
47	Montana	1,073	1,328
46	Idaho	1,402	1,350
45	Alaska	1,427	2,504
44	Delaware	1,451	2,134
43	District of Columbia	1,500	2,509

Source: U.S. Bureau of the Census 1994B, 344.

and local taxes from its own sources (ibid., 292). If democracy is to be denied the District because it is relying on the federal government rather than its own resources, then it could be argued that representation should be denied to the residents of those eighteen other states as well.

3. *Political rights are a matter of equity: an American is an American.* Why are D.C. residents any different from the other Americans who are represented in the House and Senate? This argument involves an appeal to basic fairness and equity. Any number of appeals to conscience may be brought into the discussion linking D.C.'s political inequality with past struggles for equal rights. Martin Luther King, Jr. [1963] (1976, 214), in his letter from Birmingham Jail, wrote:

> I am cognizant of the interrelatedness of all communities and states. I cannot sit idly by in Atlanta and not be concerned about what happens in Birmingham. Injustice anywhere is a threat to justice everywhere.

Sterling Tucker (1978, 139), former chairman of the District's legislative body, testified before the Senate that the issue of voting rights for District residents is linked to a chain of historical advances, noting that the right to vote was extended to blacks in 1870, women in 1920, and eighteen-year-olds in 1971. In 1913 the Constitution was amended to provide for the direct election of senators. Tucker (ibid.) stated that "the struggle for full suffrage for all Americans is not yet over."

The National Board of the League of Women Voters in 1978 congressional hearings made a similar link to women's suffrage and other voting rights gains and collected over a million and a quarter signatures nationwide for the District's cause (Fortune 1978, 143–46). Madeleine K. Albright (1991, 290), testifying as president of the Center for National Policy and who later became ambassador to the United Nations in the Clinton administration, found it ironic that many of the same national leaders who applauded the fall of the Berlin Wall and the rise of democracy around the world continue to deny to D.C. residents the same rights to help shape their own lives.

The Statehood Solidarity Committee made a similar appeal to international justice when it formally petitioned the Organization of American States (OAS), a 35-member-country regional entity of the United Nations, to rule the United States in violation of the OAS charter, which the United States ratified in 1951. An article of the charter states that "[e]very person . . . is entitled to participate in the government of his country, directly or through its representatives" and that "all people are equal before the law" (Cooper 1993). OAS Commissioner L. Valladares, after hearing D.C.'s case in February, 1995, remarked, "When I go back to my hotel room this evening and look out my window, I am going to wonder if the person I am seeing is a second-class citizen."

Former D.C. Council Chairman John Wilson, a strong voice for D.C. until he took his own life in 1993, once lectured members of Congress who opposed D.C. statehood: "When you arrive in heaven and St. Peter tells you that you've been wrong for 200 years and you can't come in, remember I warned you." On another occasion, instead of testifying at a congressional hearing, Wilson simply sang a refrain from the Supremes: "Set me free, why don't you, babe?" (*The Washington Post*, May 20 and 23, 1993).

4. *Wartime participation.* It is against American tradition to require a young person to fight for his or her country in time of war or serve in military actions to Bosnia and elsewhere without providing representation in Congress to help decide if military action should be taken. However, in Vietnam the casualty level for the District was higher than that of ten states (Best 1984, 5, citing statement of Senator Edward Kennedy). Representative Thomas Foley (1987, 31) stated that, per capita, more District residents died in military service in Vietnam than was the case with forty-seven states.

5. *The unique exclusion of District residents in comparison to residents of other nations' capital districts.* Washington, D.C., the center of democracy and capital of the free world, is unique in that it is the only capital district among all nations with elected national legislatures whose citizens are not represented in the legislative body (Best 1984, 6). Best cited Brazil as the only other such example among free world nations, but since that time the resi-

dents of Brasilia gained representation.[1] This is a unique and hypocritical situation for America, the acknowledged worldwide leader of democracy, to condone. As then-Governor Clinton (1991, 553) stated:

> You can be sure that the people of Prague have equal representation in their country's capital. So do the people of Canada, Paris and Moscow. In fact, 115 countries in this world elect or purport to elect their representatives—and not a single one of them denies this right to the people of their capital city.

6. *Democratic rights are not tied to a jurisdiction's affluence.* The District drew worldwide scorn for its abysmal experiences in the latter stages of the three-term administration of Mayor Marion Barry. Since those days the District has struggled for respectability, but was again felled by financial chaos. The crisis terminated all discussion of expanded political rights. Only a long, determined effort, guided by a financial control board, can restore hopes of greater self-government.

While the District works for the day when it can assume full authority over its own bills and budgets and prosecute its own criminal cases, it should be kept in mind that basic democratic rights—such as voting representation in Congress—are not denied in America because of unbalanced budgets, restricted government services, impoverishment in neighborhoods, or even past or present corruption. For example, affluent Orange County, California was in bankruptcy during much of the mid-1990s. Can one imagine stripping county residents of their voting representation in Congress until they learned to hire wiser money managers?

7. *An opportunity to add a greater element of diversity to the U.S. Senate.* The argument is sometimes made (as cited in Schrag 1990, 345–46, n.168) that the District's population, 65.8 percent black in 1990 (U.S. Bureau of the Census 1991, 22), is not representative of America's population as a whole. However, neither is Hawaii's, 61.8 percent Asian and Pacific Islander. For that matter, neither is Vermont's, a state that is about D.C.'s size in population and whose population is 98.6 percent white (U.S. Bureau of the Census

1. Prior to the enactment of the Federative Republic of Brazil's new constitution in 1988, the capital city, Brasilia, was administered by a committee composed of senators of various Brazilian states. Since 1988, Brasilia has continued as a federal district but has been granted representation in Brazil's national legislature. Brasilia is now represented by three senators and also has proportional representation in the lower chamber of the national legislature as well (Zandonade 1992).

1991, 22). There is, in any event, no valid reason to allocate democratic rights on the basis of a state's racial composition.

Best (1984, 78–79) evoked Madison and the *Federalist* papers in arguing that the District lacks sufficient diversity to become a state. In *Federalist* number 51 Madison wrote: "If a majority be united by a common interest, the rights of the minority will be insecure" (Hamilton, Madison, and Jay [1788] 1961, 323). Best (1984, 79) argued that the interests of the District and the federal government are one, and that the District, as a homogeneous faction consisting largely of federal workers and the government's spin-off industries, cannot serve as a check to the federal government.

The Madisonian concepts of majority domination and diversity are instructive for another reason. The majority race can dominate in America and has done so. A greater minority faction in the Senate could help "guard one part of society against the injustice of the other part" (Hamilton, Madison, and Jay [1788] 1961, 323). Voting rights in Congress for the District would further Madison's intentions, not hinder them, by adding an improved measure of racial balance to the Senate. At this writing, there is only one black member of the Senate. There have been only four senators who were black in American history, and just two since 1881. Madison (ibid., 324) desired a society with "so many descriptions of citizens as will render an unjust combination of a majority of the whole very improbable, if not impracticable." Greater heterogeneity in the Congress, as contributed by the admission first of Hawaii and perhaps ultimately of the District and Puerto Rico, would help achieve that vision. African Americans comprise the nation's largest minority, so the District's contribution to congressional heterogeneity, especially in the Senate, would be significant, whether achieved through statehood or through voting rights amendment to the Constitution.

As the qualitative research in this work indicates, of all the arguments used to expand D.C.'s political rights, Americans are persuaded the least by a call for greater racial diversity in Congress. Such an argument often elicits outright opposition to D.C. voting rights.

"Con"

Some of the major arguments used in opposition to D.C. voting rights and self-government include the following:

1. *The District is obviously a city and should not be given the same standing as a state.* The District, with its small and completely urban land area, is obviously a city, not a state. It looks, feels, smells, acts, and sounds like a city, and therefore it *is* a city. As Speaker Newt Gingrich said, referring to Con-

gress' oversight role, "We are the state for this city" (*Washington Post*, February 3, 1995, A13). One could say that the degree of congressional control should therefore not be considered unduly burdensome or interventionist.

If the nation made the District a state or gave its people the voting-rights equivalence of a state's residents, it could be argued that many large U.S. cities would want the same treatment. As Best (1984, 60) wrote: "Why shouldn't New York City be represented as a distinct unit instead of as part of a state? It has perhaps 14 times the population of the District, and it does not have two congressional committees that devote their efforts to its problems." Best does not address the fact that New York City residents have a dozen voting representatives in the House or that the city's residents may vote for two U.S. senators from the state of which they are a member. Presumably, these rights, already held, could lessen the need for a separate status for New York City residents. Nonetheless, Best's point remains: New York City residents' power could be strengthened further if they had their own two senators in Congress to accompany their twelve voting representatives.

2. *The District's small land area cannot accommodate population growth.* Even though it is possible to find a few states with population levels similar to the District's, those states have land areas much larger than that of the District. Indeed, the U.S. Census Bureau (1994, 1) projects the District's population will be last among all the states by the year 2020.

In 1801, members of Congress used the small population of the District as a reason to refuse representation for the District. At the time, the District's fourteen thousand citizens represented about .26 percent of the U.S. total of about 5.3 million people (Best, 1984, 4). In 1995 the District's 554,000 residents still represented only .21 percent of America's total of 262,755,000 (U.S. Bureau of the Census 1996, Release CB96–10, Jan. 26). Therefore, proportionally, the District's population is even less today than it was in 1801, and it has been falling precipitously.

3. *The District's residents and elected leaders have demonstrated that they are not ready for self-rule.* Some argue that there is no indication that the District's residents or its leaders are ready to govern themselves and achieve the same political standing as held by other Americans. The District's homicide rates have exceeded national averages by enormous margins and have given the District the unenviable appellation of "murder capital of the nation." Its high infant mortality and teenage pregnancy rates and other "ravages of poverty and urban decline . . . hardly make for a promising lift-off as the fifty-first state" (Raven-Hansen 1991, 161). The District's per capita expenditures for welfare in 1990 were exceeded only by California's in comparison to the fifty states (U.S. Department of Commerce, 1991). Representa-

tive Bill Lowery (R–Ca.) (1991, 37) considered statehood for the District a "distraction" and noted that the time congresspersons spent on statehood would be better spent solving the District's problems of education, crime, family breakdown, homelessness, and health care. Representative James Moran (D–Va.) (*Washington Times*, March 31, 1992, A1) cited the District's "high proportion of dependency" on social programs and added: "The District can be independent when its population can be self-sufficient. Right now, you've got a long ways to go."

Some may also argue that the District's elected leaders have not demonstrated a readiness for self-government. In the first weeks of his initial term as mayor, Marion Barry noted (American Enterprise Institute 1979, 5):

> We were confronted, on January 2, [1979] with a city government that was rather inefficiently run and with rather ineffective programs. In fact, some people here and around the country probably considered the District government the laughingstock of the nation. I have met people at conventions who were ashamed to admit they were from the District. They would say they were from Maryland or somewhere else.

Barry took control of a much-maligned government and achieved a measure of respect over several years of improved government performance, although those early years were by no means free of widely publicized shortcomings. In the latter stages of Barry's mayoral tenure (phase one), programmatic failures multiplied and two of his deputy mayors were imprisoned for misdeeds. Barry himself later became a convicted misdemeanant. During this time, Missouri Senator John Danforth said, "Some governments are corrupt but are known for their competence," while "others are incompetent but considered 'clean'." He added that the D.C. government "is seriously corrupt and hopelessly incompetent" (Jaffe and Sherwood 1994, 250).

Mayor Kelly, armed with shovel and broom, pledged a clean sweep of the old ineffective ways. She soon encountered not just an intransigent bureaucracy but unrelenting social decay in the District. Kelly bequeathed to a resuscitated Barry the District's grimmest financial crisis. Barry embarked on a sustained effort to rehabilitate the District, himself, and his image. However, his administration was soon saddled with a financial control board to make the tough choices. Many argue that after the control board completes its tasks, an extended era free from excessive urban problems, unbalanced budgets, mismanagement, and corruption is necessary before self-rule and political equality for the District can be considered. Jaffe and Sherwood said (1994, 320), "It's a political reality that the city's myriad troubles make statehood a longshot." Consequently, they said, those espousing statehood as a "panacea for the city's problems" have been engaging in "pure demagoguery" (ibid., 320, 325). With the courts controlling everything from prisons to foster care to public housing, and the financial control board and Congress scrutinizing everything else, the trend in recent years has been toward ever shrinking levels of self-government for D.C. residents.

4. *Congress provides a needed element of protection to District residents.* Some feel that the law-abiding citizens of the District themselves may need protection against the potential excesses of their elected leaders. The 535 members of the House and Senate are considered by some as necessary for maintaining this protection. For example, Congress may decide that more police officers are needed than the District's elected leaders provided in their budgets, as in fact has been decided by Congress during its budget deliberations in recent years (Harris 1989, 74).

The argument for congressional protection is one that tends to be whispered but never publicly voiced. This philosophy is also thought, at least by home rule proponents, to be prevalent in the more affluent, predominately white areas of the District. Congressional intervention may be preferred by some to a situation in which the District's fate would be determined solely by the elected representatives of the District's residents and the local government.

5. *The "they-could-always-move" argument.* During hearings on D.C. statehood, James C. Miller, III (1992), former director of the U.S. Office of Management and Budget in the Reagan and Bush administrations, reminded members of the Subcommittee on the Judiciary and Education of the House District Committee that residents of the District were well aware that they did not have the benefits of voting representation in Congress when they moved to the District. If residents were born in the District, then they could always move out when they reached voting age. They could vote with their feet. No one is forcing anyone to become or remain a District resident. As Miller (1992, 36) stated, "[F]or those who feel their protections circumscribed, they can invoke the right of unencumbered migration—to Virginia, Maryland, or anywhere else in the country. And, indeed, we do see much migration in the area, although quite rarely is this motivated by a difference in federal rights." Miller (ibid.) viewed the lack of federal rights as "akin to the prohibitions on partisan [political] activity experienced by the vast majority of federal employees under the Hatch Act." The Hatch Act constraint is a "rather minor inconvenience," and "in the event it becomes burdensome the situation is easily remedied by job relocation."

Miller (ibid.) observed that across America voting efficacy is unfortunately lacking for the most part in any event. Ordinary citizens do not have much influence over what happens in Congress; therefore, in Miller's view, the absence of congressional voting representation and other democratic rights should not be unduly regretted by District citizens. Apparently, this view holds that representative democracy is overrated, and D.C. residents should not feel chagrined by their exclusion.

6. *The District belongs to the entire nation, not just to its residents.* McDonald (1992, 225) noted that "[t]he District of Columbia, like the Constitution and the federal government, does not belong solely to the people who live there. It is the common property of all Americans." Therefore, the District should not have independent status. Former Senator Birch Bayh of Indiana once said that "[t]his city [the District] belongs to Indiana, to Rhode Island, to Virginia; it belongs to the whole United States of America." Bayh stated that he would "hate to see us [Congress] taking the Nation's Capital from . . . Hoosiers" (Best 1984, 8–9). The District is said to have a special status to be enjoyed by all, and all should have a voice in its operation.

7. *Congress, not the District, is responsible for protecting the federal interest.* Congress has an obligation to protect the interests of the federal government, which is housed in Washington, D.C. Washington, D.C.'s origins sprang from an incident in 1783 involving a band of about eighty soldiers who stormed Congress in its Philadelphia location, demanding back pay that was due them. The Pennsylvania Executive Council refused to order the local militia to protect Congress on the grounds that the militia may not have been responsive to the Council's orders. The mutiny continued for three days, and the number of troops involved swelled. As a result of this incident, Congress abandoned Philadelphia and planned a more secure location, a site at which the federal interest would be protected (McDonald 1992, 221). The federal interests may be more intricate today than ever but, it is argued, just as in need of protection.

Raven-Hansen (1991, 173–74) countered that the federal government for an extended era has acquired the moral and physical power necessary for it to perform its duties. For example, the Supreme Court reaffirmed in 1990 the federal government's authority to command the operation of state militias (ibid., 174); the federal government no longer must beseech state governments to protect it. Nonetheless, the actions of a self-governed entity that would literally surround the federal enclave would inevitably profoundly affect federal operations.

8. *Control is needed to guard against a potential expansion of the District's taxing powers that would be experienced under an alternative political structure.* If granted full state-type taxing authority, the District would

undoubtedly enact a nonresident income tax, as all fifty states as well as fifty-one cities with populations over fifty thousand currently have the authority to impose. This new tax would create an additional burden upon the residents of Maryland and Virginia who work in the District. Residents of these states feel they have enough difficulty supporting their state governments as it is. If the District were allowed to enact a nonresident income tax, and if a credit on the home state's income tax were provided, then the state governments of Maryland and Virginia would have to enact tax increases or eliminate the jobs of state workers. Such a circumstance would likely cause some financial hardship in the Maryland and Virginia state governments.

9. *The District has an "unrepresentative" population.* The District's population is said to be "too liberal, too urban, too black, and too Democratic," and is therefore not representative of America's population (Senator Orrin Hatch quoting Senator Edward Kennedy in the foreword to Best 1984, vii). This argument is usually cited by advocates of expanded D.C. political rights characterizing how they believe their opponents feel. Nonetheless, Republican party strategist Ed Rollins has indicated that Republicans generally do not favor full voting rights for the District because "you're going to get two liberal Democrats [in the Senate] and keep getting them for the next 100 years" (Schrag 1990, 345, n.167).

10. *The District clearly lacks economic diversity.* The argument is sometimes made (Best 1984, 74) that the District is a "company town" revolving around the federal government. Of the 687,900 jobs located in the District in 1990, only 220,400 or 32 percent were federal government jobs (D.C. Office of Policy and Program Evaluation 1991, 171). However, Best (1984, 74) estimated that another 25 percent of the District's jobs were in "service industries closely associated with the federal government." Best likely included the District's large tourist industry in her calculation. If she is correct (or even close), then over half the jobs in the District are "directly or indirectly dependent on the federal government" (ibid.).

Best (ibid.) quoted Senator S. I. Hayakawa as calling the District a kind of "fairyland":

> There is no seaport. There is no industry. There is no agriculture. We have no automobile factories like Detroit, no golden fields of corn like Iowa or Indiana, no dairy farms like Wisconsin, no shipping like New Orleans, Baltimore, Seattle, or Galveston, no clothing industry like New York, no movie studios or wineries or orchards like California, no wheat fields like the Dakotas, no pineapples and sugar cane like the glorious islands of Hawaii, no mineral resources like Alaska, no lumber

> resources like those of Alaska and the state of Washington. There is just no wealth-creating business here in Washington, but only one great money-spending entity, the Federal Government.

Indeed, instead of wheat fields, the District has six times the proportion of public administrators than the nation as a whole, five times the concentrations of economists and statisticians, four times the public relations specialists, and more than three times the concentrations of computer scientists, reporters, and lawyers (*Washingtonian* magazine, December 1992, 15). However, some may argue that even Washington, D.C. lawyers are Americans and are entitled to the benefits of full citizenship. Moreover, the District's economy and labor force have changed since Senator Hayakawa's 1978 statement. Between 1980 and 1992, federal government employment in the District grew by 2,200, or less than one percent, while private sector employment in services grew by 56,500 jobs, or 17 percent (Office of Policy and Program Evaluation 1991, 171; and 1994, 155). By 1992, 58 percent of jobs in D.C. were private sector jobs (ibid.). Moreover, the number of federal government jobs has been declining in recent years, and the decline has been greater in the District (-9.2 percent between 1992 and 1995, *Washington Post*, December 25, 1995, A18) than in suburban Maryland (-4.8 percent) and Virginia (-2.4 percent).

District residents often express concern that they do not receive a sufficient share of the federal government jobs in the District, and the jobs for which they are hired are disproportionately lower-paid, non-policy jobs. Indeed, whites hold 88 percent of the highest paid jobs in the federal government and 92 percent of the very highest salaried positions (*Washington Post*, December 6, 1993, A21). Most of the federal jobs in the District, and especially the good ones, are held by suburbanites who have full democratic rights. If this is the case, then the argument sometimes heard that U.S. senators and a voting representative from the District of Columbia would represent the "overwhelmingly homogeneous factional interest" of the federal government in Congress (Best 1984, 76) may be of lessened concern.

Indeed, the data show that D.C. residents only hold 10.5 percent of federal jobs that are located in the Washington, D.C. metropolitan area (*Washington Post*, December 25, 1995, A18). D.C. residents do not even fare particularly well when one examines who holds the federal government jobs that are located inside the city limits. The 1990 Census (Metropolitan Washington Council of Governments 1993) revealed that of the 220,400 federal government jobs located in the nation's capital, 48,639 or 22.1 percent were held by residents of the District, with suburban Maryland and Virginia residents holding the vast majority of the remaining jobs. The District's share is declining. According to the 1980 Census (U.S. Bureau of the Census 1984, 126), D.C. residents held 28.1 percent of federal jobs located in D.C.

Employment statistics demonstrate that the District's labor force is becoming increasingly oriented toward the private sector. In 1980, D.C. had 297,293 employed persons in its labor force, and 29.3 percent of the employed D.C. residents worked for the federal government, while 59.5 percent worked in the private sector or were self-employed. By 1990 the number of employed D.C. residents had increased to 303,994, and 67.7 percent were either working in the private sector or were self-employed. However, the number of D.C. residents who were employed in the federal government declined by more than 25,000 people, and federal government workers comprised only 20.4 percent of the employed D.C. labor force (Metropolitan Washington Council of Governments 1993). Moreover, local elected officials have a history of conflict, not sympathy, with their federal guardians (Weaver and Harris 1989). Should the District achieve a form of political independence, it would be unlikely that the two entities would join forces against the interests of other Americans to a greater extent than Maryland and Virginia delegations currently support pro-federal government initiatives.

It is not altogether clear that all current states would meet Senator Hayakawa's diversity standards. According to the U.S. Department of Labor (1991, 66), the state that had the greatest concentration of employment in any single occupational category in 1990 was Nevada, with 35.9 percent of its employment in services. (No breakdown is provided on the percentage of these jobs that were in tourism-resort-gambling industries and spin-off employment related to those jobs.) In this report (ibid.), the District had 33.1 percent of its employment concentrated in services and 31.1 percent in government. Nevada was also one of five states, including the District, having agricultural employment under 1 percent of total employment (ibid.). Additionally, Nevada was said by a witness (Raven-Hansen, 1992) at congressional hearings on D.C. statehood to be dependent almost completely on mining at the time of its admission to the Union in 1864; it was a "one horse" territory, he said.

To take another state that may have diversity "problems," Alaska and the District in 1990 had similar proportions of their employment in agriculture (.6 percent vs. .2 percent, respectively), manufacturing (3.9 percent vs. 3.2 percent), and construction (4.0 percent vs. 3.3 percent), while Alaska's proportion in government at 26.3 percent was not considerably less than the District's 31.1 percent. The District had a much greater proportion of its jobs in services (33.1 percent) than did Alaska (18.6 percent), while Alaska held the advantage in trade (17.6 percent vs. 10.3 percent) (ibid.). It would be difficult to say from these statistics which state was more diverse in its 1990 employment characteristics. However, the District's statistics did not include government spin-off employment data. As Best pointed out, if such jobs were considered, the District could indeed have an exceptionally low diversity quotient. In favorably reporting a D.C. statehood bill, the House District Committee (U.S. Congress 1987, 12) stated that

> [w]ithin the District of Columbia earnings by industry are very diverse and rank higher than many states in several categories. In finance, in insurance, [and in] real estate activities the District of Columbia ranks higher than 14 states. In hotel and lodging, it ranks higher than 27 states of the Union. In business services, it ranks higher than 41 states. . . . There are 1,800 trade associations in the District of Columbia; 18–20 million tourists visit the District of Columbia every year. The benefit to the District of Columbia from tourism is larger than the Federal payroll.

Regardless of how one interprets the above data, the concern likely persists among many that the federal presence would be too strong an influence in a newly created state. As Best (1984, 77) stated, D.C. "could come perilously close to being the state whose sole business is to govern, to control all the other states."

CONSTITUTIONAL QUESTIONS

During the period the District government is under supervision by a congressionally legislated control board, possibilities for self-government are nil, although prospects for an expansion of political rights are better. However, once financial solvency is restored, a wide variety of options for the future will be considered. The ultimate in independence and political rights is statehood, although this form carries with it constitutional questions. Such concerns were regarded as "unpersuasive" by one legal analyst (Schrag, 1990, 349–50); nonetheless, the same writer regarded those legal arguments as "politically weighty." The arguments would "provide good camouflage for a President" who wanted to oppose statehood (ibid.). However, Raven-Hansen (1991, 166), a statehood advocate, wrote: "No one who has troubled to explore the issues with an open mind could claim in good faith that the answer to the constitutional conundrum of D.C. statehood is clear and unequivocal. It does not have to be. It is enough that there is no clear constitutional barrier to statehood. . ." During hearings on D.C. statehood, the U.S. Department of Justice (Valentine 1992) outlined four principal "serious constitutional questions" about statehood. A counter-argument is also provided to each concern.

Legal Concern #1. During the Bush administration, the Justice Department (Valentine 1992, 89–94) testified that Congress may not permanently surrender its exclusive authority over the District without a constitutional amendment. Its representative (ibid., 92) stated: "Like a State, the district established as the seat of government pursuant to Article I, section 8, clause 17 became a fixed juridical entity under the Constitution. Congress cannot abolish that entity, even if in the process a new entity is created, absent a constitutional amendment" (ibid.).

Response. Raven-Hansen (1991, 169–70) pointed out that should the District become a state, the remaining federal enclave would be considered a much smaller version of the District. Congress would retain complete control over that enclave, and the constitutional requirements would thus be satisfied. Raven-Hansen noted two historical precedents where the District's size was changed by congressional legislation: (a) retrocession in 1846 to Virginia of what is now Alexandria and Arlington, an action which the U.S. Supreme Court declined the opportunity to reject in 1875; and (b) some changes in the District's southern boundaries in 1791. Thirteen of the original framers of the Constitution signed the latter law, including James Madison, and they evidently did not believe a constitutional amendment was required to effect the change.

Legal Concern #2. The Justice Department (Valentine 1992, 94–96) asserted that the Constitution, specifically the twenty-third amendment, recognized the District as a permanent entity. The amendment provides for the District to have three electors in presidential and vice presidential elections. To reduce the District to a small federal enclave with virtually no one living there would effectively nullify the twenty-third amendment, which only another constitutional amendment could do. Thus, as pointed out by Howard University law professor Adam Kurland (1993), no matter how liberally one interprets the Constitution, some amendment to it will be required if D.C. is to gain statehood. If D.C. were granted statehood by an act of Congress without first repealing the twenty-third amendment, then in essence Congress would be forcing the states to ratify the repeal, which in Kurland's (1993, 4) view, would "cheapen the constitutional amendment process." Kurland recommended that D.C. statehood be adopted contingent upon the states' approval of a repeal of the twenty-third amendment. Kurland (1993, 9) viewed such an approach as "constitutionally appropriate," although he did not argue that it was constitutionally mandated.

Response. Schrag (1991, 348–49) concluded that the twenty-third amendment empowered Congress to "direct" the manner in which electors from the District are to be selected and, in the words of the amendment, "enforce this article by appropriate legislation." Implementing legislation would determine whether the new federal enclave would have three electors. Therefore, should Congress approve D.C. statehood by simple majority vote, "Congress may use its discretionary powers under the twenty-third amendment and [the Constitution's] District Clause to unplug the now-obsolete machinery for organizing the District's electoral college" (Raskin 1993, 2). Subsequently, Congress "at its leisure" could propose repealing the twenty-third amendment, which would have no further utility (Schrag 1991, 349). American University law professor Jamin Raskin (1993, 1) predicted:

> Such a Constitutional amendment will sail through both houses of Congress and the states in a matter of weeks, if not days. There would be no political constituency to oppose it, since every state in the Union, including New Columbia, would oppose having a handful of people living in the environs of the White House casting three electoral votes.

Raskin (1993, 7) responded to Kurland's (1993) suggestion that D.C. statehood be made contingent upon repeal of the twenty-third amendment by noting that New Columbia would be the only state in American history to be admitted by constitutional amendment, which requires ratification by three-fourths of the states. Raskin (1993, 7) added: "Many states, perhaps most of them, never would have gotten into the Union with such steep odds." In any event, this may be a constitutional matter pertaining to the new federal enclave and not the state of New Columbia.

Legal Concern #3. The Justice Department (Valentine 1992, 96–97) stated that the consent of Maryland "might" have to be secured before the District could be admitted to the Union. The Justice Department (ibid., 9) stated that "[e]recting a new State or territory originally ceded for the purpose of establishing a seat of government would, at least arguably, nullify the cession." Maryland originally ceded the land that is now the District for purposes of creating a national capital.

Response. Raven-Hansen (1991, 177–83), in reviewing the wording of the cession, stated that the Maryland grant of land was unconditional. Even if the intent were implied that the land could only be used for purposes of creating a nation's capital, the fact that the land was used for that purpose for two hundred years "may" have constituted "substantial compliance" with the original intent (ibid., 182).

Legal Concern #4. The Justice Department expressed concern that statehood for the District would conflict with the original intent of the Constitution's framers, who clearly envisioned a nation's capital "to be located on neutral ground, outside the borders of any State, to avoid, in the words of Virginia's George Mason, 'a provincial tincture to ye Natl. deliberations'" (Valentine 1992, 98–99; United States Constitutional Convention [1787] 1966, 378). A federal district was devised as a means by which the federal government would remain independent of the states and, in turn, the states would remain independent of the federal government (Valentine 1992, 99). Statehood for the District "would forever change the balance between the States and the Federal Government the Framers so carefully struck in Philadelphia" (ibid.). Currently, no state has the power to prevent the federal government from performing its duties; however, the Justice Department had concern that a state of New Columbia surrounding a small federal enclave could excessively and independently influence such performance.

Response. Raven-Hansen (1991, 162–66) agreed with the "originalists" that the framers indeed intended that the district comprising the seat of government would be permanent, and, further, that the framers never intended this district to become a state. However, he observed that the district would not be eliminated; it would simply be shrunk to a small enclave of federal buildings. The remainder would then become the state of New Columbia (ibid., 163). The statehood concept is thus not inconsistent with federal intent, he argued. Moreover, Raven-Hansen (ibid., 173–74) argued that the federal government has developed sufficient power and authority so as not to be threatened by the proximity of any state.

Governor Bill Clinton (1991, 555), testifying as a presidential candidate at congressional hearings into D.C. statehood, agreed that a constitutional amendment would be required if "there were no Federal enclave left." However, if an enclave would remain, he felt D.C. statehood "could be handled legislatively." Clinton (1991, 556) stated his preference to handle the matter with legislation, since "the less we amend the Constitution the better." Clinton (1991, 550) acknowledged:

> I know there has been some disagreement over the intent of our country's framers . . . [but] for the life of me I can't imagine that the same people who fought to free the colonies from Great Britain ever wanted to disenfranchise over 600,000 Americans—a number greater than the population of three other states—just because they grew up in the shadow of the Capitol Dome, or because they came to Washington to serve their country.

Raven-Hansen (1991, 164) introduced an additional matter of original intent to this discussion. He stated that the framers failed to enfranchise future District residents because the framers "naively believed" that the residents' location contiguous to the national government would adequately substitute for electoral representation. In fact, James Madison believed that this contiguity would provide an advantage to District residents over the residents of the states because of the ease of access and influence such proximity would provide. Raven-Hansen (ibid.) wrote: "This quaint vision of representation by neighbors has not materialized." President Andrew Jackson stated in 1831 that the interests of the District "are much neglected," and that "the people [of the District] are almost afraid to present their grievances [to Congress], lest a body in which they are not represented and which feels little sympathy in their local relations should in its attempt to make laws for them do more harm than good" (ibid., citing Jackson's *Third Annual Message*).

OTHER LEGAL ISSUES: THE BUILDING HEIGHT LIMIT AND FEDERAL PAYMENT

Two other legal concerns were subjects of 1993 hearings in the House. First, how can the nation be assured that the District, if it achieves greater political independence, would not alter a congressionally imposed height limit of 160 feet on downtown buildings? And second, would a politically autonomous District still be entitled to a federal payment, which it currently receives in compensation for federal tax-exempt land and other federal tax restrictions?

The District, known for its "horizontality," has a "distinctive roominess, filled with direct light and fresh air by comparison with taller, darker, more crowded cities" (Medish 1993, 2–3). This special quality has been protected by a 1910 act of Congress. The District, if it ultimately achieved self-rule, would be unlikely to alter its essential character and jeopardize its tourist trade, but Americans have no guarantee that the District, free from direct congressional control, would not do so.

Medish (1993, 9–12) suggested a constitutionally sanctioned way to preserve the height limit. The Constitution's fifth amendment contains an eminent domain clause allowing for private property to be taken for public use with just compensation. A common means of aesthetic and historic preservation on the federal and state levels is taking or condemning property as a scenic easement. Just as scenic vistas and historic buildings are protected through eminent domain, the air rights above the current 160 foot height limit could similarly be preserved for all times by the federal government. There would be no need for compensation to be paid by the federal government to D.C. building owners, since the value of the buildings would not decrease merely by preserving the existing height limit.

Another legal question involves the federal payment. Economist Robert Ebel (1993, 6–7) advised that the government has provided statutory consent for the application of fifty-seven instances (from a 1979 study Ebel performed with the U.S. Advisory Commission on Intergovernmental Relations) of federal payment-in-lieu-of-tax or PILOT programs. Under the PILOT programs, the federal government compensates states and localities for federal ownership and use of land in these jurisdictions—for example, for national parks, forests, and wilderness areas. Ebel (1993) found it appropriate for the District to receive PILOT funds—with the formula to be developed by a transition commission—should D.C. statehood or some other form of greater self-rule be approved. In developing the formula's methodology, the commission "need look no further than to what Congress has already repeatedly done for other states and local governments in the United States" (Ebel 1993, 8).

TEN POLICY OPTIONS

Strengthened congressional control or statehood are only two of several potential policy outcomes for the District's structure. Public opinion will help shape the policy ultimately chosen by Congress. V.O. Key, Jr. (1961, 14) defined public opinion as "those opinions held by private persons which governments find it prudent to heed. Governments may be propelled toward action or inaction by such opinion; in other instances, they may ignore it."

The District's political structure is an obvious example of an issue that government has found easy to ignore, perhaps because public opinion on the issue has not formed. Key noted (ibid., 557) that "[m]ass opinion is not self-generating; in the main, it is responsive to the cues, the proposals, and the visions propagated by the political activists." Since national political leaders have not made D.C.'s political structure a prominent issue, it is easy to understand why Americans have not formed thoughtful opinions on the subject. The lack of representation for the District in the Congress has reduced leadership opportunities to spotlight this issue for the public, for such elected leaders would be the ones most likely to educate the public. This lack of voting representation also lessens the likelihood of legislative trade-offs that could improve D.C.'s political status in exchange for other concessions.

The strategies to achieve greater levels of self-rule are not fully formed, either among D.C. elected officials or D.C. residents. As Schrag (1990, 351) stated, "Gradual reform through incremental improvements may be much easier to achieve than statehood, but it may make the achievement of statehood impossible." That is, by removing some onerous restrictions on the District, the drive toward statehood could be diverted. Schrag went on to state (1990, 351, 193): "It is possible, of course, to make exactly the opposite argument, that statehood would become more likely after a period in which America became accustomed to a fully self-governing District of Columbia, particularly one that voted in Congress." After such equivocation, Schrag favored the statehood strategy; nonetheless, this is the type of dilemma D.C. may face once a financial structure is devised that assures viability.

This research reviewed various structural options with focus group participants. These ten options are not mutually exclusive and include various combinations of voting rights and self-rule authority:

1. *The Status Quo.* Once the financial control board concludes its work, the current form of government, termed limited home rule, would continue, with a nonvoting delegate in the U.S. House.

2. *Revocation of Limited Home Rule Authority.* Edwards and Keating (1995, ix) wrote: "After twenty years of attempted 'home rule' in the District of Columbia, it's time to admit that the experiment has failed." These authors (ibid., xvii) believe that generous government schemes designed to help the poor destroyed individual responsibility and economic opportunity by creating dependent populations. Their blame is unequivocal: "Bloated, plodding government brought about the decline of Washington, D.C."—not Congress, D.C.'s successful neighbors, "the establishment," or anyone else except the electorate who voted the squandering public officials into office (ibid., xiii, xvii). Representative Tom DeLay (R–Tex.), who went on to become majority whip in the Republican Congress, held this same view in 1989: "Let's either revoke or drastically restructure home rule—let's finally help the unfortunate residents of this festering liberal hellhole" (Schrag 1990, 345, n.167). Home rule revocation could be complete or partial—for example, the congressionally legislated financial control board could continue indefinitely.

Thus, while D.C. residents' political status is much lower than that of other Americans, even this tenuous democratic thread can be snipped at any moment. For example, the head of the House Appropriations D.C. Subcommittee, James T. Walsh (R–N.Y.) (*Washington Post*, January 27, 1995, B3), warned: "Home Rule is contingent on the submission of a balanced budget to Congress," strong words from a member of a body that had not balanced the federal budget for a quarter century. Nonetheless, D.C. residents have grown accustomed to such threats. Any of 535 overseers may become perturbed over the District's real or perceived misconduct (they are seldom distressed over the nation's mistreatment of D.C. and other urban centers). If enough members are angered, D.C. residents could find their local rights to be as barren as their status in Congress.

3. *Downsizing to a Municipal Government.* The District is currently a state-county-city form of government without many typical state resources (see chapter 2). Instead of attempting to expand the District's resources (e.g., through nonresident income taxation or repeal of other special congressional tax exemptions), perhaps the District should be nothing else but a city government. The federal government could assume responsibility for D.C.'s prison, its mental health facilities, its courts, and various state licensing and regulatory functions. Other current state functions could be terminated altogether, including the university, law school, hospital, and nursing homes. Perhaps the federal government could assume greater responsibility for welfare and medical costs.

Such downsizing would place the District on sounder financial footing. Downsizing could severely limit future statehood possibilities, and it is a favored option of many who oppose all but the weakest forms of self-rule. However, downsizing would not necessarily compromise D.C. residents' goals of achieving voting rights in Congress, which could be implemented with a constitutional amendment. Downsizing, however, would involve federal government assumption or termination of hundreds of millions of dollars of services against the wishes of D.C. residents' elected leaders—or many services could be contracted out to the state of Maryland.

4. *Gradual Improvements.* Much of the District's political fate hinges on how well it performs in managing its financial crisis of the mid-1990s. If it performs well by achieving balanced budgets in cooperation with the control board, the District's self-government status could be gradually improved by Congress through enhancement of the District's authority in several areas:

(a) *Full Budgetary Autonomy.* Currently, the District's annual budgets are recommended to the District of Columbia Council by the mayor and revised and adopted by the Council after extensive public hearings, debate, and compromise. Then the budget, if not modified by the control board, goes to Congress for additional public hearings and potential further revision (Harris 1989; Weaver and Harris 1989; Schrag 1990, 340–342). During the congressional review process, numerous appropriation riders have been attached to the budget by the House and Senate that have forbidden or required the District to take specific actions (Harris 1989, 73–78; Schrag 1990, 355–71). As Schrag (1990, 340) stated, "For purposes of budget approval, Congress treats the District as though it were a federal agency rather than a local government."

By eventually granting the District budget autonomy, the District would be treated as if it were a state government. Congress provides the District with a federal payment, amounting in fiscal year 1994 to $647.9 million or 19 percent of the budget. Provision of a federal payment carries with it, in the minds of some, congressional budget review responsibility (Schrag 1990, 341). Nonetheless, this payment could be considered merely as compensation for federal tax-exempt land and other congressionally imposed tax exemptions, such as the restriction on taxation of nonresident income, as well as compensation for services provided by the District to the federal government rather than as a "subsidy," as some analysts deem it (ibid.). Moreover, P.L. 102–102, adopted in 1991, provided for a formula-based federal payment; authorizations for fiscal years 1993 through 1995 were based on a fixed percentage (24 percent) of audited local revenue levels. Such a predictable formula, if implemented on a long-term basis, complements the concept of budgetary autonomy. The congressional review role is diminished when a formula is implemented; Congress need only appropriate the authorized level provided by the previously adopted formula and leave the budgeting to the District.

(**b**) *Legislative Authority.* Legislation is enacted by the D.C. Council, usually after well-attended and televised public hearings, extensive debate, and two votes. The enacted legislation, if not overturned by the control board, then proceeds to Congress, which may repeal the statute by joint resolution—a process that also requires presidential concurrence (Schrag 1990, 328–29). No other city or state is required to present its legislation to Congress for approval (ibid., 329).

Congress has retained full control over the District's local laws, including initiation of legislation, in three areas: criminal law, criminal procedure, and treatment of prisoners (ibid.). Moreover, Congress has expressly denied the District certain other legislative powers. The District cannot tax nonresident income, cannot reorganize the structure or jurisdiction of the courts, and cannot revise the congressionally imposed height limit on D.C. buildings (ibid.). The latter restriction is sometimes viewed (Standen 1992, 167) as adding to the amount of territory in the District that is effectively controlled by the federal government. Land devoted to the federal and foreign governments plus various other land exempted by acts of Congress comprise over 51 percent of the total land in the District, (D.C. Office of Policy and Program Evaluation 1991, 93), even without adding anything extra for the federal height restrictions.

Greater legislative autonomy involves removing or lessening these restrictions. If restrictions against nonresident income taxation were removed, then potentially the federal payment could be eliminated or sharply reduced as well (Farber 1990, 25). Even if a nonresident income tax were imposed at only a fraction of the rates applicable to District residents, enough revenue could be yielded to offset much of the federal payment, even allowing for the likelihood that Maryland and Virginia would tax the income of District residents working in those jurisdictions as well (computed from D.C. Office of Policy and Program Evaluation 1991, 121). To the extent a federal payment is retained, as a federal Payment-in-Lieu-of-Taxation (PILOT) program, the burdens on the treasuries of Maryland and Virginia would be lessened (e.g., the amount of the nonresident tax would be lowered to 2 percent and consequently the tax credits granted to Maryland and Virginia residents when they paid income taxes to D.C. would also be lower).

(c) *Judicial Nomination Authority.* Currently, the president of the United States nominates the District's state judges and the U.S. Senate confirms them (Schrag 1990, 342–43). This responsibility could also be turned over to the District as if it were a state.

(d) *Control over Criminal Prosecution.* Except for the District, every state and city selects the officials who prosecute local crimes (ibid., 343). In the District, the U.S. Attorney holds this responsibility in what Schrag (ibid.) terms an "insult" to the District. In another measure of gradual improvement, the District could be placed on the same status in this regard as other states and cities.

All of these gradual improvements imply trust by Congress of D.C. residents and their elected leaders—trust that is assumed for other citizens across America but which must be built in D.C.

5. *Nominal Statehood: Voting Representation in Congress.* The District could be granted full voting authority in Congress (one representative and two senators) without the need to create a new state (Harris 1989, 80). This option is sometimes referred to as nominal statehood (Best 1984, 25–62).

This reform could be accomplished, according to one legal analyst (Schrag 1990, 325), with congressional legislation and without a constitutional amendment. However, another analyst (Best 1984, 25–62) asserted that such a measure may be challenged as unconstitutional since it violates article 5 of the Constitution which provides that "no State, without its consent shall be deprived of its equal Suffrage in the Senate." Diluting a state's power by adding one or two senators from a "nominal state" could be interpreted as affecting equal suffrage, according to Best (ibid.).

A "symbolic compromise" to this option would be to provide for one representative and one senator (Harris 1989, 80; Schrag 1990, 325–26). The measure could be made more politically palatable by simultaneously enacting a modest increase in the number of U.S. representatives beyond the current 435, so that states would not lose power in the next round of reapportionment (Weaver and Harris 1989, 46). D.C. Councilmember Kevin Chavous (1993) commented to this writer that a "symbolic compromise" of one senator and one representative amounted to fulfillment of the clause of the U.S. Constitution (article 1, section 1; subsequently repealed by the fourteenth amendment) that allowed slaves to be counted as three-fifths of a person for the purpose of representation. Chavous said, "It shows that for purposes of representation in the federal system that we count more than animals but not as much as the other Americans. We are in the middle somewhere." Indeed, if one were to assign the relative value of senators as two points and representatives as one point, then D.C. would have exactly three-fifths of a share in the federal system if the "symbolic compromise" of one senator and one representative were implemented. On the other hand, this three-fifths "slavery-level representation" would be an infinite improvement over the current zero-fifths.

The lowest level of representation in Congress would allow the District's nonvoting delegate to attain full status in Congress as a voting representative. This measure would give D.C. residents greater political standing than held by residents of American territories and is thought by some to be an answer to the "taxation without representation" question. It would not provide D.C. residents with one or two powerful senators. Consequently, the policy has bipartisan appeal.

6. *Retrocession to Maryland.* Another option is retrocession of the District of Columbia to Maryland, which in 1788 ceded the land to the federal government for the purpose of creating the nation's capital (Schrag 1990, 318). Best (1984, 63–83) regarded retrocession as a constitutionally valid option to nominal statehood. Retrocession is also preferable to full statehood in Best's view (1984, 71–77) because "[t]he District lacks the political attributes of statehood: diversity of interests and financial independence" (ibid., 72). Representative Dana Rohrabacher (R–Ca.) (1991, 45) observed that adding the city of "Washington, Maryland" would "hardly be overwhelming to Maryland," as it would constitute only the fifth most populous jurisdiction (counting cities and counties) in Maryland.

In 1990, former Maryland Governor Schaefer indicated that "he would have no trouble with D.C. becoming a part of Maryland" (*Washington Post* February 26, 1990, A6). However, as Schrag (1990, 319–20) pointed out, a governor cannot act unilaterally to enlarge his or her state. Retrocession would require an act of the state legislature. In a 1990 survey (Schrag 1990,

319), 82 percent of the Maryland state delegates and 92 percent of state senators who responded indicated that they would reject retrocession even if Congress provided Maryland with a substantial subsidy.

Republican congressional leaders have stated their intention to explore retrocession of D.C. to Maryland, to allow D.C. residents to vote in Maryland, or to have Maryland control the District's social services and motor vehicle registration functions on a contractual basis. These ruminations prompted Maryland Governor Parris Glendening to say, "I think the District of Columbia's financial problems ought to be clearly assumed by the sixth district of Georgia," referring to House Speaker Gingrich's district.

While it is clear that Maryland does not want the District, there is also the matter of the wishes of the District residents, who have already voted for statehood (ibid., 319, n.49). Perhaps the main policy options, after much public discussion, should be placed before the voters of both jurisdictions (ibid., 352). The District's elected shadow senator Jesse Jackson termed retrocession a "Bantustan concept" (ibid., 319, n. 50)—that is, placement of a majority black enclave into a white state. Whether most District residents would be concerned about dilution of their local power and whether they could identify with the customs, traditions, and practices of Maryland are matters that only a public referendum could likely clarify with certainty. Raskin (1990, 439, n.102) contended that the populations of Maryland and the District are both "fiercely and justifiably proud of their own historic political communities and boundaries," and retrocession is therefore "probably not politically feasible."

7. *Enable District Residents to Vote in Maryland.* Under former Representative Stan Parris's (R–Va.) National Capital Civil Rights Registration Act of 1990, the District government's status would remain as is, while District residents would be empowered to vote in Maryland congressional elections (Raskin 1990, 438–40). As an "outspoken foe of District autonomy" (ibid., 439), Parris's proposal was not well received by District leaders at the time of its introduction (Schrag 1970, 327–28, n.87). Nonetheless, one writer sympathetic to statehood (Raskin 1990, 439) stated that the Parris plan "may offer the best intermediate tactical step to full statehood" for the District.

An advantage of the Parris plan, according to Raskin (ibid.), is that District residents would have voting representation in Congress and thus have "real leverage . . . while preserving whatever amount of integrity remains with their local government." Under this plan, D.C. residents could vote in Maryland elections and run for the House and Senate as quasi-Maryland residents. Since persons campaigning for U.S. Senate seats could become partly dependent on District resident votes, District residents may be able to trade their support in exchange for a pledge from the prospective senator to work for improvements in D.C.'s political status.

8. *The Panacea of No Representation, No Taxes.* There is a flip side to the demand for representation on the grounds that D.C. residents pay their fair share of federal taxes: since few want to give D.C. residents full representation, then it is only fair to remove their federal income tax burden as well. D.C. would join Puerto Rico by having commonwealth status. How much is congressional representation and self-rule worth to a D.C. resident? And how would a Maryland or Montana citizen respond to the same deal? An individual could be tempted to go for it, but the cumulative effect of the "no taxation, no representation" deal, were a majority of Americans to accept it, would be a loss of democratic rights. This calamity would place all of America in the same situation that D.C. residents experience—they would be on the outside looking in to someone else's government, wondering what it is going to do to them next.

Thus, while the deal is absurd from the viewpoint of political rights, it is no more absurd than the level of rights D.C. residents now hold. The concept makes economic sense. As George Washington University President Stephen Trachtenberg wrote (*Washington Post*, December 4, 1994, C4), "Mismanagement aside, the D.C. government has been placed in the impossible situation of having responsibilities without the commensurate authority or resources to meet them." If D.C. were a tax-free zone, the reduction in overall tax burden would inevitably attract prodigious new investment, stimulate jobs, expand the long-term tax base, and enhance D.C.'s economic environment and quality of life, Trachtenberg said (ibid.). Edmonds and Keating (1995, xi, xii) termed the notion a "magic potion" that would re-energize D.C. virtually overnight. They envisioned "a truly multi-racial and economically diverse society that attracts the middle class as well as the poor."

The District would become the nation's most successful empowerment zone and would experience the ultimate in supply-side economics. The District, now abandoned by many, would suddenly become America's most desired place to live and to locate one's business. The District would have the opportunity to increase its local tax rates because of the absence of federal income taxation. But the increase in jobs, income, and property values would undoubtedly enable local tax rates to be lowered over time. The District would gain the resources to confront its socioeconomic problems at their roots. The policy is as close to a panacea for the District as can be imagined.

The only problem is that the rest of America would have to compensate for the District's tax exemptions. America's resentment toward the District, already sky-high, would go through the ionosphere if Americans paid a tax increase for this experiment. Yet many claim the District is already a net drain on federal taxpayers. If supply-side remedies are therapeutic (and not voodoo economics), then halting the drain would benefit U.S. taxpayers before long.

The proposal has an added benefit for those D.C. residents who prefer retention of congressional control over D.C. bills and budgets. Under the tax-free zone plan, such D.C. citizens not only have reduced overall tax liability but continued freedom from local self-governance—the best of both worlds from their viewpoint. Over a longer term, however, the economic momentum ensuing from a tax-free zone could produce the population and economic stature needed to win self-government.

Should D.C. residents gain partial representation in Congress (e.g., a voting representative but no senators), then one could rationally argue for partial federal taxation. Reduced federal tax rates could prove as much of a supply-side elixir as no federal taxation at all and would (a) partly compensate D.C. residents for their unequal political standing compared to other Americans, and (b) avoid much of the hysteria that would ensue if D.C. residents, who already are thought to feed from various federal troughs, were absolved of all federal income tax responsibility.

To true believers in the District's cause, all such deals are akin to trinkets for Manhattan. Charles Cassell, a cofounder of D.C.'s statehood party a quarter century ago, remarked to this writer (May 27, 1995) that if the devil offered people fame and riches, asking their souls in return, most would ask, "What's the catch?" Cassell was not willing to sell out so easily, but he is correct in thinking that most D.C. residents would gleefully take the deal. It's an obvious choice for a D.C. resident who has long lacked basic democratic rights in America without receiving any compensation.

9. *The Beltway State.* Another option, developed by the late D.C. Council Chairman John A. Wilson in an interview (1993), and by the Harrisburg focus group, would be to create an "inside the Beltway" state. Geographically, the highway ringing the District encompasses the affluent Maryland and Virginia suburbs of the District as well as the District itself. "Inside the Beltway" is a mythical land characterized by its residents' obsession with politics and policy to such an extent that they are thought out of touch with real American life in the vast continent "beyond the Beltway." As long as this state of mind exists, why not go the rest of the way and make it a state? Of course the main reason for not doing so is practical. Article 4, section 3 of the Constitution requires consent of the state legislatures when a new state is to be formed using parts of other states' lands. If Maryland is likely to resist

widening its borders to accept the District, then it is even more likely to resist sacrificing its affluent suburbs to the Beltway state, as would Virginia—unless an enormous payoff could be concocted to satisfy the remaining residents of Maryland and Virginia. While one cannot wish away overwhelming practical difficulties, it could make sense to create a state with far greater population, land area, and economic resources than the District now possesses.

10. *Statehood.* The primary advantage of statehood is that "it provides the District with political rights fully equal to those of residents of the existing states" (Schrag 1990, 345), in contrast with several other options which offer improvement but not full equality. Moreover, statehood assures that these rights would be "permanent rather than subject to reversal when the political coalition that had produced reform began to dissolve" (ibid.), as could be the case with respect to some of the incremental reforms. Further, D.C. statehood is not dependent upon the actions of any other states that would have to agree to change its borders, as would apply in retrocession or formation of a "Beltway state." Thus, statehood is the most politically pragmatic of those options that provide for equal political standing of D.C. residents with other Americans.

Statehood requires different conditions than those prevailing in recent years; that is, it assumes D.C. financial stability with a structure that assures long-term economic independence from the federal government. The original home rule deal of 1973, which required the provision of state and county services with only municipal resources from which to draw, would have to be junked. D.C. statehood also requires evolution of a political climate that is empathetic to political equality for District residents.

THE CRITERIA FOR STATEHOOD

Congress has articulated three standards for admission of a territory or other entity to statehood (U.S. Congress 1959, 7):

> (a) that the inhabitants of the proposed new State are imbued with and sympathetic toward the principles of democracy as exemplified in the American form of government;
> (b) that a majority of the electorate desire statehood;
> (c) that the proposed new State has sufficient population and resources to support State government and to provide its share of the cost of the Federal Government.

Relative to the first criterion, involving a commitment to democracy, Raskin (1990, 440) asked, "[W]ho could question the democratic devotion of more than 600,000 citizens who continue to pay federal taxes, fight and die for their country, and obey national laws, but in 1990 have no voting representative in Congress and no real powers of self-government?" Raskin (ibid.) added that "[t]he real question to be posed is not whether the citizens of the District are committed to democracy, but whether the rest of the country is in fact committed to democracy for the citizens of the District."

The second criterion has been at least partly answered in the District's voting booths, when in 1980 District voters by a 60–to–40 percent margin approved an initiative calling for a constitutional convention and, in 1982, by a 53–to–47 percent margin, approved the state constitution resulting from the convention's work (Schrag 1985, 3; Schrag 1990, 351, n. 195). Schrag (1990, 351), however, pointed out that neither vote necessarily could be construed as "a *strategic choice* in favor of statehood or as a genuine, deep, and continued commitment to a new political order" (Schrag's emphasis), since alternatives such as retrocession to Maryland or gradual improvements in political rights were not presented to voters.

The third criterion is open to considerable interpretation and debate. The District's population size, while relatively small, does not seem to be an impediment to statehood. Moreover, District residents' per capita federal tax payments would indicate that the District provides its share of federal government revenues. The point of contention is whether the District has the resources to support a state government without major restructuring of its financial authority. Best (1984, 76) argued that "the entire population [of the District] is dependent upon the federal payment, a direct grant annually given to the District by the federal government." Best (ibid.) pointed out that this payment amounted to 28 percent of the District's budget in 1978, a proportion that had shrunk to a still sizable 19 percent by fiscal year 1994. Jesse Jackson (1990, 308), who was elected in 1990 by District voters as a "shadow senator," argued that the federal payment "is for services rendered [by the District government to the federal government] and in lieu of taxes that are not being paid by the Federal Government on 41 percent of the land it occupies in the District." If one were to take the value of these services, tax exemptions, and restrictions, then according to Jackson (ibid.), "[T]he District is, in fact, subsidizing the Federal Government." The District government has calculated the value of the federally imposed tax exemptions (see table 2.5, chapter 2) and placed the federal tax exemptions and restrictions at triple the magnitude of the federal payment received by the District.

In a report to the D.C. Commission on Budget and Financial Priorities, Farber (1990, 3, 11–13, 25) estimated that the fiscal effects of statehood would produce a net gain to the District of $323 million. Thus, statehood could prove a vehicle that enhances financial independence of the District government from the federal government.

Smith (1974, 277) wrote:

> The argument that the new state could not support itself is a familiar one in the history of statehood movements. It was one of the major reasons cited for opposition to Alaskan statehood. Yet it has been repeatedly true that new states have been aided towards self-sufficiency through special grants of monies and, more dramatically, immensely valuable lands. Statehood, in fact, may be considered almost a prerequisite to financial self-sufficiency for units of the federal system. In order to be financially equal, one must first be politically equal.

Smith (ibid.) noted that Alaska, for example, received 103 million acres of federal lands, $28.5 million in transitional grants, and 90 percent of the proceeds from federal mines. Washington, D.C. contains numerous parcels of land now held by the federal government.

Raskin (1994) noted that congressional debates over the admission of Nevada, New Mexico, Arizona, Alaska, Florida, and Mississippi were "filled with predictions that economic underdevelopment would make it impossible for them to be self-sustaining." In testifying before the Senate, Raskin (1994) reminded the committee chair, John Glenn, that Ohio's territorial governor, prior to his state's admission, observed that "[s]uch a multitude of indigent people are ill qualified to form a constitution and govern for themselves." Raskin (1994) noted that in every case Congress reiterated its support for its decision of July 13, 1787, in which it unanimously rejected a wealth requirement for new states.

Should the District reach the point where statehood is once again considered, transitional help could be needed, not necessarily for the people of the District, but for the state governments of Maryland and Virginia. Once the District gains taxing authority for nonresident income earned within the District's borders (as the fifty current states have authority to do with respect to income earned within their borders), the state treasuries of Maryland and Virginia would be depleted to a degree. This is because those states would give a credit on the home state's income taxes for taxes paid by those state residents to the state of New Columbia. To avoid this tax shock, federal transitional help to Maryland and Virginia may be needed.

Even without such federal transitional help, however, the tax rates in those states—including financing of the new income tax credits—would not have to climb to levels currently experienced by District residents. The current D.C. tax levels are disproportionately high in major part because the District does not presently have access to nonresident income earned within its borders. The question becomes where to place, or to disperse, the economic hardship. The trend has been to give D.C. the problems and bemoan its mismanagement of them.

Smith (1974, 277) noted that the new state would also benefit by added leverage in Congress: "One of the basic traits of Congress is a reluctance to undercut the special interests of its members." Smith added (ibid.) that it would be hard to conceive of Congress deliberately alienating the District's senators and representatives over a dispute of, say, $20 million in the federal payment. Currently, Congress has no pangs of conscience when its oversight alienates D.C. residents.

Bond analyst Claire Wadlington (1992, 43–44) testified before Congress that the fifty states tend to have stronger credit ratings than do cities because they have greater predictability of revenues and greater control over their sources of revenue. The District could achieve a higher bond rating as a state than it has as a city, a prospect that could help reduce financing costs and enhance self-reliance. Standard & Poor's (1993, 54) elaborated on the District's financial prospects under statehood:

> This new independence could enhance the credit worthiness of the state or detract from it, depending on how it is used. With sound planning, New Columbia might be able to sustain an atmosphere conducive to long-term economic growth. The revenue-raising flexibility of a state could give it tools to add to or diversify its revenue sources, thus strengthening the revenue mix and developing a firmer, more predictable base. . . . One revenue enhancement that would be possible for a state is a tax on the income of non-residents. . . . The new state probably would use this tax in conjunction with the revision of other taxes to encourage economic activity and balance the tax burden of its own residents.

Standard & Poor's (ibid.) cautioned that the District's federal payment "would be subject to question" under statehood, and its bond rating as a state would depend on resolution of this question, along with its pension liability outlook.

Much of the District's huge pension liability was accrued during pre-home rule years under direct federal control, and these funds could be subject to renegotiation with Congress. The D.C. Commission on Budget and Financial Priorities (1990, xi–xii), known as the "Rivlin Commission," stated that the federal government is only contributing 25 percent of funding of the pension liability that accrued during pre-home rule years, leaving the District to pay over $150 million a year for "a liability it did not incur." The Commission (1994, 14) called the inherited $2.0 billion tab at the end of 1974, having an estimated $5.4 billion value in 1994, "the single largest imminent threat to the District's budget." The Commission (1990, xii) also noted that "the federal government forced the District to assume an over $300 million operating deficit" when home rule began in 1975. The Commission (ibid.) noted that federal decisions clearly caused the deficit in the pre-home rule years. Federal assumption of its pre-home rule financial responsibilities is a practical option under any scenario.

Thus restoration of financial viability for the District would be a precondition to statehood, and statehood itself would help the District meet Congress' third criterion of self-sufficiency. Patsy Mink (1987, 37–52), former Hawaiian congressman, described Hawaii's substantial economic growth ensuing from statehood, including tourism, construction, commercial enterprise, and population. Mink (ibid., 48) indicated that statehood advocates feared that Hawaii would lose its territorial "glamour" once it became a state, but the effect was "quite the opposite." Mink (ibid.) thought that the District could experience a similarly favorable result.

Because of the District's high poverty rates and related socioeconomic problems, as well as the extensive proportions of tax-exempt land in its borders, the District is vulnerable to charges that it cannot sustain itself independently and must therefore remain under federal control. However, Jackson (1991, 82) pointed out that President Bush promoted statehood for Puerto Rico, even though that island's 1990 per capita income was approximately $6,000 per year, compared to the nation's $19,000 and the District's $24,000.

4

The Role of Race in Determining D.C.'s Political Status

> *"You ache with the need to convince yourself that you do exist in the real world, that you're a part of all of the sound and anguish, and you strike out with your fists, you curse and you swear to make them recognize you. And, alas, it's seldom successful."*
>
> Ralph Ellison, *Invisible Man*, 1952

Jack is an insurance agent residing and working in Maryland. His neighbor, Julia, commutes into D.C. where she is a clerk-typist for the U.S. Department of Agriculture. Cynthia, also an insurance agent, is a D.C. resident who works in Jack's office in Maryland. Bob, a clerk-typist with Julia in Agriculture, is a D.C. resident. All pay federal taxes and none is particularly political. Why do Jack and Julia have the usual American political rights, while Cynthia and Bob lack them?

This writer has been a resident of the District of Columbia for twenty years, in five of the District's eight political wards, and has been heavily involved in D.C.'s self-government discussions the entire time. From this experience, it can be stated with assurance that most black residents of the District routinely assume that race—that is, the fact that D.C. has nearly three-quarters African Americans and other minorities in its population—is the unspoken, underlying, yet predominant reason why the District has not achieved equal political standing with other Americans. Many whites involved in racially integrated living and working situations also adopt this opinion. However, many white D.C. residents who lack racially integrated lifestyles have been more reluctant to accept an explicit connection between race and an unequal political standing for D.C. residents.

Americans in general may be aghast that anyone could target race as a reason why some Americans today would be politically diminished. Consequently, other reasons—such as the wisdom of the founding fathers or D.C.'s irresponsible leaders—are offered as rational reasons behind the exclusion. Many whites envision a race-neutral society, in D.C. and elsewhere, as an achievable goal—if only liberals would stop seeing race as a factor in every political discussion. Many blacks, on the other hand, cannot figure out when or how race became irrelevant.

After reviewing the history of D.C.'s drive for political equality and statehood, civil rights historian and *Washington Post* writer Juan Williams (1993, 16) observed:

> But underneath all the hoopla, then and now and maybe forevermore, is the question of race, and white people's fear that black people—poor and poorly educated for most of the city's history—will gain power over political life in America's capital. It is that racial antagonism that feeds today's consensus among black Washingtonians that statehood is a civil rights issue and as such is a must for the District.

It proved impossible to locate a recently published statement advocating denial of equal political treatment for the District on the basis of race, although U.S. Attorney General John Mitchell's reference in the Nixon era to the District government as the "Amos and Andy Cab Company" (Jaffe and Sherwood 1994, 100–01) captures the flavor of some critics. Jaffe and Sherwood (1994, 24–25) stated that "it's impossible to dismiss the fact that raw discrimination against blacks was for years at the root of Congress' relationship with the District of Columbia." As an example, these writers (ibid.) unearthed an 1890 quotation from Alabama Senator John Tyler Morgan explaining why Congress had removed self-government from D.C. residents:

> Now the historical fact is simply this, that the negroes came into this District from Maryland and Virginia and other places . . . and they took possession of a certain part of the political power of this District . . . and there was but one way to get out—so Congress thought, this able committee thought—and that was to deny the right of suffrage entirely to every human being in the District . . . in order to get rid of this load of negro suffrage that was flooded in upon them.

These writers (ibid., 23–30) cite several other racist remarks over the years, including those of Senator Theodore Bilbo of Mississippi, chair of the District Committee, who proposed shipping blacks out of the District and back to Africa or placing blacks in a "self-liquidating" stadium. Bilbo used his chairmanship to deny funding of efforts to ameliorate poverty among blacks (ibid., 28).

Of historical interest is a 1945 statement by Jesse Sutter on behalf of the Citizens Joint Committee on National Representation for the District of Columbia at a congressional hearing on national representation for District residents (Noyes 1951, 173). Sutter stated that "[t]he objection most frequently raised against the proposal to give the people of the District representative participation in the National Government" is one that is "seldom heard above a whisper." This objection is "based on the theory that the Negro is not fit to be the political equal of the white citizen." Sutter added that continuing to deny the District representation "would mean that three white voters must be denied the vote to keep one Negro from voting," since at the time the District's ratio of whites-to-blacks was three-to-one. Sutter curiously added, "Surely that would be carrying race prejudice to an illogical extent." Sutter's implication is that race prejudice that merely denies voting rights for blacks may be acceptable, but it becomes unreasonable once white votes are denied in the process. Another writer of that era (B.M. McKelway in the foreword to Noyes 1951, 13) reviewed obstacles to national representation for the District and said, "Many, though not all, members of Congress are skeptical still of the Negro vote, and hostile to his right to vote." Jenkins (1993, 20) commented on the historical conflict between D.C. and Congress:

> But for many District residents, even the subtlest congressional involvement in local matters hits a raw nerve, exposing passions rooted in history. Many D.C. citizens recall a time when southern lawmakers who opposed integration used the District as a convenient target. Even today, race is seldom far below the surface when city and national leaders clash.

Whether resistance to voting rights or self-government for the District is at least partially racially motivated, as it was said to be for decades in the case of Hawaii, is difficult to ascertain. Such difficulty should not necessarily produce dismissal of this hypothesis. In their studies of Americans' evolving racial attitudes, Hochschild and Herk (1990, 321) concluded: "The point is not that whites want blacks to have a depressed quality of life—quite the contrary. The point is that some combination of structural obstacles, history, and the aggregation of white views combine to inhibit" the achievement of improved life chances for minorities, "despite what whites want." The authors (ibid., 320) point to "a pattern of resistance in a pluralist political system with many veto points." This pattern "stymies every policy move beyond tokenism, even though many (most?) individual whites might not object to a given policy initiative." It is not out of the question to link inertia in the District's political rights movement to such complexities in societal thought.

Many D.C. blacks are insulted when they hear comments that D.C. residents are not ready for self-rule or representation in Congress. They feel as ready as any other Americans and tend to interpret such comments as part of the ageless question of who will control this minority-populated jurisdiction. Election data from 1980 help to assess whether one's race affects one's preference for congressional rule or self-rule over D.C. laws and budgets. In 1980, Ward 3, the area of the District to the west of Rock Creek Park, was 91 percent white in its adult population and had a median household income that was 55 percent above that of the District as a whole (D.C. Office of Policy and Program Evaluation 1991, 44). This ward voted against the initiative to establish a statehood constitutional convention by a 38–to–62 percent margin. In 1980, none of the other seven wards of the District had a majority white population; these wards voted in favor of the initiative by a 66–to–34 percent margin. The District-wide vote in favor of the initiative was 60–to–40 (D.C. Board of Elections and Ethics 1980, election returns by ward).

A *Washington Post* (February 20, 1994, C5) poll further delineated the racial split. District-wide, 51 percent of D.C. residents polled favored D.C. statehood, compared to 41 percent opposed (and 8 percent "don't know"). However, D.C. white residents opposed D.C. statehood by a 39–to–55 percent margin, while D.C. black residents favored statehood by a 58–to–33 percent margin. Thus, D.C. blacks (by definition of statehood) favored self-government, while D.C. whites seemed less inclined.

A year later, after revelations of the District government's financial collapse, D.C. residents opposed statehood (by a 45–to–48 percent margin) for the first time ever in a *Washington Post* (March 5, 1995, A17) poll. However, even in this latter poll, black D.C. residents still favored statehood by a 51–to–42 percent margin, while D.C. whites opposed statehood by 36–to–57 percent. The *Post* poll also indicated that D.C. whites favored the congressionally legislated financial control board by a 70–to–26 percent margin, although D.C. blacks opposed the legislation 31–to–62 percent. One point of unison in the poll was the overwhelming opposition by both races to permanent congressional control over D.C.

The O.J. Simpson trial taught America how differently the races can view the same issue; only 34 percent of whites agreed with the verdict and 49 percent thought the largely black jury ignored the evidence, while 85 percent of blacks agreed with the verdict and only 13 percent of blacks thought the jury ignored the evidence (*Washington Post*, October 8, 1995, A34). Each "side" in the debate thought the other incoherent or worse. A point that is assumed as rational, valid, and objective to some may be the subject of hot dispute among many members of another racial group. Columnist Bill Rice (*Washington Post*, November 27, 1994), who wrote that the District could not manage all of its state functions with current resources and needed to downsize to a true municipal government, observed:

> Shedding the statehood fantasy, never a very deep one judging by the low level of popular emotion it evoked, gets us out from under an issue that needlessly divided us, antagonized many on Capitol Hill and angered our suburban neighbors.

If everyone would simply unite behind the prevailing (white) viewpoint regarding D.C.'s self-government aspirations, surely antagonism would be reduced. It may be correct to assume that statehood has evoked little support in D.C., but before solidifying that conclusion qualitative research is needed. An exploration of black D.C. residents' views on voting rights and self-rule may well tap into deeper support for all forms of equal political standing than may be assumed in white communities.

When columnist Richard Cohen referred to D.C. as a banana republic (*Washington Post*, April 6, 1995), when Mary McGrory (*Washington Post*, March 26, 1995) wrote that the District deserved its return to the colonial status of pre-home rule days, or when the *Economist* (February 25, 1995, 24) called D.C. government employees "uniformly indolent," were such viewpoints received differently by members of different racial groups?

Lines of racial thought are not precisely drawn, but patterns have emerged over the years. Many whites tend to see a bloated D.C. bureaucracy dispensing jobs that are little more than welfare in disguise. For example, columnist Steve Twomey (*Washington Post*, August 21, 1995) questioned the term D.C. worker: "Come on, only a foolish few have actually *worked* for the District. Tens of thousands do take home paychecks, though" (emphasis his). The jobs may have limited value as employment of last resort (for the otherwise jobless). However, their main purpose, many feel, is to build a dependent political base, even though the District cannot afford to live beyond its means. Many whites offer individual responsibility as the remedy for urban poverty, not government jobs and other handouts.

African Americans readily agree that D.C. is on the urban critical list, but many are less likely to conclude that the patient made herself ill through government obesity and other self-inflictions. Many suspect, instead, that the patient was poisoned. Blacks, more than whites, are likely to recognize that no government has coped well with the ravages of discrimination that relegated millions of Americans to urban poverty over many decades and which continue today. At least the D.C. government seems to try, albeit clumsily, and the efforts are more likely to be appreciated in black than in white communities. Even in affluent black communities, many residents have a cultural or familial bond with those who have not escaped. The bond is not so strong in white communities.

D.C. government managers and workers have been demeaned and demonized for decades. Many blacks, more so than whites, tend to read (and to filter out) much of the vilification as a subset of a larger pattern of racial antipathy. There is nothing in the D.C. water supply that makes its workers incompetent while government workers in nearby affluent counties are seen as efficient. D.C. employees may be just as outraged as their numerous critics over the failure of the D.C. government to cope with urban conditions, but the employees, and blacks in general, are more likely to see other culprits too. Conditions of poverty did not just happen, nor were they produced entirely by overly generous D.C. government programs.

To many black D.C. residents, a manager in the D.C. government may be just another neighbor, as credible as anyone else and not some buffoon. Someone who collects the trash, plows the snow, or repairs a pothole in the driving rain deserves thanks and respect, as does a social worker who through sheer guile may beat the system and keep a family off the streets or place a child in a caring home. Individual successes achieved by a D.C. school teacher are recounted in neighborhood gatherings along with the overall low test scores, school dropouts, and poor support from public school administrators. Black D.C. residents are more likely than whites to see the details beyond the stereotypes, and the details are positive in part and negative in part. Regardless of how awful the D.C. government may be, the constant references to it as a third world republic, banana'd or otherwise, are offensive. Many blacks (more so than whites) also link the daily characterizations of D.C. workers' laziness, corruption, rudeness, and ineptitude to centuries-old racial indignities; they have heard it all before. Besides, where else is participation in the American democratic system tied to the level of efficiency of the residents' government?

D.C.'s mayor, Marion Barry, personifies D.C.'s profound racial schism. Many whites see Barry as an atrocious role model for young people in a city inundated with drugs. They wonder how someone who so thoroughly abused the public trust and bespattered the District's image could have been so highly rewarded with his re-election. Many blacks respond to such "role model" arguments by pointing to Barry as an inspirational example of how one can overcome past failings, no matter how devastating they may have been, and lead a successful life. It is not that black Washingtonians are unaware of Barry's flaws; they know them all too well. Howard University political scientist Ron Walters (*Washington Post*, September 18, 1994) placed the matter in perspective:

> Many blacks simply don't see Barry in the one-dimensional terms of the crackhead that the Vista [hotel room] video suggested. They see a man who made a mistake, but they also see him as someone who has delivered much needed services, especially in his first two terms as mayor. Barry balanced the budget, spent money in public housing, increased the welfare budget, instituted a nationally recognized summer youth jobs program and youth leadership program and helped seniors with housing and transportation services. He also facilitated downtown business interests, supporting the office building boom of the 1980s by focusing on simplifying the business licensing process, among other things.

The racial splits are not unanimous, of course. For example, *Washington Post* columnist Juan Williams, a much-awarded black writer with credibility among all races, charged Barry with having "sold out the city's political independence, . . . divided the races and chased off the middle classes, [and] . . . trapped the poor in shameful schools" (December 3, 1995, C2). Many blacks, however, find no shortage of other factors that caused these conditions. While Barry received under 7 percent of the vote in the District's largely white political Ward 3, he nonetheless was elected mayor in the 1994 general election by a comfortable 56–to–42 percent margin. The varying racial perceptions of Barry were startling. While 73 percent of D.C.'s blacks thought Barry would do a good or excellent job in reducing corruption in the D.C. government, only 14 percent of D.C.'s whites thought so. Among D.C.'s blacks, 67 percent thought he would improve D.C.'s race relations (compared to 21 percent of whites); 74 percent thought he would improve D.C.'s image nationally (6 percent of whites thought so), and 60 percent thought he would do a good or excellent job in dealing with Congress (11 percent of D.C. whites agreed). Moreover, 83 percent of blacks believed that Barry was a "changed man" (31 percent of whites agreed), and only 22 percent of D.C. blacks surveyed were embarrassed by Barry's victory (79 percent of whites were) (*Washington Post*, October 2, 1994, A19).

In a discussion with this writer (November 29, 1994), Barry noted that blacks view the D.C. government more warmly than do whites, and said, "I suspect they would also view statehood more favorably because they put the two together." In contrast, he said, whites see an ineffective, inefficient government and thus, when asked about statehood, say, "No way, José." Moreover, Barry noted that people who are in the minority—in D.C.'s case, whites—"feel they have no power over what happens in their lives." Barry disagreed that whites lack power in D.C., but he acknowledged the feeling as a reason why many whites "rebel" against a largely black-led government, statehood, and other forms of local political control. This racial schism, along with D.C.'s homicide rates, its middle-class flight, its budget crisis, and Republican congressional control all combine to cloud D.C.'s prospects for greater self-rule, Barry said. Barry's citation of race as one factor among many for D.C.'s inferior political status is a conclusion many people of all races would accept.

Perceptual differences are found not just between the races but among D.C. and its suburbs as well. As the Wirthlin Group (1994, 46, 67) found, D.C. residents are much more likely than suburban residents to favor outside answers to the District's problems—for example, increased federal payments for D.C.'s state services, a 2 percent nonresident income tax, and reduction of federal taxes in the District—while "suburban residents, on the other hand, feel the burden falls squarely on the shoulders of the local D.C. government to improve things." D.C. residents are more than twice as likely as suburban residents to rate D.C. government public services as "very good" or "good" and are much more likely to support D.C. statehood (ibid., 35, 54). Much of the difference in viewpoint is due to the race of the respondents (ibid., 55, 56). D.C. and suburban residents alike used negative words and phrases to describe the District, with suburbanites doing so in greater proportion (72 percent) than D.C. residents (56 percent) (ibid., 11).

All of these gulfs in viewpoint, race-to-race and city-to-suburb, make the District's climb to political equality mountainous, especially since a "dominant ideology" may exist in American thought, as discussed later in this chapter, which assigns greater credibility to the views of the majority population than to minorities' views.

This research assesses, among other objectives, whether focus group participants make an explicit or implicit association between race and D.C.'s political status, and if so, how such an association influences their opinions. This chapter reviews research into political behavior to determine whether people tend to operate on the basis of self-interest, group interest, or national interest. The extent to which people's political actions and views are influenced by their identification with a group will be particularly reviewed—for example, to what extent does identification with a racial, gender, occupational, or other group (such as senior citizens) influence how people view issues?

Whites are generally viewed as too massive and heterogeneous a population to constitute a "group," although one may say the same about African Americans. Nevertheless, there are certain common sociotropic themes that Americans, and especially many white Americans, hold. These will be summarized, including a review of research into whether a dominant ideology exists in the American culture—that is, whether there are commonly held explanations for inequities in the distribution of economic and political goods. The policy implications of a dominant ideology, to the extent that one exists, will be examined along with the potential association of a dominant ideology with D.C.'s political standing. For example, Kluegel and Smith (1986, 183, 275) found that one consequence of a dominant ideology was unsympathetic attitudes toward racial minorities, who are blamed for their own lack of progress and whose demands for change are often viewed as illegitimate. A body of research linking "affect" (emotional response) and race will also be summarized in this chapter. Research also indicates that racially oriented policies are more easily supported in principle than in implementation (Schuman et al. 1985, 103–4, 205–11), and this possibility will be considered relative to D.C.'s political future.

A ROLE FOR RACE IN QUALITATIVE RESEARCH

Jennifer Hochschild (1981, 52, 70–75, 198–203), in her analysis of American beliefs about justice in the distribution of economic goods, found that just distribution of economic goods may depend on ascriptive traits: those which are fixed at birth, easily ascertainable, and subject to a value ranking. Race is one such ascriptive trait, along with gender, age, class, and religion. Hoschschild (1981, 144) found that her study made it "clear that many poor as well as rich respondents see the very poor as members of an alien race, culture, and style of life, which they neither understand nor approve of."

The District is far from a low-income society, border-to-border. Nonetheless, if ascriptive perceptions pertain to low-income societies, can they also pertain to societies such as the District in which minorities are actually in the majority? Are such ascriptive perceptions prevalent enough to influence focus group panelists' opinions about D.C.'s political future? Do people make individual judgments in forming opinions, or do they form opinions based on identification with a larger group's interests?

BASIC BELIEFS AND COMMON THEMES

Kinder and Kiewiet (1981, 132) attempted to determine whether voters were influenced by their own pocketbooks—the "trials and tribulations of their own economic lives"—or whether they were moved more by "sociotropic" information. Citizens so moved "support candidates that appear to have furthered the nation's economic well-being and oppose candidates and parties that seem to threaten it." The sociotropic voter asks political leaders not what they have done for her or him lately, but what they have done for the nation lately, and what they are likely to do for the nation in the future (ibid., 156).

Iyengar and Kinder (1987, 47–53) also found that personal predicaments contributed "rather little to beliefs about society and the nation." For example, in their study, victims of violent crime did not regard crime as more serious than those untouched by crime. Nonetheless, people who are personally affected by a particular problem are more likely to be sensitive to news about it. They are "predisposed" to accept the problem as a serious one (ibid., 48). Moreover, in their study of the role of emotional reactions in evaluations of the economy, Conover and Feldman (1986, 75) found that "personal well-being" is a key indicator of how people will evaluate government performance in managing their economy.

Graber's findings (1988, 259–60) "support the contention that people take an altruistic approach to many social problems rather than judging them purely from self-centered, pocketbook perspectives." However, Graber also found limitations to such a sociotropic argument. Schemata contain "personal" as well as "public welfare" concerns. The personal concerns tend to predominate when people feel seriously threatened (ibid., 260). Such a conclusion supports the similar, earlier finding of Sears et al. (1979, 382) that self-interest can take over in "highly charged atmospheres."

On balance, political researchers have found a continuing role for self-interest in shaping political attitudes and behavior. However, many researchers have found an even stronger role for a public-regarding or sociotropic orientation. Researchers have also been attempting to determine the role of group identity, which resides somewhere between self-interest and sociotropic orientation, in shaping public attitudes.

Despite a plethora of competing views, Graber (1988, 66) found that "a number of basic beliefs were steadfast and shared by nearly all panelists." The common beliefs are constantly reinforced and have "the quality of political religion, learned early in childhood and never questioned." In her study, Graber (1988, 222) correctly anticipated that she would find "uniformity among people's schemata that involve basic cultural orientations because these are part of the common heritage taught children by their parents, their teachers, and their religious and social advisors." Graber (1988, 222–23) observed that "accepting readily available schemata is a way to economize on intellectual effort." After all, she said (ibid., 214), "When shared stereotypes suffice, why should the panelists go to the trouble of thinking independently?" Despite the capacity for interschematic clashes, Graber's (1988, 252) basic conclusion remains: "All [of her panelists] had adopted culturally sanctioned values as the schematic framework into which schemata covering more specific matters were embedded."

In their examination of racial attitudes involved in the issue of busing school children, Sears et al. (1979, 381) made it clear that whites had not been "socialized" as children to oppose busing. Rather, the racial imagery surrounding this issue was enough to evoke racial attitudes. The authors (ibid.) observed that the clearest cases of symbolic politics are those which present the symbols that are most similar to the original socialization and which therefore can elicit the strongest responses.

One must be cautious in attributing racial motives in cases where they may be lacking. For example, as Schuman et al. (1985, 178) pointed out, white opposition to busing approached 90 percent at the time. If this opposition reflected a new form of racism, that of "symbolic racism," then virtually all of the white population and a substantial part of the black population would have been characterized as racist. Schuman et al. (ibid.) believed that Sears et al. (1979) may instead have uncovered "symbolic antiracists"—that is, the small (10 to 15 percent) portion of the white population willing to defend busing when almost no one else is willing to consider busing as a practical tool to achieve racial balance. Schuman et al. (1985, 178–79) questioned the need to find a new form of racism, the "symbolic" kind, when so much of the old-fashioned, garden variety of racial intolerance still exists.

"Symbolic racism" is a polarizing term. We live in a polite society where, for the most part, we respect others' sensitivities. From time to time, however, an institution or person crosses a line and is considered so egregious by many that the rules of civilized society no longer apply. Anything goes in colloquial chatter about such symbols. Examples include the U.S. Post Office, the D.C. Government, welfare mothers, Jesse Jackson, and Marion Barry. A collective judgment is reached that obscures some of their positive qualities. This judgment may be considered symbolic, although the degree of racism involved is debatable. Many blacks see whites' reactions to these symbols as racially amplified; however, many whites are offended by such perceptions.

As observed by Sears and Citrin (1982, 214), some scholars and many blacks see racism in the midst of a great many political issues, including those "that had little manifest racial content." In their examination of the California tax revolt of 1978, these authors (ibid.), employing factor analysis, found that "surprisingly" the most influential of the longstanding symbolic predispositions that boosted support for tax revolt was, in their view, symbolic racism, "even though almost no explicit discussion of race took place during the tax revolt." General political conservatism and Republican party identification were two other major symbolic predispositions.

Sears and Citrin (1982, 185) wrote:

> The blunt truth is that race remains a central issue in American domestic policy today, as it has been virtually throughout American history. It plays a powerful role in the public's decisions even on issues with no manifest racial content and in campaigns with little explicit reference to race, as is the case of the tax revolt. Large numbers of whites remain fundamentally opposed to special government efforts to aid blacks, and that opposition was a central determinant of white support for the tax revolt.

The findings of Sears and Citrin could lead one to hypothesize that general political conservatism and symbolic racism (or at least exaggerated attribution) could be expected to play roles in D.C. political structure discussions as well. As Graber (1988, 222–23) observed, "Accepting readily available schemata is a way to economize on intellectual effort." Whether D.C. issues would tap into a readily available schema of "opposition to special government efforts to aid blacks," as in the above Sears and Citrin (1982, 185) excerpt, is one of the objectives of this research.

AFFECT AND RACE

The prominent role of affect, or emotion, in the shaping of public opinion is discussed in appendix G (Sniderman et al. 1986; Conover and Feldman 1986). Sniderman et al. (1986, 428) concluded that people need to know very little about politics; rather, they only need to know whether they like or dislike a group and whether a particular policy is intended for the group's benefit or not. This observation, if accurate, could have significant impact on focus group panelists' opinions on D.C.'s political options.

Sniderman et al. (ibid., 429) found that some people tend to "reason backwards." For example, in arriving at a position on whether blacks should receive government assistance, people will start with their feelings toward blacks, then skip to the end of their reasoning chain to a position on the policy of assistance for blacks. Inference on this policy proceeds "more or less immediately" from feelings straight to a policy preference. Their final step is to reason "backwards" from the policy preference to an explanation of why blacks are worse off than whites in the distribution of economic goods. This explanation is then offered in support of the policy preference. Sniderman et al. (1986, 408) indicated that liberals might say that the reason behind socioeconomic disparities is discrimination, while conservatives might assign more of an individual responsibility (e.g., failure of blacks to work hard) to explain disparities between the races.

People reason in this way not to disguise their motives but to complete missing links in their chains of reasoning. A more ideologically based chain of reasoning, with all links in the chain intact, would be to arrive at an explanation of why blacks are worse off economically than whites and to use this knowledge in determining a policy position on government assistance for blacks. Affect eliminates the need for completed links. The reasoning chains of the less educated are especially affect-driven (ibid., 417). Sniderman et al. (ibid., 426–30) stated that the well educated, in developing their opinions on racial policy, are more likely to take into account both ideology and their feelings. In any event, their research attributed a large role to affect in public opinion development. Without the knowledge of the role of affect and the manner in which affect is applied, "it would be quite inexplicable how people so often figure out what they think about political questions given how little they so often know about them" (ibid., 430).

A northern California based group called Americans Against D.C. Statehood attempted during the presidential campaign of 1992 to link Bill Clinton in the minds of voters with statehood advocate Jesse Jackson as a means of dissuading Californians from voting Democratic. A spokesman for the group, speaking of D.C. statehood, said, "It's the sort of issue people say they never heard of, but when they think about it for a split second, they say, 'That's ridiculous'" (*Washington Times*, October 21, 1992, A5). Is such split-second reasoning affect-driven, ideology-driven, or both?

Predispositions are related to affective responses and often precipitate them. Sears, Hensler, and Speer (1979, 370–71) found that "people acquire in early life standing predispositions which influence their adult perceptions and attitudes." These authors held that a person's "stake" in an issue "triggers long-held, habitual responses" (ibid.). In particular, political symbols such as "integration," "blacks," or "Harlem" trigger "underlying predispositions," such as the person's level of racial tolerance or, conversely, prejudice (ibid.).

GROUP IDENTIFICATION RESEARCH

As discussed earlier in this chapter, researchers have demonstrated that citizens' orientations are often beyond self-interest. Are these orientations truly national or sociotropic? On the other hand, is the reference often subnational—that is, not sociotropic in the all-encompassing sense but oriented toward an ethnic or economic group with which an individual is associated? If the orientation is often "ethnotropic," and if such an orientation is evident with respect to D.C.'s political status, then race could indeed be a factor in citizens' support for or opposition to D.C. political autonomy or voting rights—as many D.C. citizens suspect it is. Group identification research is of assistance in answering this question.

Campbell et al. (1960, 301–21) found that "the higher the identification of the individual with the group, the higher the probability that he will think and behave in ways which distinguish members of his group from non-members." A group enjoying high member identification is said to be a cohesive group. As stated by Miller et al. (1981, 495), group consciousness "involves identification with a group and a political awareness or ideology regarding the group's relative position in a society, along with a commitment to collective action aimed at realizing the group's interests." This group consciousness involves acceptance of the belief that fundamental differences exist between the interests of one's own group and the interests of the dominant group. Group consciousness is mobilized group identity, politicized by feelings of power deprivation and the attribution of blame to the larger society for the group's societal position (ibid., 498–503).

POLITICAL BEHAVIOR OF PARTICULAR GROUPS

Welch et al. (1975, 375) stated, "Clearly generalizations made about one group at one time are not applicable either to that group at another point in time or to other groups in reasonably similar situations." With this caution in mind, the following is a review of some of the research conducted for several particular groups: blacks and other minorities, women, the aged, and blue-collar workers. This review concludes with a review of what appears to be limited research on the group identification and group consciousness of whites.

Blacks

Over the past several decades, political science research has found blacks to have strong group identification. Campbell et al. (1960, 316) found that blacks outside the South, along with Jews, were the most distinctive as a group in their voting tendencies for Democrats. They also stated, "We have found the Negro community to be the most cohesive," a characteristic of groups with high group identity.

Verba and Nie (1972, 160) stated that "[b]lacks are separated from white society by a variety of social norms that make communication across the racial barrier difficult. And they are separated, in addition, by the sense of group consciousness." This high group consciousness is associated with a higher level of political activity than is the average for whites when one corrects for income class. Controlling for socioeconomic status, Verba and Nie found that blacks held a nine percentage point edge over whites in political participation and held a twenty-three percentage point lead in participation when matching whites against blacks of similar socioeconomic status and with a high level of group consciousness (Verba and Nie 1972, 159–61).

Gurin and Epps (1975, 264) elaborated upon the characteristics of black group consciousness. They stated that blacks have traditionally been shackled with responsibility and guilt for their poverty. However, if blacks can "externalize the guilt, transferring responsibility from themselves to the broader society," then blacks will have a healthier self-image. This self-image produces a greater sense of "personal efficacy" as well as mistrust of the political system. In their study (ibid., 264–66) of students at historically black colleges, they found that those students attributing responsibility for one's class status to the system rather than to the self were nearly twice as likely as self-blaming individuals to become involved in political activity.

Bryan Jackson (1987, 639–44) cautioned against developing a monolithic view of the black community. There are several such communities. In fact group awareness on the basis of race competes with class and religious identity among blacks. Nonetheless, Gurin et al. (1980, 35) found that group identification among blacks is the most widespread of all the groups studied, followed by other groups who identified on the basis of age, income class, and gender. Blacks as a group had the highest proportion of power discontent (83 percent), followed by older citizens, the working class, and women. Blacks also led the field in advocating collective action to change societal strata, followed by other groups: the working class, older citizens, and women.

Other Groups

Other groups besides African Americans tend to act as a group. For example, Gurin (1985, 154–58, 161) found rather strong levels of growing group consciousness in her analysis of women's attitudes between 1972–1983. The younger, college-educated, employed, and unmarried women in particular demonstrated growing political consciousness and the need for collective action (ibid., 154–58).

With respect to group consciousness among older Americans, Gurin et al. (1980) found that the discontent of those aged sixty and above approximated the level expressed by blacks and was stronger than the discontent of women and blue-collar workers. Group discontent contributes to group consciousness. Miller et al. (1980, 699) concluded that "[a]ge group consciousness, when coupled with a feeling that the elderly can increase their influence in society, promotes political participation which goes well beyond what could be expected. . . ."

Additionally, Gurin et al. (1980, 35–41) found the blue-collar working class to follow only blacks in their advocacy of collective action (as opposed to individual responsibility) as a means of improving socioeconomic status. However, on the whole, blue collar workers' class consciousness was found to be considerably weaker than race consciousness, and it also did not exceed age consciousness. Campbell et al. (1960, 309, 379) found that, among blue collar workers, high group identification is more distinct among union members than among non-union members. They also found that unionism leads blue-collar workers to a more accurate self-identification—that is, as the working class.

Whites as a Political Group

The above research has established that people identify themselves as part of a group: as women, the elderly, blue-collar workers, blacks and other minorities, or more than one of the above or other groups. Are whites a group? If so, do white Americans identify with whites as a group, and does such group identification help shape political opinion?

The Campbell et al. (1960, 333–80) theory of status polarization refers to mutually antagonistic positions. Many researchers on group political behavior subsequent to Campbell refer to dominant or superordinant groups (Kluegel and Smith 1986). Statistically these groups are largely white, affluent, and, for the most part, suburban-residing in largely segregated neighborhoods. These communities are characterized by white-collar employment, low unemployment, and relatively high economic security, with little need for a government-woven social safety net. These citizens can usually afford the cost of health care insurance or have employers who provide health care. The citizens usually provide their own private means of transportation. Crises or emergencies are usually financed through their own family resources. The population is well educated, often through private schools; even many of the public schools in affluent neighborhoods resemble private schools. Children are, to a greater extent than is the case in cities, from two-parent households. Crime and drug abuse, while excessive everywhere, are still less prevalent in suburban than in urban neighborhoods.

These suburban communities are rapidly growing. By the 1990 census (U.S. Bureau of Census 1993, 1), 60 percent of all metropolitan area residents lived in suburbs, compared to 40 percent who lived in cities. In 1950, those proportions were reversed. Jobs are rapidly locating in the suburbs as well, especially in high-growth, high-tech industries (Meyers 1986, 36–40). Labor Secretary Robert Reich (commencement address, University of Maryland, December 22, 1995), spoke of a "secession" of successful America, which has walled itself off from lower-income populations by hiring private security guards, working in industrial parks far from urban centers, and shopping in secure suburban malls. Even the middle-income suburban populations that lack the affluence of the higher income communities tend to share the American Dream; they are often more desirous of joining higher socioeconomic status communities than they are of identifying with their current status.

American suburbs contain about 115 million people, or 46 percent of the U.S. population (U.S. Bureau of Census 1993, 1). The proportion of eligible people who vote is much higher in suburbs than in large cities by virtue of the relationship between socioeconomic status and turnout, and political participation is higher in other respects as well. Because developers target homebuyers by income strata, suburban residents tend to cluster with those of similar income levels. Many common values have likely evolved in these optimistic, affluent, growing, and often racially homogeneous areas. A key question to answer, from a research standpoint, is whether there is sufficient commonality among these populations to constitute a group.

Miller et al. (1981, 501) concluded that the feasibility of extending the group consciousness model to dominant groups is less than conclusive. They examined two dominant groups, whites and businessmen. They found higher levels of group consciousness for businessmen than for whites as a whole. Businessmen have highly developed networks that engage in participatory politics. Whites, however, were considered to be a "large, heterogeneous and socially dominant stratum that has not been systematically mobilized en masse against any competing group's interests." Gurin et al. (1980, 35) found that only 5 percent of whites closely identified with whites, while 58 percent of whites did not identify with whites as a group. They also found (ibid., 45) that power discontent and advocacy of collectivism were both greater among closely identified members of lower than of higher income strata of society.

This research adds to the conclusion that there is no one homogenous "group" known as whites; there are many subgroups. Bryan Jackson (1987) reached the same conclusion for blacks. The research also confirmed that there are several distinct groups within white communities; there is no lack of group identification among whites with respect to these distinct subgroups.

SOCIOTROPIC VS. ETHNOTROPIC BEHAVIOR

The wealth of research on group identity and political behavior seems conclusive. Americans are not likely to place group interests and differences aside and base their political decisions solely on what is good for the nation. Conover (1985, 151) found that evaluations of group and national well-being are relatively independent. The vast majority (65 percent) of Americans view themselves as being part of an economic group, whether it is businesspeople, women, the working class, farmers, or many others. Members of groups view group interests in a more pessimistic light than they view national interests (ibid., 61). Discontent has been widely found to contribute to group consciousness. Group well-being has more personal relevance for an individual, Conover stated, than do assessments of national well-being (ibid., 140). Conover concluded that "falling between the broad spectrum of national well-being and the narrow range of personal self-interest is a middle ground occupied by social groups and their particular economic interests" (ibid.). Attraction to and association with those interests may be called "ethnotropism," or in the case of purely economic groups, "group-tropism."

Miller et al. (1981) demonstrated that white America is composed of heterogeneous strata, and Conover and Feldman (1984) observed a variety of distinct groups within the strata. However, the finding that there may be relatively little white group identification and consciousness (e.g., Miller, 1981; Gurin, 1980) should be questioned. This nation could not have been formed, displacing and nearly eliminating existing cultures, without such identity. Racial slavery and subsequent segregation could not have been maintained without this identity. Black and Black (1987), in their analysis of southern politics, found numerous commonalities in white middle- and upper-class political behavior in the South. In contrast to the findings of Miller et al. (1981), Black and Black found high levels of mobilization of whites in reaction to black interests (for example, in opposition to Great Society programs of the 1960s).

Whites do not need to identify themselves as whites. Since they are in the overwhelming majority, they need only distinguish themselves as Americans, in their view. Perhaps this perception may account for the low identification levels for whites as whites. Likely there is no deficiency of ethnotropism among whites. As was accomplished in the Black and Black (1987) analysis of southern politics, several other studies reviewed below have distinguished a clear white identity, distinct from black and other perspectives, on a variety of issues.

A DOMINANT IDEOLOGY

As discussed above, overarching cultural values internalized early in life account for a substantial consensus in American politics (Graber 1988, 254–55). Moreover, issues relating to race (as well as party identification) are among the strongest residues of many Americans' early socialization (Sears, Hensler, and Speer 1979, 381).

These findings are supported by Kluegel and Smith (1986), who observed a "dominant ideology" (after Huber and Form, 1973) in America. Kluegel and Smith (1986, 11) stated that the "American culture contains a stable, widely held set of beliefs involving the availability of opportunity, individualistic explanations for achievement, and acceptance of unequal distribution of societal rewards." These beliefs "generally dispose people toward conservative attitudes toward inequality-related public policy."

Many Americans, and especially whites, tend to rationalize inequalities or not to acknowledge their existence. For example, Kleugel and Smith (1986, 49) found that Americans believed that people "who grow up in poor families" have an average or better chance of getting ahead than does the average person in the United States. Similarly, only 28 percent believed that blacks are disadvantaged by the socioeconomic conditions in which they find themselves, compared to 73 percent who believed that blacks' chances of getting ahead are average or better. Whites tended to favor individual explanations for wealth and poverty (whether one works hard, takes risks, and practices thrift) as opposed to blacks, who offered structural explanations (such as lack of inherited wealth, lack of available jobs, and poor schools) considerably more than did whites (ibid., 94–102). Kleugel and Smith (1986, 187) stated that "there is a strong element of blaming blacks for their lower average level of socioeconomic status relative to whites." For example, 90 percent of whites in a 1976 survey agreed that "blacks haven't prepared themselves enough" to take advantage of opportunities. For several decades, a majority of the southern white population attributed greater intelligence to whites than to blacks (Schuman, Steeh, and Bobo 1985, 125).

It should also be noted that whites over time have observed considerable improvement in blacks' socioeconomic status, while blacks have had a much more pessimistic view of their race's standing during the same time period (Kleugel and Smith 1986, 185–191; Schuman, Steeh, and Bobo 1985, 141). Kleugel and Smith (1986, 185) concluded that "[m]any white Americans seem to believe that a reduction in individual prejudice against blacks is sufficient to provide opportunity for blacks equal to that of whites." Because opportunities have improved so significantly over the years for blacks in the minds of many whites, blacks presumably no longer have an "excuse" for their economic deprivation.

The Kleugel and Smith study demonstrated that the vast majority of whites believed that blacks no longer faced unfair employment practices, and that blacks on the whole had worse jobs, income, and housing because blacks lacked "the motivation or will power to pull themselves out of poverty" (Kleugel and Smith, 1986, 188–91). Inequality in the minds of most Americans is "just in principle" (ibid., 141). Kleugel and Smith (1986, 275) noted that "[t]he consequences on the societal level of widespread belief in the dominant ideology include unsympathetic attitudes toward the poor and racial minorities, for they are blamed for their own lack of progress."

American society has not advanced much since the days of that study. In a 1995 *Washington Post* article (October 8, 1995, A26, 27), 58 percent of whites (and 23 percent of blacks) thought that the average African American was "as well or better off as the average white person" in terms of employment, and 56 percent of whites (compared to 29 percent of blacks) thought so in terms of education. Those whites who were uninformed about actual socioeconomic standings were much less likely than informed whites to support a variety of national actions to cope with urban problems (ibid.).

POLICY IMPLICATIONS OF A DOMINANT IDEOLOGY

Kleugel and Smith (1986, 175) stated that the relationships of dominant ideology beliefs to policy attitudes are "strong and systematic." Individual explanations for poverty "influence attitudes almost across the range of policies considered." The authors (ibid., 182–83) observed a real decline in traditional or "old-fashioned" race prejudice (i.e., pro-segregationist, white supremacy sentiment). However, whites may not find it unfashionable to express opposition to equal employment programs, and such sentiments could be considered "disguised social prejudice," in the authors' view (ibid.).

The authors (ibid., 303–4) noted that the persistence of economic differences in jobs, marked by race and sex distinctions, and a strong and continuing theme of social liberalism (aided by the civil rights movement) have provided support for social policies that address inequities. However, these trends are counteracted by other factors, primarily "racial affect," which is assessed as stronger than the economic self-interest that arises when whites compete with blacks for jobs. Some whites will oppose those policies that are identified as primarily benefitting blacks, such as affirmative action or welfare, because of "racial animosity." Many whites believe that government gives disproportionate attention to improving conditions for minorities and the poor, who are often thought of as undeserving, while the problems of the majority are overlooked (ibid., 183–84). The authors (ibid., 183) stated:

> Specifically, white Americans see blacks as a major disruptive force in society and as making demands for change that violate cherished values such as individualism and self-discipline. Many whites blame blacks for social problems such as crime and the "welfare mess." As a consequence, blacks are viewed as undeserving of government assistance, their demands for change are viewed as illegitimate, anger results, and the opposition to equal opportunity programs for blacks follows.

The focus groups on D.C.'s political status help assess whether racial affect is demonstrated by panelists, and whether D.C. political equality is viewed as an illegitimate demand of blacks.

Kleugel and Smith (1986, 293–94) indicated that public policies that are compatible with dominant ideology beliefs may be supportable. On one end of a continuum are policies which enunciate a goal of equal opportunity, and these policies may have broad public acceptance; however, on the other end of the continuum are income redistribution policies which are often resisted. For example, the public may accept antidiscrimination laws and job training programs, while they may oppose hiring goals for minorities. The continuum may also apply to D.C. political equality. Equality of political rights with other Americans may be a policy that has widespread acceptance. However, what may be considered "special treatment" for a small, minority-governed jurisdiction—for example, the granting of statehood, whereby D.C. might gain the same degree of power in the U.S. Senate as would residents of a large state—may not gain acceptance. The focus groups help determine where on this continuum the D.C. political rights issue falls.

Schuman et al. (1985, 211) remind us that "racial change has always involved some element of conflict and resistance." The probability of acceptance is often a factor of the extent and type of implementation sought (ibid., 205). The authors observed (ibid., 103–104) that whites are much more likely to support the principle of racial progress than the implementation of means to achieve that progress. For example, whites have for years supported an end to overt employment discrimination. While discrimination was condoned in the early 1940s and before, such support had virtually vanished by the 1970s. *Implementation* of the principle to eliminate employment discrimination is another matter, with under 40 percent supporting intervention by the federal government to assure fair treatment of minorities in obtaining jobs (ibid., 196, 88–89). The same is true of the widespread support for the principle of equal educational opportunity compared with low support for busing and other neighborhood intervention strategies (ibid.).

Verba and Orren (1985) agreed that Americans advocate the principle of political equality even though implementation of this principle is more difficult to achieve. Verba and Orren (ibid., 214) stated:

> American leaders take an egalitarian view of political influence. Their attitude reflects adherence to a general norm of political equality. Where they perceive wide disparities in influence, they would reduce or eliminate them. This attitude is consistent with an antipower ethic.

While Americans approve of equality and "actively seek it through the powers of the state and the actions of individuals," it is the form of equality that "arouses debate" (ibid., 266).

The focus group discussions were designed to assess whether consensus on the principle of political equality for the District is more easily achieved than agreement over the form of implementing the principle, and this hypothesis was indeed manifested in the focus groups.

5

Public Opinion Patterns on D.C. Policy Options

> *"It seems to set up a kind of barrier to say you have to meet certain criteria in order to be allowed to vote. That's not true anywhere else in the country. People get to be as dumb, as foolish, as passionate, as disinterested, as whatever, as they want. All you have to be is old enough and a citizen. That's it."*
>
> Jeanie, Iowa Focus Group

Now it is time for research results. This chapter discusses *what* the focus group panelists thought about D.C.'s political status, while the next chapter discusses *how* panelists processed information and *why* they developed their opinions.

The protagonists are average Americans. For this research into D.C.'s political options, five focus group sessions were held in various locations in the nation during 1992 and 1993: Montgomery County, Maryland; Austin, Texas; Van Nuys, California; Harrisburg, Pennsylvania; and Des Moines, Iowa. Appendix F describes these sites as well as the research procedure. By the time of the focus group sessions, all of the focus group participants had heard about the District government's numerous problems and those of its people. They knew all about Marion Barry and Jesse Jackson, or thought they did. They knew about the "corruption" of the District's government and what they viewed as the District's pathetic lack of resources. They knew that a rather high percentage of D.C. residents were "on welfare" or in prison. D.C. was universally known as America's murder capital. It amazed this writer how the phrase "bloated bureaucracy" cropped up in each focus group.

Many focus group panelists did not restrain themselves, characterizing D.C. as a "cesspool" and full of "scum areas," governed by bureaucrats who, in the minds of many panelists, did not know what they were doing. The District was not viewed as an all-American city; its flaws were described with facility.

Panelists also were aware of urban problems in Los Angeles, New York, Detroit, Cleveland, D.C., and elsewhere. Urban America had lost its charm to many of the panelists. Cities were dangerous areas to many, to be avoided if possible.

Such negative perceptions about D.C. and other urban centers have been years in the making. The predispositions shaping the perceptions were developed over the course of panelists' lifetimes. The research results produced variations in outcome depending upon the composition and location of the focus groups and when the sessions were conducted. The results were influenced by latest news events about the D.C. government or its leaders to the extent that panelists followed this unformed issue. As demonstrated by Bryan D. Jones (1994, 70–77, 225–30), contextual changes inevitably cause shifts in an issue's dimensions that are emphasized or de-emphasized over time. Largely, however, because predispositions take years to evolve, the panelists' comments were reflective of an extended era that will continue until the District is able to dispel negative perceptions about its government, its leaders, and the magnitude of its urban problems. A long-term era of stability and relative prosperity would be needed to produce a true perceptual difference. The District is a long way from such a new era at present.

OVERVIEW OF FOCUS GROUP PANELISTS

Focus groups do not "represent" anyone. Rather, focus group panelists provide insights into how at least some people consider various topics. Even though it is not valid to generalize focus group results to a broad population, it helps to have participants who as a group are rather representative of the universe (in this case, the American voting majority). If the groups in this study had been mostly Democrats, predominantly black, or had other liberal characteristics to a disproportionate degree, then an ensuing crescendo of appreciation for D.C. political equality would not have been worthy of much analysis. Similarly, conservative groups of religious fundamentalists, strict constructionists, or those harboring deep racial distrust would predictably and vociferously oppose D.C. political equality.

The sixty-one people assembled were fairly representative of reasonably thoughtful and politically involved Americans with one significant exception. Fifty-eight were white; one in Austin was a newly arrived Hispanic, one in

Van Nuys was a well-assimilated Hispanic, and one in Harrisburg was a well-assimilated Asian American. This composition was chosen based on guidance from focus group literature, discussed in appendix F, that indicated that many white Americans will not be open in expressing their true viewpoints in the presence of minorities. On a racially charged topic such as D.C.'s political structure, many white participants could be expected to place a check on their opinions that related to African Americans. Thus by structuring focus groups where viewpoints could flow freely, richness in information from these panelists was captured. Nonetheless, it should be acknowledged that by artificially structuring focus group composition in this respect, the views are slanted to a degree in a more conservative direction away from a policy position favoring full D.C. political equality.

With this one major exception, the groups' compositions met the goal of thoughtful representation. Appendix A is a reference guide for readers who would like more information on those expressing opinions. In the text that follows, reference will be made to participants by name and state—for example, (Ben, Tx.). Characteristics of the participants can be found in appendix A.

In appendix B, a summary is provided of these panelists' responses to presession questionnaires. Twenty-five of the sixty-one participants identified themselves as Democrats, twenty as Independents, and fifteen as Republicans; the Austin group had one Irish citizen who had lived in the U.S. for fifteen years and who had no party identification. The panelists were for the most part strong party identifiers, giving themselves a 74 out of a feeling thermometer scale designed to elicit how warmly they felt about the goals of their party (100 = warmest). All five of the groups had strong party identifiers, with Austin the lowest at 65 and Bethesda the highest at 86. This high strength of party identity is helpful in producing focus group data, since aschematics or followers who would have little to contribute to the group discussion would likely be apathetic about their party of choice.

Similarly, the focus group participants were disproportionately college graduates having rather high incomes. This characteristic was also helpful in producing data. As a generality (that does not always hold), the well-educated tend to have an ideological structure and are opinion leaders more so than the less-educated (Verba and Nie 1972; Campbell et al. [1960] 1976). They have much to offer in focus group discussions. Of the sixty-one panelists, forty-three were college graduates, with eighteen holding advanced degrees. Only in Van Nuys were college graduates in the minority. Nearly half, or twenty-eight, of the panelists had family incomes of $50,000 or greater. The focus group payment for participation (forty dollars) was relatively high so that all income levels could be attracted. Nonetheless, there was still a large segment who had not graduated from college (eighteen) and a few unemployed and lower-income people as well.

The numbers of women (thirty) and men (thirty-one) were in balance, although Austin had a women/men ratio of four to nine, while in Des Moines it was eight to five. A little over half (thirty-four) were married, and thirty-seven were suburban (nearing the national proportion). The average age was forty.

As a short cut way to gauge panelists' political leanings, they were asked to score, on a feeling thermometer of 0 to 100, how warmly or coldly they felt about various national figures. Martin Luther King, Jr. came closest to universal acceptance, scoring an average of 73. Clinton and Gore did well, scoring 64 and 63 respectively, as expected in the months following the presidential election. Perot (50) was the only other politician who was received warmly enough to reach the midpoint. The rather liberal Pennsylvania group was the only one to give Jackson a score (55) that was over the midpoint, although this group regarded Bush more warmly (55) than average as well. Oliver North (29) was inserted to help assess personality types and fared poorly on the whole.

Panelists felt warmly (76) toward treating blacks more equally; however, fourteen of the sixty-one gave a 20 or greater score to the notion that whites are better than blacks at running things and should be allowed to do so.

Panelists were also tested about their knowledge of D.C. Twenty-three thought that D.C. residents were already represented in the House (fifteen), or didn't know (eight). Seventeen thought that D.C. residents were already represented in the Senate (eight), or didn't know (nine). The panelists guessed on average that 29 percent of D.C. residents were receiving welfare—not a bad guess considering that 13 percent of D.C.'s population and 46 percent of D.C.'s children were in AFDC families in 1993 (*Washington Post*, June 29, 1995, D.C.3). Iowa panelists were highest in this regard, guessing 36 percent; this group as a whole also demonstrated the most hardened attitudes toward D.C. residents' aspirations for political equality. On average, the panelists guessed that 39 percent of the people who live in D.C. work for the federal government, nearly double the proportion of D.C. residents in the labor force who actually work for the federal government. In Harrisburg, the panelists guessed 50 percent. Nonetheless, many D.C. residents who do not work for the government do have jobs that service government workers and tourists; thus, these guesses cannot necessarily be regarded as off-base. The panelists thought that 57 percent (as an average guess) of D.C. residents are black, with Maryland panelists guessing the correct figure of 66 percent on the button. Several panelists had wildly high guesses in these categories, often picking the identical high percentage for blacks and welfare recipients.

Panelists were also asked whether D.C. residents were out of touch with the rest of America. Many gave this sentiment high marks on the feeling thermometer, with 45 the average score (and without much intergroup variation). Eighteen panelists favored D.C. statehood, while eighteen were opposed; the others had no opinion in the pre-session questionnaire.

PANELIST TYPOLOGY

No one fits into a neat category; most of us are much too complex for that. Yet an analysis of the transcripts reveals that some panelists drew upon certain schemata more than others. Patterns emerged. By categorizing the panelists into six types, the findings of this research have greater application than if overall conclusions are solely presented. Policy leaders may learn what arguments are most effective in producing schema change in various types of people and target their messages accordingly. The six categories of panelists from this study are as follows:

1. *True Believers/Emphathizers.* A true believer was someone who favored full political equality for D.C. residents, including statehood, before the session began or at an early stage during the session. She or he had a reasonably accurate knowledge of the District and attributed positive as well as negative traits to the District. The true believer not only liked Martin Luther King, Jr., but also Jesse Jackson and Ron Brown. A strong motivating force in a true believer's life was human rights. These were "symbolic anti-racists," in the words of Schuman et al. (1985, 178); that is, people willing to speak out against injustice, real or perceived, at every opportunity without much concern about bruising the feelings of those to whom their remarks are directed.

An empathizer exhibited many but not all of the characteristics of a true believer. For example, she or he may not have been fond of Jesse Jackson. Cheryl (Ca.) was typed an empathizer because she seemed caring and insightful about the District's difficulties and efforts, even though she gave a rather high score of 40 on the feeling thermometer to the notion that "whites are better than blacks at running things and should be allowed to do so."

Appendix E summarizes the types of panelists. There were four true believers, all for D.C. statehood, and thirteen emphathizers, who on average awarded 72 political equality (or "PE") points on a scale of 100 (see appendix D as well as the narrative that follows later in this chapter for an explanation of PE points).

2. *Pragmatists.* Unlike true believers, originalists, and some of the others, pragmatists were not primarily ideology-driven. They were actively engaged in the group discussions, they were open-minded or considered themselves to be, and they were concerned with seeking solutions. Pragmatists often viewed true believers, the racially troubled, and originalists as extremists. As compromisers, pragmatists sought a middle ground. Often a compromise would involve eliminating the District altogether, giving it to Maryland, for example, or allowing D.C. residents to vote in Maryland. While realizing that such courses of action could cause anguish among many in Maryland and the District, many pragmatists believed that such a policy would be accepted in the long run. Pragmatists were also leaders in producing the popular compromise of giving D.C. residents some—but not full—representation in the U.S. Congress as well as a reduction—but not elimination—of congressional control over D.C. budgets, laws, and judicial appointments. A pragmatist could be a member of any political party or ideological group. The sessions had fifteen pragmatists, who awarded an average of 32 PE points.

3. *Anti-Big-Government.* To these panelists, government exists for its own benefit. Among government's nefarious side effects are excessive taxation and interference in the daily business of honest people who are struggling against the odds. Some government is a necessary evil, but for the most part society would function much better with less government. Those holding this schema were likely to be skeptical of Washington, D.C., the capital of American bureaucracy with its own reputation for having a bloated and allegedly corrupt work force. On the other hand, adherents of this schema were likely to abhor congressional interference into local affairs of the District. Nine anti-big-government types emerged from these sessions, and they awarded an average of 56 PE points.

4. *Originalists.* These types held the founding fathers schema most dearly. They were political fundamentalists and strict constructionists. To originalists, those who framed the Constitution were prescient and approached omniscience to the extent that any political leaders could. If one element in the Constitution is changed, the entire carefully crafted system could be endangered. If we chip away at the Constitution bit by bit, even for something as ostensibly minor as changing the District's status, then it will not be long before other rights begin to crumble. Originalists knew that they were in a small minority and were accustomed to criticism by pragmatists, true believers, and others, but they defended America's heritage for the benefit of all. Originalists were principled, thoughtful conservatives. Only four

originalists emerged (the same number as their counterparts, the true believers), and they scored, on average, 9 PE points.

5. *Racially Troubled.* Just as empathizers were not quite true believers, the racially troubled were not quite originalists. They did not pass all the litmus tests. The racially troubled usually attempted a principled stance, but often fell or tripped back on racially oriented motives when discussing policies as racially laden as D.C.'s political options.

These were the panelists whose views were most easily labeled "racist" by true believers, empathizers, and occasionally liberal pragmatists. The racially troubled gave high scores on the feeling thermometer to the statement that "whites are better than blacks at running things and should be allowed to do so." They were contemptuous of Jesse Jackson, and many of the racially troubled did not have high regard even for Martin Luther King, Jr. The most quotable examples of emotionally driven attitudes about the District were from this type. Six racially troubled types emerged, and they awarded an average of 38 PE points.

6. *Followers.* These were aschematics not only about D.C. matters but most other political issues as well. Followers had an insufficient ideological structure to contribute to the focus group discussions. To nearly all the panelists outside of the Maryland group, the D.C. policies issue provided new information. Nonetheless, the other five types of panelists were able to match new with prior information; followers were not. They tended to be apathetic in the focus group. Followers had inconsistent patterns in assigning degrees of warmth on the feeling thermometer to Oliver North, Jesse Jackson, Bush, Clinton, etc., basing their judgments on personality more than ideology. Followers tended to know little about D.C. or any issue discussed. They did possess a pro-democracy schema, but the other schemata were thinly textured or nonexistent. Followers gladly joined in any consensus and welcomed the session's end. There were ten followers who awarded an average of 54 PE points, which reflects how well followers joined the opinion of their fellow panelists; the average for all sixty-one panelists was 52 PE points.

POLICY IMPLICATIONS

Panelists' initial impressions of the District tended to be superficial and mostly negative. Panelists' opening comments in the focus groups were reflective of an era of national media comment on D.C.'s performance that dates from about the mid-1980s and will likely extend well into the future until stability can be restored in the District's political, economic, and social conditions. As the issues and options were discussed in the sessions, the following patterns emerged:

A. *An Active Interest in the District's Political Status.* All five of the focus groups became lively, interactive sessions where the panelists developed a genuine interest in the District's political status. Most participants readily acknowledged that at the outset they had not given much or any thought to the fact that U.S. citizens living in the District are treated so differently from other Americans. While the reactions and proposed solutions varied, no more than ten of the sixty-one would be described as aschematics—that is, those who basically played follow-the-leader and did not develop a coherent viewpoint about the District. The panelists produced considered, well-informed, high quality discussions, not at all on a lower level than the ones heard, for example, in Congress on this topic.

B. *Few Adherents to the Status Quo.* The views of the sixty-one panelists were in disharmony with congressional policy over the last two decades on the District's political status. By the end of the session, only three panelists—one each in Van Nuys, Des Moines, and Bethesda—favored the status quo for the District.

Since there were only three advocates of the status quo, let us see who they were. Sid (Ia.), an originalist, strong Democrat, and college professor, thought that D.C. would have nothing to gain from voting rights or statehood, since he thought that the 535 U.S. senators and representatives who live in and around D.C. already look out for D.C.'s interests. George (Md.), an originalist, Republican, successful attorney, and thoughtful historian, opposed D.C. statehood and other forms of autonomy on constitutional grounds. He also said that D.C. is not open to Republicans and Independents, that D.C. is too dependent on the federal government, and that he questioned whether whites would feel represented under statehood. Dell (Ca.), a Republican investor typed as "racially troubled," thought that D.C. residents are not ready for political autonomy, pointing to failed black African governments as indicators of why D.C. could not function independently from federal oversight and observing that he would not tolerate blacks "ruling over" him. That was the extent of panelists' support for the status quo.

When informed that the District's nonvoting delegate to the House could at that time vote in the Committee of the Whole, but that her vote would not count if it would help determine the outcome, all five panels erupted into "only in America" laughter. They seemed to feel that some attempt was being made to include D.C. into the federal political system, albeit a clumsy one.

C. *A Pro-Representation Landslide of Opinion.* Much more representative of the focus group panelists was Al (Tx.), who said, "As time goes on, the whole idea of people paying tax to a federal entity without some type of representation just doesn't hold water." Willie Bob (Tx.) agreed, saying the current structure "is sort of a setup; it is asking for trouble," implying a mass rebellion by D.C. residents because there are "lots of social problems, and then on top of that there's a feeling that you are not really being heard, that no one's really looking out for you."

Nearly everyone (fifty-seven of sixty-one panelists) who considered D.C.'s political status favored some sort of representation in Congress by the end of her or his focus group session. It is rare to find any issue in which such a high ratio would be willing to overturn an existing policy. The panelists' stance on representation in Congress was not achieved through arduous consensus building. The conclusion followed rather easily once the panelists discussed the facts. Howard's (Md.) comment was typical: "I don't think anybody's going to argue with the fact that these people need to be represented. The big problem is how are they going to be represented." Ashley (Pa.) expressed a prevalent theme that D.C. citizens "should have the same rights, privileges, and responsibilities as everyone else." Others such as Margaret (Ia.) cautioned that the "city of D.C. does not have to be a separate state just to have representation."

Many people evoked the restorative powers of democracy, as in this exchange between Christine and George in Maryland reveals:

> CHRISTINE: I think the [congressional-D.C.] relationship could be responsible for some of the unhealthy stuff that's going on, the crime, the social ills, that prevent the people from feeling full integrity about themselves or as a legal entity. It is paternalistic. I think people need to feel that they can have full participation in the government.
>
> GEORGE: Are you saying that some hustler who robs somebody on the streets is reacting to, "Gee, we're not a state, I don't have a senator, so. . . ."
>
> CHRISTINE: I think he is a symptom of something much more complex. I don't think he can make that direct connection. That's much too simplified.

Representation in Congress did not automatically translate into support for D.C. statehood. El (Md.) did "not know whether it was the chicken or the egg": are D.C. residents "capable" of performing their democratic functions under statehood or would they become capable "once you give them statehood and they begin to act like a state?" Various options were supported in the sessions, but the underlying conviction was indestructible that all Americans should be represented in Congress. Full representation in Congress received less support; still, thirty-five of the sixty-one panelists favored at least one U.S. senator for D.C.

D. *Greater Autonomy for District Residents.* After participating in the focus group discussions, over two-thirds of the panelists (forty-two of sixty-one) thought that D.C. residents should have greater self-rule. As Herb (Md.), a congressional lobbyist and prototypical pragmatist, said:

> I would like to see, at the very least, for the District to have true home rule without Congress' heavy hand over it, and that would mean Congress could not have the right to veto what they do.

Many panelists were concerned about big government in general needlessly meddling in the daily lives of ordinary citizens. As Lynn (Tx.) said:

> I think it's ridiculous that they don't have control over their own city. I mean, there would be hell to pay if Houston decides they wanted to spend their budget this way and the state of Texas says, "No, we really don't think you should spend it like that." It would be a nightmare, in essence, what we are doing to the city of Washington right now.

Lynn feared that congressional control could be interpreted as a sign that "democracy is not working and D.C. needs somebody, a father figure, to take care of them."

Not everyone favored a complete hands-off policy; in fact, less than half (twenty-five) favored full self-rule. While a majority would remove congressional controls over local laws and budgets, many others were concerned that Congress should be able to protect what they termed the national interest. They believed that the District in many ways belonged to the nation and "should be kept up to a certain standard" (Willie Bob, Tx.).

Al (Tx.) spoke of a "magical" feeling he gets and of being "politically star-struck" every time he visits Washington. When traveling up and down the East coast on I-95, he would go an hour and a half out of his way "just to see the monuments lit up." He therefore felt "very strongly that the folks there should not hold the rest of us hostage for a place that means so much to so many people in the country." Al said that "it's probably nothing that would ever happen, but there's always that possibility."

Ways to accomplish some sort of oversight ranged from a "coterie of governors from across the states to serve as powerless consultants to this fledgling state" (Christine, Md.) to retention of some or all of the current congressional powers.

E. *Low Levels of Support for D.C. Statehood.* As noted above, nearly all of the panelists (fifty-seven) favored representation in Congress for D.C. residents, and a clear majority (thirty-five) favored representation in the Senate as well as the House. Two-thirds of them (forty-two) favored greater self-government. Despite such substantial movement away from the status quo, only a little over a quarter (sixteen) of the panelists favored D.C. statehood after participating in a two-hour discussion.

What seemed striking was a frequent, self-admitted deficiency by panelists who supported full voting rights and self-rule in explaining why they could not bring themselves to a position of accepting statehood, as typified by Jeanie's (Ia.) bewilderment:

> I don't think I'm in favor of statehood, and I wish I could be more articulate about why. It doesn't feel right. It probably has something to do with the fact that it's just this city and nothing else. It probably has something to do with . . . I don't know what it has to do with. It doesn't seem like a state. That's dumb. There must be something else there, but I don't know what it is. But I do feel passionately about the representation issue, and I think that needs to get solved, somehow. I also would not have the Congress review judges or D.C. laws or anything like that.

If one favors full congressional representation for D.C. residents and greatly reduced congressional control over D.C. affairs, as Jeanie did, then one is for all practical purposes for statehood. Herb (Md.) acknowledged this inconsistency:

> What else has to change? It would be exactly like a state, except what's in a name? A rose by any other name still smells as sweet. . . . We're not going to call you a state, but hey, you are a state.

Al (Tx.) said the difference is "the title—it's like giving someone a job and a salary, but we're not going to give you the title." And Jeff (Md.): "They would have the representation, but not the glorification." Jeanie, Herb, and Al would not spring for statehood—even though they advocated policies that would produce *de facto* statehood—while Jeff was consistently pro-statehood.

George (Md.) gave a more hardline reason for opposing statehood:

> D.C. has really severe problems, and the energy and time these D.C. politicians spend on this issue should really be directed at the school system, the potholes, the inefficiency of the bloated government. It's just a smoke screen. It's a way for more patronage, more jobs, more layers of bureaucracy.

Rick (Ca.) thought that "giving D.C. complete statehood and all the responsibilities could very well compound the problems they already have now." Mia (Md.) expressed a similar concern that the District as a state would "have to maintain their own budget, get their own tax base, and pay for their own programs. Is the District in a position to do that?"

Other panelists proposed alternative solutions to the heavy congressional control and lack of representation. For example, Chris One (Ia.) said, "I think it would be nice if Maryland would just take them in." Realizing the impracticality of this suggestion, she went on to favor "nominal statehood," which would give D.C. congressional representation but retain full federal control.

F. *Fluidity in Panelists' Positions: A Group-by-Group Review.* Panelists exhibited considerable strength of conviction in their views on democracy, representation, and big government. However, on an issue as little known as D.C.'s structure, much fluidity in position taking remained by the end of the two-hour sessions.

The interaction, consensus building, and leader effects of focus group participation were easily observable. Those holding the most coherent and well-articulated views, and those who exhibited status in the group resulting from perceived income and educational levels—and to some extent age—tended to emerge as opinion leaders. Such emergence is observed in society in general. By design, the focus groups had a disproportionate share of opinion leaders to capture ideologically rich data. Nonetheless, many panelists seemed content in varying degrees to follow the group opinion leaders and join in a consensus.

While discussions on the issues of representation and self-government were lively, the option of D.C. statehood was seldom regarded as crucial. In Austin and Van Nuys, a strong leader could have persuaded the group toward statehood without great difficulty, while in Harrisburg the group did advocate statehood. The Des Moines, Iowa and Bethesda, Maryland groups, however, would have presented obstacles to leaders of any stature who advocated any policy approaching full autonomy for the District. The Des Moines participants had no clear schema about D.C. residents, and what they did know, most did not like. The negative affect likely precipitated a policy favoring some congressional control over D.C. Nonetheless, even in Des Moines, nine of the thirteen panelists were in favor of representation by D.C. in the U.S. Senate—a major policy shift—and 12 favored voting representation in the House. Even this most hardened group was several light years removed from the status quo.

Unlike the other groups, Bethesda, Maryland participants knew D.C. well, or thought they did. They had familiarity with the topic and were rather less fluid in the policy positions than were the other states' panelists. In Maryland, several had fixed positions which were not subject to much refinement during the discussion. Still, even in Maryland, the majority were rather flexible. Of the eleven Maryland panelists, seven favored greater D.C. self-rule and seven would allow for representation by D.C. in the U.S. Senate. Ten would provide some sort of voting representation in Congress for D.C., and Maryland's lone advocate of the status quo would "not be against" a constitutional amendment to allow D.C.'s nonvoting delegate to become a voting representative.

Many in the Van Nuys group empathized with the District's lowly political status. Twelve of the thirteen panelists were for greater self-government, and eleven favored some sort of voting representation in Congress. Three held fixed positions against supporting D.C. in any form throughout most of the discussion, yet the others felt generally friendly—some occasionally passionately—toward D.C.'s self-rule efforts.

After a discussion of policy options, two opinion leaders in Van Nuys found a way to solve, at least in their own minds, D.C.'s situation. They advocated keeping Congress out of D.C. affairs and allowing D.C. residents to vote in Maryland elections. This well-intentioned policy did not give much consideration to the wishes of D.C. or Maryland residents. Actually, it was a time-driven policy outcome, coming at the end of the session when some solution seemed in order. A consensus among nearly all the group members was readily achieved by the opinion leaders; even one of the focus group's severe critics of D.C. joined in.

The Austin group was also empathetic with the District's political status. Two in the group were typed racially troubled, demonstrating negative racial affects toward the District which influenced their policy choices. However, the major theme in Austin, not surprisingly for Texans, was a desire for citizen independence—to keep the federal government off the backs of Americans. A greater proportion of people in the Austin group (ten of thirteen) than elsewhere favored complete D.C. self-government. All favored voting representation in Congress of some sort, with eleven favoring representation in the U.S. Senate. The panelists fully acknowledged the contradiction of wanting to give D.C. all the powers of statehood but not the title, and they enjoyed mocking their own cognitive shortcomings in this regard. The Austin group would be ripe for presidential leadership on behalf of any of the major policy options from retrocession to statehood.

The Harrisburg group, on its own initiative, achieved a consensus in favor of D.C. statehood by an eight-to-three margin. Nearly half (five of eleven) of the group were Republicans or Independents and some were self-professed conservatives, but it was generally a rather liberal group. Supporting full political rights for D.C. was not a difficult stretch for this group. Generally, the Harrisburg group would not only be receptive to presidential leadership on this issue, but ready to give the president and Congress tips on how Americans could be educated to support D.C. statehood. None in the group favored the status quo. The three panelists opposing statehood favored full political rights through Maryland's absorption of D.C. Unlike Van Nuys, where the participants seemed naive to the ramifications of allowing D.C. residents to vote in Maryland elections, in Harrisburg the three hold-outs against statehood were aware of the political upheaval Maryland absorption would cause. They knew the idea would be distasteful to Maryland residents and thought that Marylanders should be told to "eat your broccoli" (George, Pa.). Absorption of D.C. would be like forcing Maryland to take "a nuclear waste dump," but Maryland residents would get over it after a few decades, when the enlarged state would be fully accepted by all (George, Pa.). Less consideration by the three panelists was given to the feelings of D.C. residents about being absorbed into Maryland.

POLITICAL EQUALITY POINTS

As a shorthand summary of focus groups' policy outcomes, "political equality points" or "PE points" were assigned to the judgments of each panelist, each focus group, and each type of panelist and then totaled for all sixty-one panelists. Appendix C summarizes the stances of panelists and the points assigned, while appendix D is an explanation of how PE points were assigned. Appendix A includes an assignment of PE points for each panelist.

PE points were assigned on a 100 point scale, with 0 = status quo and 100 = statehood. For each senator a panelist was willing to give D.C., 30 points were assigned, and 15 points were given for a voting representative. (D.C. is entitled to only one representative by virtue of its population size.) If a panelist concluded that "one or two senators" were warranted for D.C., then 5 points were assigned for the panelist's consideration of the second senator.

Ten points were awarded for allowing D.C. residents to vote in Maryland elections. Under this policy option, D.C. residents would have many of the same advantages of representation as other Americans, including their own voting representative. D.C.'s residents could also, against long odds, run for the Senate. The plan does not encourage D.C.'s cultural identity, and it is difficult to say whether such a policy would assist or block D.C.'s long-term drive to statehood. Giving D.C. outright to Maryland is worth 0 PE points, since D.C.'s efforts toward autonomy and independence would be permanently ended. Such a policy would be worth many points on some other scale (e.g., a congressional representation scale), but not on a D.C. scale of political equality. Americans are accustomed to retaining their cultural identity; absorption by another state sacrifices cultural integrity. In the long run, of course, the new Maryland residents would accept their new identity, but so could any state's residents if they were absorbed into another state.

Fifteen points were awarded when a panelist advocated an end to congressional control over D.C. laws and budgets, with 5 points assigned for reduced control from the present level.

The average number of D.C. PE points assigned to the 61 panelists was 52. This means, for example, that the panelists would be for a voting representative, a U.S. senator, and reduced congressional control over D.C. affairs (actions which together total 15 + 30 + 5 = 50 points) with a couple points to spare. Such a policy position is about midway between statehood and the status quo.

The highest average PE points were awarded to the Harrisburg (73) and Austin (70) focus groups. These groups would on average approve, for example, two U.S. Senators, the one voting representative D.C.'s population level would allow, and reduced congressional control over D.C. affairs. These actions together total 70 points. The lowest total of 22 statehood points was awarded to the Van Nuys group. This is a somewhat misleadingly low score. Most of the Van Nuys panelists were rather friendly toward D.C.'s political ambitions. Most panelists clearly wanted the Americans who live in the District to have the same democratic rights as the Van Nuys panelists have. The solution these panelists chose—to have D.C. people vote in Maryland elections—was intended as a helpful gesture. This is a case where presidential or congressional leadership or persuasive (rather than objective) moderator leadership clearly would have produced a better policy outcome from D.C.'s perspective. Significantly, the Van Nuys group was among the most assertive in desiring an end to congressional control over D.C. bills and budgets.

OPINIONS AMONG TYPES OF PANELISTS

Earlier in this chapter and in appendix E, a typology of panelists was presented along with an assessment of the degree to which each type advocated political equality for D.C. residents. The true believers and empathizers tended to favor statehood, as expected, while anti-big-government types gave statehood and other forms of greater autonomy for D.C. residents some support. Originalists and the racially troubled tended to oppose D.C. statehood and other improvements in D.C.'s political status.

There were no differences in opinion patterns between men and women. Similarly, Democratic and Republican panelists were identical in their support for D.C. equality, with each awarding 47 PE points. The twenty Independents in the groups awarded an average of 57 PE points. Because of the small sample size, and because qualitative research results cannot be generalized, one cannot draw conclusions from such data. Nonetheless, it is of interest to note that the panelists who were Democrats did not simply view D.C. voting rights or D.C. statehood as a means to strengthen their party in Congress, nor did the Republicans view these policy outcomes as a threat to the erosion of their party's strength.

Older panelists tended to be somewhat more willing than the young to accept changes in D.C.'s political status (older citizens, 54 PE points; middle-aged citizens, 52 PE points; young citizens, 47 PE points), although this pattern, to the extent that there is one, has no statistical significance.

Clearer trends among the panelists emerged with respect to education and income. The lowest income panelists (those with family incomes under $30,000/year) awarded 65 PE points. Those in a middle income range ($30,000–59,999/year) awarded 54 points. Those in a higher range ($60,000–100,000/year) awarded 46 points. Panelists in the highest income range (over $100,000/year) awarded 42 points. Thus, at least among these panelists, the higher a panelist's income the less likely she or he was willing to support greater political autonomy for D.C. citizens. This tendency is confirmed in the research literature; for example, Kluegel and Smith (1986, 169) found decreased support for redistributive social and economic policies as income of their respondents increased.

On the other hand, as education among the panelists increased, support for improved political autonomy also increased. Those without college degrees awarded an average of 45 PE points. Panelists with undergraduate degrees awarded 48 points, while panelists with graduate degrees awarded 57 points. Again, while the small sample size limits the data's statistical significance, this tendency is confirmed in the research literature. Nie, Verba, and

Petrocik (1976, 37) demonstrated that education is a source of one's commitment to a democratic creed. Moreover, they found (ibid., 275–77) a greater level of political involvement and interest, which could imply a greater interest in exploring changes to the status quo, among the more highly educated. Kluegel and Smith (1986, 92) noted that like income, education is an indication of status. However, they observed that "[i]t may be that the socially liberalizing effects of education counter the status effects. . . ." The more highly educated are generally better able than the less educated to see flaws in theories that assign blame to the poor and minorities for their poverty status. Similarly, Schuman, Steeh, and Bobo (1985, 172–75) found greater tolerance among the more highly educated for the principle and implementation of racial integration.

METHODOLOGY FOR ANALYZING FOCUS GROUPS

Several useful guides facilitated an analysis of the focus group sessions (Krueger 1988; Stewart and Shamdasani 1990; Templeton 1987; Merton, Fiske, and Kendall 1956; Johnson and Joslyn 1986). A review of the policy highlights from focus group discussions, as summarized above, enables one to go beyond opinion polls to see policy outcomes when some groups of Americans encounter a little-known issue, process information about the issue, and form an opinion. In a similar vein, analyzing focus group discussions beyond the policy highlights makes it possible to gain a fuller understanding of opinion outcomes by examining the ideological conceptions that helped produce the outcomes. In this way, one may uncover the ingredients of public opinion, find what caused people to change their minds, and, of particular interest to political leaders, assess ways to mobilize public opinion for or against a political issue and target strategies.

Even though most of the panelists never gave a second's thought to D.C.'s political status prior to the sessions, they were nonetheless prepared for the discussions. They interacted with their fellow panelists and the moderator based on inferences they had previously drawn, collected, and assimilated. Most treated the topic with facility, providing startling insights that this writer (who has lived with this topic for many years) had not previously encountered.

Appendix G discusses schema theories, political cognition, and the research design. Graber provides a working model. Schemata, Graber (1988, 28–29) said, "contain conceptions of general patterns along with a limited repertoire of examples to illustrate these patterns." The examples are obtained from one's own experience, through others vicariously, and from the media. The schemata may be linked to one another, they may overlap one another, or they may be "morselized"—that is, isolated or embedded in limited contexts. The latter condition is often found among the majority of people who lack complex, overarching belief structures (ibid., 28–29, 188–214).

To arrive at a stage where schemata could be identified, the focus group discussions were transcribed and reviewed for common themes. Following research guidelines developed in appendix G, the transcripts were coded for (a) affect and priming; (b) policy implications; (c) thresholds of policy acceptance; (d) heuristics employed by the panelists; (e) potential schemata and their various dimensions and themes; (f) instances of schema change and potential catalysts to schema modification; (g) categorization of panelists; and (h) causes of schema change within the panelist categories.

SCHEMATA HIGHLIGHTS

Six schemata emerged from the focus group discussions:

1. *Democracy Schema.* Panelists believed that the full rights of democracy should be extended to all Americans. "Taxation without representation" was an especially persuasive theme, and some panelists regarded this theme as the "only" argument in D.C.'s favor. Democracy was viewed as a great leveler among the rich and poor, all races, both genders, and all geographic areas. The restorative powers of democracy were often cited; that is, political participation was felt to improve the individual, society, and government. This schema was strongly held by all the panelists, and it was the best understood and most textured of all the schemata.

2. *State Schema.* A majority of panelists had difficulty in matching what they knew about D.C. with their concept of what a state should be. This schema was often employed when the option of statehood was discussed. D.C.'s geographic size was thought to be too small, especially since it would not accommodate massive population growth (as Alaska's or Wyoming's sizes would). Panelists thought that D.C. does not "look like a state" and lacks economic diversity. It was thought by many to be a government town. Unlike the democracy schema, which largely went unchallenged, a panelist's state schema was vigorously contested by others. Because of the variety of sizes, shapes, occupations, and cultures in the existing states, no one state schema prevailed.

3. *D.C. Schema.* This schema was shaped by two themes. First, D.C.'s image was primarily negative to panelists who pointed to crime, drugs, corruption, welfare, and some unpopular (to the panelists) D.C. politicians. Second, aside from these negatives (many of which were generalized to all major

cities), panelists tended to be aschematic toward D.C. To most, D.C. had no identity aside from the negatives. Several thought that D.C. did not even have a clear identity among its own residents. Perhaps this schema facilitated policy solutions such as giving D.C. to Maryland or other states, or allowing D.C. citizens to vote in Maryland or other states. Such solutions are more palatable when it is perceived that D.C. has no cultural identity to be sacrificed.

This schema could not be pushed too far. If panelists indicated, for example, that D.C. residents could move if they wanted full democratic rights, or that D.C. residents are "not ready" for self-government, they would invariably receive a healthy dose of ideology from other panelists employing the democracy schema.

4. *Special Treatment Schema.* Many panelists voiced the opinion that D.C. residents are already advantaged without their political rights. D.C. residents receive federal jobs, federal grants, and welfare benefits, it was said, more than residents of other states do. D.C. residents already were said to govern the United States through their federal jobs, and adding senators and a voting representative would provide for "double representation" and special treatment.

A minority of panelists were concerned about the diminished political power of whites if they were subjected to a black-controlled government and no longer had Congress to overtly or subtly control the local government. Excessive taxation and reduction in services for the D.C. white population were the most frequently voiced concerns about greater self-rule for D.C. This latter theme was usually challenged successfully by the democracy schema.

5. *Anti-Big-Government Schema.* The second most prevalent schema among panelists was an anti-big-government schema. The vast majority of panelists questioned what value they received from their federal tax dollars. Moreover, the federal government was thought to interfere too much in state and local affairs. This schema worked to D.C.'s advantage, since several panelists were outraged over congressional control of D.C.'s laws and budgets. However, D.C. has its own image problem in that its bureaucracy is thought of as wasteful, inept, and often corrupt. This latter theme counteracts some of the beneficial effects of this schema.

Many panelists felt that Congress has a legitimate role to play in protecting federal interests in D.C., and that granting D.C. autonomy would undermine this responsibility. Others thought that Congress has so many explicit and implicit controls over states that special control over D.C. is unnecessary.

6. *Founding Fathers Schema.* A minority of panelists led by originalists felt passionately that D.C.'s place in the federal system was fixed in the

Constitution by the founding fathers, and that to alter their work would endanger freedoms beyond the D.C. political rights issue. All of the panelists revered the founding fathers; however, some more than others were unwilling to accommodate change to the original design.

SUMMARY: POLICY THRESHOLDS AND INTERSCHEMATIC LINKS

Sears, Hensler, and Speer (1979, 382–83), in their analysis of white racial attitudes, discussed the concept of "easy" and "hard" tests, with the former involving, for example, equal treatment in hotel accommodations, and the latter including, for example, friendships across racial lines and support for affirmative action programs (see chapter 4). Sears and Citrin (1982) also found such policy thresholds pertaining to ostensibly nonracial policies. In their examination of tax revolt schemata in California, an easy test involved advocacy of smaller government, while a harder test involved acceptance of budget cutbacks in specific programs that could affect respondents' daily lives.

In this analysis of public opinion on D.C.'s political future, the easiest test of all was voting representation of D.C. residents in the U.S. Congress, which nearly all panelists accepted as a basic American right. A majority even allowed for at least one senator from D.C. A harder test was full voting representation in the Senate and House, with the frequently voiced concern that such a policy would dilute a panelist's own vote. Statehood was the hardest test of all, supported by only a quarter of the panelists. There was some concern not only about dilution of the panelists' vote but also about taking away the nation's capital, which was said to belong to all Americans.

Schuman et al. (1985, 88–89, 196–211) identified an additional factor in public opinion formulation that could well pertain to shaping policies for D.C. Schuman et al. found abundant support for the *principle* of racial progress (e.g., an end to overt job discrimination), but their respondents could not as easily support *implementation* of means to achieve racial progress (e.g., federal intervention to assure fair staffing patterns). Their respondents experienced little pain of dissonance when realizing that their opposition to effective means of implementation would result in failure to achieve the principle. Issues of race aside, Verba and Orren (1988, 214, 266) observed that Americans actively support and seek political equality, while it is the *form* of equality that "arouses debate."

In this study, panelists supported with ease the principle of equal political rights for D.C. residents, but experienced great difficulty in supporting a form by which equality could be implemented. The status quo was clearly intolerable. Probably the most accepted solution to D.C.'s lack of representation was to provide D.C. with partial representation in Congress while retaining some lessened degree of congressional control over D.C. affairs. This compromise was a rather precise middle ground (50 political equality points on a 100 scale) between the status quo and full statehood rights.

In most groups, the pragmatists led the way in seeking solutions that had the least negative impact on the panelists' home state. In California, the state farthest geographically from D.C. among the five focus group states, there was unanimous support for allowing D.C. residents to vote in Maryland elections, and there was some support in other groups for absorption of D.C. by Maryland. However, in the Bethesda group, there was almost no support for using Maryland to solve D.C.'s political problems.

While self-interest was clearly a factor in panelists' decisions, a "dominant ideology," conceived by Huber and Form (1973) and statistically confirmed by Kleugel and Smith (1986), may have been more significant. Kluegel and Smith (1986, 11) demonstrated a belief system that disposes people toward inequality-related public policy. Kluegel and Smith (1986, 212) found from their survey "and several other surveys and polls"

> a pattern of majority support for programs that involve changing individuals to fit the existing stratification order and majority opposition to programs that appear to call for change in the stratification order itself.

Policies that pass what Sears et al. (1979, 1982) termed an easy test are those that are compatible with dominant ideology beliefs—for example, equal employment opportunity, voting representation of all Americans in Congress, and other such principles involving equal treatment. On the other end of the continuum are the hard tests which do not conform to the dominant ideology. As discussed in chapter 4, Kleugel and Smith (1986, 187) found a prevalent belief that blacks are to be blamed for their lower average socioeconomic status relative to whites because, for example, blacks are said by most whites not to have prepared themselves sufficiently to take advantage of opportunities that have been presented to them. This theme surfaced in panelists' discussions with respect to the failure of D.C. citizens and their elected leaders to take advantage of their self-rule opportunities.

The harder test of D.C. statehood is not "passed" by many panelists partly because of a negative D.C. schema and a special treatment schema that produced skepticism over D.C.'s drive to political equality. Moreover, the state schema and founding fathers schema are as equally powerful as the two racially charged schemata in producing opposition to D.C. statehood. In contrast, the democracy schema is clearly the most dominant one of the six, and when this schema worked in partnership with the anti-big-government schema, panelists advocated substantial improvement in D.C.'s political status.

6

Americans' Six Schemata on D.C. Policy Options

> *"How would you feel if we didn't have senators or congressmen representing us in the state of California? We have to remember that there are six hundred thousand American people who want to vote, want that representation, want to feel like us, and want to be accepted."*
>
> Pete, California focus group

Average Americans from around the nation have analyzed the District's unique situation in a more in-depth manner than any opinion poll could ever provide. This chapter presents the panelists' views on D.C.'s policy options, in their own words and through the six schemata emerging from the sessions.

Most schemata had from two to four themes. A theme may be thought of as a way in which a schema is manifested. Subthemes also emerged, which were not as strong or as prevalent as themes, and which were derivatives of the main themes. These will also be discussed. Finally, this chapter will discuss schema change—that is, how panelists' concepts about D.C. policy options changed during the course of the focus group sessions and what information or arguments tended to produce the changes. In chapter 5, panelists were categorized into several types (true believers, originalists, etc.). This chapter will discuss how each panelist type tended to process information and how each type experienced schema change. In the processing of new information, panelists often employed various heuristics (see appendix G) or shortcuts, and these will be described as well. Appendix H presents an easy reference guide of how the six schemata, their themes, and subthemes are organized.

1. The Democracy Schema

By far the most prevalent schema of the panelists was their core belief in democracy, the political infrastructure of a free and fulfilling way of life. All the panelists possessed this schema without any reservation.

Universality

The most predominant theme within the democracy schema was universality. It was assumed that all adult Americans (felons serving time excluded) should participate in the political process. The District's political status obviously presented blatantly contradictory information. Almost no one could reconcile her or his strong emotional attachment to democracy with D.C.'s lack of congressional representation, although originalists and the racially troubled (see typology in chapter 5) had sufficiently strong competing schemata—namely, founding fathers and special treatment, respectively—to accommodate divergence.

A few panelists tried to find other exceptions from American political participation. For example, Pete (Ia.) observed that American Indian reservations constituted their own nations, with their own settings and rules. However, he later acknowledged that the reservations' residents have voting representation in Congress. Information was presented to panelists about Puerto Rico, Guam, the Virgin Islands, and American Samoa. Each of these territories is on the same political plane as the District (they each have a nonvoting delegate in Congress), even though the latter three have much smaller populations than does the District and all lack the District's historical location among the original states. The information was designed to see if panelists would draw a distinction between D.C. and the territories. Surprisingly, it had an opposite effect on several people who thought that residents of the territories should be represented in Congress as well as D.C. residents. The democracy schema was triggered. As Ben (Tx.) said:

> I feel that we got a little dilemma when we have people who are American citizens, who happen by accident or geography not to have that right [of representation], but I feel more and more strongly, going through this discussion, that we've got five problems on our hands, not one.

Or as El (Md.) said, referring to the territories, "I don't think D.C. is unique." El and Ben employed a representativeness heuristic (appendix G), a shortcut form of reasoning that enabled them to match new information about D.C. with information they had previously received about U.S. territories.

The democracy schema was strong enough to compete effectively with other schemata. For example, Christine (Md.) did not appreciate many of the arguments that she heard against D.C. statehood: "What bad stuff could happen to those people [if they gained statehood]? I want to know. What corruption or repercussions?" As Mary (Pa.) said, "Why eliminate just those people who live in D.C.?"

The universality theme of the democracy schema helped counter the special treatment schema discussed below. Those with a special treatment schema expressed concerns, among other things, that D.C. whites would suddenly become powerless if the black majority of D.C. residents receive their full democratic rights. Such concern invariably would elicit a comment as to why "a white minority should set out rules for the majority" (Pete, Ia.). As Natasha (Md.) said, "Why shouldn't D.C. residents have a black senator who is very militant? They should!"

As discussed below, concepts about the District conflict with many panelists' schemata of what a state should be, especially because of the small land area. Nonetheless, the democracy schema and its universality theme prompted Marlene (Tx.) to remark (to laughter), "I'm sure that the six hundred thousand people in Washington, D.C. feel just as strongly about their land, whatever it is." Moreover, to the argument that D.C. residents may not be ready for full democracy, Molly (Tx.) said, "Those types of statements can get us into a lot of trouble." Mary (Tx.) agreed: "Yeah, it's scary, because then you can say, 'Well, women can't vote; people with AIDS can't vote; gays can't vote; and that's just opening up a whole can of worms." Mary also employed the representativeness heuristic, concluding that judgments about whether D.C. citizens can vote or not are representative of statements she has often heard with respect to minority groups. Pete (Ca.) summed up his view of D.C.'s situation:

> The problem is we have this mass of people who are unfortunately in the wrong spot [laughter]. These people are here. But still and all, these people are important because they are Americans like everybody in this room. . . . We can't forget about those people.

Taxation without Representation

Strongly supporting the democracy schema is the theme of taxation without representation. This is a theme that, for many, also helps counter the founding fathers schema held so tenaciously by originalists and many others as well. Taxation without representation was thought of as an obvious injustice. In fact, it was regarded by two panelists (Sid, Ia.; Willie Bob, Tx.) as the "only" argument D.C. had in its favor for greater political rights.

Several panelists mentioned the other side of the taxation-without-representation coin. As Al said, "If you really want to help D.C., take the noose from around their necks on paying the federal taxes." Three focus groups initiated this solution to D.C.'s politically inferior status. If the nation is not going to allow D.C. residents to have representation in Congress, then Congress should simply free D.C. residents from paying federal taxes and wealth would pour in. As Ben said, "I would buy my D.C. real estate before they trigger that." All three focus groups were simultaneously jocular and sincere in offering this solution. All recognized (again only half-jokingly) the policy's only drawback—that everyone else would gladly trade their democratic rights for freedom from paying federal income taxes. Discussion of this theme also sharpened the panelists' distinction between D.C. and the other federal territories in that D.C. is the only one with a nonvoting delegate in Congress whose residents pay federal income tax. As such, D.C. resembles a U.S. colony more than a territory.

Equal Political Power for All

A core belief of the democracy schema is that all U.S. citizens should be equally empowered—rich and poor, women and men, people of all colors, new citizens, and Americans of many generations. While elements of this theme favored improved D.C. political status, several panelists questioned how residents of a city, even a rather large one, could have power equal in the Senate to those of their own state. As Barb (Md.) said:

> You don't have to be a rocket scientist to figure out that in committees and everything else, senators are very, very powerful. That's the answer to why people are worrying about adding two senators [for D.C.]. It's not the population or the land mass, it's the fact that senators are very powerful.

A few panelists talked in terms of the "dilution" of their votes if two new senators from D.C. were added. It was difficult for a Texan such as Ben to accept parity for jurisdictions having great size differences. Texas, after all, is 3,950 times larger than D.C. in land area and 29 times larger in population. Ben, like others, observed that Vermont, Wyoming, and Alaska—states with smaller voting age populations than D.C.'s today—could likely accommodate growth better than D.C. could. The major concern was over a "skewing of power" (Mary, Md.).

Concerns over disproportionate power if D.C. gained full congressional representation arose in every focus group and in each instance were countered when it was pointed out that the U.S. Constitution provided for a bicameral legislature. This basic civics lesson was recited in each group by someone who said that the smaller states were given equal power in the Senate, while the larger ones received their just due in the House. Each group had a panelist who knew approximately how many representatives her or his state had. Someone in each group also pointed out that Los Angeles, for example, does not have to become its own separate entity because its residents already have voting representatives and senators.

Restorative Powers of Democracy

Numerous panelists pointed out that full participation in the American democratic system by D.C. residents would not solve the District's many socioeconomic problems. Many others, however, cited the restorative powers of democracy, as the Austin discussions demonstrated. Mary (Tx.), for example, said, "I think we have problems there to be solved, and I think they will be solved better if those people are represented in the federal government." When David (Tx.) noted that some "quick solution" such as statehood would not be the answer to D.C.'s problems, Marlene (Tx.) replied, "But it might be a step in that direction." David (Tx.) tried again by saying that if you gave people a choice between representation and a thriving economy, the latter would win out every time. He called statehood a "misguided effort." Another panelist (Molly, Tx.) responded to David by citing democracy's restorative powers:

> I really believe that when people are given the chance to speak out or feel that they are being listened to, that things change. But if they feel like they have no voice they will say, "What the heck, it doesn't matter anyway" [and the problems continue]. So I would favor statehood, if that's what they would like.

Willie Bob (Tx.) also thought that "statehood might actually solve some problems. If nothing else, it would be a change. Maybe it would give them a chance."

Other focus groups responded similarly. Natasha (Md.) viewed D.C.'s problems as "a symptom of their needing a different form of government." Laura (Pa.) cited D.C.'s problems as proof that the current system has not worked for two hundred years. In Van Nuys, Dawn, a supporter of the status quo for D.C. for much of the session, seemed to shift gears and join in a consensus for D.C. self-government and for a vote in Maryland elections by calling upon democracy's restorative powers:

> We need to look at someone who for a period of time has had no representation. Apathy begins to set in after a while. They don't care anymore, and they don't feel like they can have any effect, so they don't try. And then you end up with a generation of illiterate people, people who may not even be able to read a ballot. . . . History hasn't proven this, but [with congressional representation and self-government] there might be a resurgence of hope to some degree. People would say, "Yes, I can make a difference now, I do have some say, and this is my life to choose my laws."

Of all the schemata, the democracy schema was the one most dearly held and the most textured. It was seldom, if ever, successfully challenged in any of the focus groups. An interchange from the Maryland group provides a humorous insight into the power of this schema:

> HOWARD: People who move into the District, do you think they really care whether they lost their vote or not? I'm just curious.
>
> JEFF: I would guess it's not a major concern, but it's at least a minor concern.
>
> ABBY (former D.C. resident): I thought it was real annoying.
>
> NATASHA (another former D.C. resident): I was constantly going to write my senator or congressman. Only, I didn't have one.

The simulation heuristic (appendix G) was employed by Abby, Natasha, and other panelists. They had experienced or witnessed the benefits of democracy in the past, and they believed these benefits would be simulated in the scenarios they constructed for D.C.'s democratic participation. One may speculate that democracy's benefits are especially appreciated once they have been removed.

2. The State Schema

While the democracy schema helps the District's cause, the state schema damages at least the statehood component of D.C.'s efforts. To panelists, a state consists of mountains, prairies, cities, suburbs, rural areas, and people holding a wide variety of occupations. As Americans, D.C. residents may be entitled to full democratic rights, but they may lack a vehicle to obtain these rights if D.C. cannot be a state. Hence the frequent use of the word "dilemma." A decided minority thought the people themselves may not be worthy of the rights other American enjoy because D.C. people are viewed as unproductive; that is, they are viewed as either welfare recipients or employees in the federal government, a slightly more respectable form of welfare. However, most panelists considered D.C. residents, as Americans, worthy of full democratic rights. It is the jurisdiction, not the people, that many question. In contrast to the strong and consistent democracy schema, for every argument emanating from a state schema, a counterargument was often devised by another panelist.

Size and Shape

The primary theme in the state schema is size—of population and of resources. As Herb (Md.) said, referring to the constitutionally designed size limit on the District, "It's hard for people living in Ohio, Iowa, and California to conceive of a 'ten miles square' city as being a state. I don't agree with it, but it is a psychological problem." Closely related to size is shape. Pete (Ca.) asserted, "States are mapped. That's a state." As Tony (Md.) said, "It would be the only state that's just a dot on the map and has nothing but the city."

Tom (Pa.) summed up the size issue by saying that D.C. "does not have the physical stature as many of our other states do." Often in the groups, Rhode Island was mentioned as a "parking-lot-size state" (Jeff, Md.) or some such term, at which point someone would observe that it takes much more time to drive across Rhode Island than it does the District. Just as inevitably, someone would respond that there is nothing in the Constitution specifying that a state has to meet a minimum size requirement. A panelist would then add that it is the people residing in the state who count, not how long it takes to drive across it. Lynn (Tx.) observed, "I think we are discounting peoples' value just because they live in a small spot, and I think that is unfair."

One concern that arose in all the groups was the consequence of granting statehood to D.C., since New York City, Dallas, Philadelphia, Chicago, and other cities might also want to become their own states. There was a mild fear that at a "fracturing point" (Glenn, Pa.) the nation could no longer function. The nation would be destroyed if Dallas, Philadelphia, New York, D.C., and others all could become states. Employing the "anchoring and adjustment" heuristic (appendix G), they anchored on allowing D.C. statehood and adjusted by considering the effects of such a policy on other cities. This fear was usually not allowed to take root in the focus groups, however. For example, in Harrisburg, Tom observed that "[w]e are not breaking the country down, we are building it up" by bringing into the federal system "people who are disenfranchised there." Sue (Pa.) also countered: "I don't think there is going to be a domino effect, because the other cities already have their representation, so there's really nothing for them to break down for."

The District's relatively small population size was factored into discussions about how many senators D.C. deserved. Population size was not a major impediment for many. As Christine (Md.) said, "Wyoming would never be a state if it was population" that comprised the criterion. However, an area's future population did matter to others. David (Tx.) said:

> I don't think it's hardly disproportionate right now. But looking down the road fifty years, Wyoming is going to have a lot more people, and how much bigger can D.C. get? Well, obviously it may get to a couple of million, but I can't see it really growing. Texas is still going to keep growing and keep growing.

This latter argument usually arose in the groups and gained some acceptance.

In two of the groups, a subtheme evolved that it is not just D.C.'s population size that is in question but its "certain kind of population" (Howard, Md.). Not only is D.C. just a city, according to Howard, but it is a truncated city; the outer parts of what would ordinarily be part of the city are instead in Maryland and Virginia. Howard said that the "cream" of the city moved out, with the "worst part" in the middle left over. Tony (Md.) was responsive to this point, saying that D.C., as a result, is "lacking in so many of the demographics that make up other states." Others were offended by the thought that poverty could affect democratic rights. In Austin, the point was also made that the suburbs of Texan cities isolate themselves from the problems of urban centers, while in D.C. this phenomenon is exacerbated by the effects of the state lines: "You can really completely turn your back on the center [D.C.] of this hub and cross a line" (Ben, Tx.). To Molly (Tx.) the result is that

> probably the more affluent don't live in Washington, D.C. They are able to live in the outlying areas and they have representation. So what you end up with is you have all these poor people living in one area without representation.

Sufficiency and Diversity of Resources

The moderator gave panelists Congress' criteria for achieving statehood (see chapter 3), and panelists particularly noted the third criterion, which requires an area to have sufficient population and resources to support a state government and contribute its share of costs in providing for the federal government. The Des Moines group particularly expressed this concern, though several other groups' panelists did as well. Danny (Ia.) bluntly stated:

> I don't think they got the resources to contribute financially to the country like most other states do, because my feeling is it's mostly government workers or a lot of welfare recipients.

Sid (Ia.) added:

> I don't believe Washington, D.C. could survive without federal funding and all the services that are required, and they are still going to need federal funding whatever they are.

Some of the panelists in other groups pointed out that the nation currently has states that are struggling economically. For example, Herb (Md.) said, "This society [D.C.] can support itself better than the state of Mississippi can, probably right now." In Des Moines, however, Sid countered this argument seemingly to the satisfaction of most members of this group by saying that Mississippi "became a state under the criteria for statehood, and they contributed in the past." Even though Mississippi lacks abundant resources now, "I don't think there is a mechanism to take away statehood," Sid said. Danny (Ia.) added: "Can Mississippi make it on their own or is it all government that is keeping it together? The U.S. government is not located in Mississippi." In the Bethesda group, El noted that other states rely upon considerable federal assistance, but questioned whether "we want to build that in at the beginning" by making D.C. a state. Barb (Md.) countered that "if D.C. is in such a horrible state, then maybe the federal government has an obligation to make it viable as a state."

Many of the concerns expressed about D.C.'s resources related to their lack of diversity. In Des Moines, where this schema was the most hardened, Gary noted:

> In Iowa, if corn prices are down, we hope our insurance industry is doing well, whereas in D.C., if it starts going down it just spirals. There's nothing there to offset a downturn. . . . That's an argument against making any city a state.

The concerns appeared elsewhere—for example, in Van Nuys:

> DELL: It wouldn't be comparable to other states would it? You wouldn't have any farming community.

FRANCINE: You wouldn't have any industry, other than government.

DELL: It could be all special interest groups, all or mostly government.

Dell (Ca.) noted that in the states you have "pastures and forests." At such points, someone invariably would ask whether we are forgetting about the people of D.C. Herb (Md.) was among the strongest in countering other panelists' state schemas: "I don't care about the land, parks, or anything like that; there's six hundred thousand people." And Sue (Pa.) argued that "[i]f you consider resources as being human resources," then the District would have a sufficient supply.

The panelists seemed to know that the content and boundaries of a state schema were up for grabs. Christine (Md.) listened to George's argument that "50 percent of the employment is the D.C. or federal government or the post office" and responded:

> D.C. doesn't have mining, it doesn't have natural resources, but it's got the federal government. Why can't it live off the federal government? There's business to be done in support of the government.

She did not see this type of employment as disqualifying an American from full democratic rights. Pete (Ca.) observed:

> Maybe if there was representation there, then maybe industry might come into Washington. Maybe they might start a computer chip factory there. Maybe they might start exporting stuff.

Again, the restorative powers of democracy came into play, this time helping to shape a state schema.

In Des Moines, Jeannie attacked some of her fellow panelists' state schemas by pointing to the lack of diversity in other states. After Gary argued that a state should have a "diverse economy, with urban and rural areas," Jeannie said:

> If that's going to be a problem, we are going to have states that will wither and die because they have no urban areas, and all they are is rural. You can look at Montana, where urban areas are simply dying. Does Montana get not to be a state because they do not have urban areas anymore?

Herb (Md.) had a similar thought:

> For many years, Nevada was nothing but a bunch of desert, so we got Las Vegas and built it into a gambling capital. Otherwise, we would have two senators representing a lot of sand.

Land areas and the numbers of people in them evolve over time, and several panelists urged others not to adopt a fixed view of what constitutes a state. Sue (Pa.), a young Asian American, said she couldn't remember when Hawaii became a state, but remarked:

> I'm sure, though, that the people who were around then had trouble handling the fact that it had become a state. To me, it's a state, it's virtually always been a state, and I think the same thing would hold true with D.C.

Indeed, Hawaii is far out in the Pacific, and with a large population of Asian origin, became a state less than two decades after Pearl Harbor.

There was no commonly held state schema, probably because the fifty states are so diverse. On average, most of the panelists had difficulty conceptualizing D.C. as a state, but their views of what a state should be were conflicting.

3. The D.C. Schema

Closely related to panelists' state schema was their D.C. schema. A D.C. schema was rather well developed among the ten panelists who at some point had lived there. The D.C. schema was bidimensional among those who have visited D.C. or who merely depended upon news images. Even among those who had lived in D.C., the transient, federal worker component of Washington was often emphasized. As many panelists observed, D.C. is really two cities, an affluent part—which in the minds of panelists is largely white and composed at least in part of people who come to D.C. for government-related work and then head elsewhere after a brief stint—and a largely black, low-income area with numerous urban problems where generations of families are more likely to live. This schema is incomplete and in many ways inaccurate. Even in the largely white, affluent areas of D.C. there is more racial integration than one finds in many other states and cities, and there are several affluent, predominantly black areas of D.C. as well.

The focus groups revealed two major themes within the D.C. schema. One theme is largely negative. The other is surprisingly absent of much content, as if one does not expect to find a distinctive character and the elements of "home" in Washington, D.C. Many panelists were aware that D.C. was not all crime, corruption, and welfare, but could not conceptualize the remainder.

The panelists' D.C. schema would seem to work against the District's aspirations for improved political rights. Nonetheless, since this schema is so poorly developed in the panelists' minds, it is the schema that can most easily be influenced by political leaders. By adding substance of any kind—about the neighborhoods, occupations, universities, D.C.'s state-type government structure, and the like—the negative images could be reduced more closely to their proper proportions, and the "void" perhaps could be erased altogether for those who might care enough to listen.

Negative Images

About one-fifth of the panelists' images about D.C. were quite positive. Panelists' views of democracy and its capital were intertwined. Some claimed to be mesmerized by the monuments and by the power of events that take shape in Washington. Others expressed disenchantment with politics, which tarnished the capital city's sheen. For example, Ivana (Tx.) remarked, "It's like not wanting to go to Hollywood because I'm not starstruck. I'm not impressed with Washington because I'm not impressed with politicians."

Primed with so much negative news coverage of D.C., it is not surprising that panelists' views of D.C. were about four-fifths negative. The sessions were conducted just three years after the massive news coverage of Mayor Marion Barry's troubles, while the earlier, generally successful Barry terms received little national notice. As Bruce (Ca.) said:

> Marion Barry kind of summarizes Washington, D.C. up in a lot of people's heads. You know, he was that leader who got in trouble with drugs and appeared to be irresponsible. I think a lot of people form their impression of Washington, D.C. based on him.

While Bruce is probably accurate in thinking that for now Marion Barry serves as a proxy for many Americans' impressions about D.C., it is also likely that D.C. itself serves as a proxy for panelists' stereotypical views about low-income minorities.

The overriding feeling emerging from the sessions, with the racially troubled and originalists leading the way for this schema, was a view of Washington, D.C. as a cherished placed honored by all Americans which has fallen into the hands of D.C. residents, who have usurped the splendor and accessibility. To many, the capital should belong to all the people. The capital city is a place that should symbolize America, but instead has become something else entirely. Crime, corruption, welfare, and a general "mess" were emphasized in all of the sessions. For example, to George (Md.), D.C. "sounds like a basket case that nobody wants." The conservatives in the groups placed primary responsibility for the mess upon the D.C. government or the low-income people themselves, who created their own demise, while the liberals attributed causes of the problems to the federal government and society in general. Regardless of blame, there was some feeling that the nation's capital was no longer quite theirs anymore. For some, self-government for D.C. residents was an extrapolation of a trend that was already unsettling for them—D.C. is slowly being taken away. The notion of an enclave of federal monuments and buildings under federal control helped ameliorate the concerns to a degree. Panelists also lamented the decline of their own areas' central cities, such as Dallas, Houston, Los Angeles, and Philadelphia, pointing out that D.C. was not alone in its socioeconomic conditions.

D.C.'s negative images emanated from several sources. To the racially troubled, D.C. would be a "very black state" (Mia, Md.) with "a lot of scum areas" (Francine, Ca.). Francine elaborated, "Their citizenry is predominantly black, so you have a whole different kind of thinking there." By this Francine meant that the D.C. people

> seem to be illiterate and not able to really take care of themselves emotionally and physically. . . . You say they can't get off welfare—hey, they don't want to get off welfare. . . . Criminals go commit a crime so they can get back in jail so they don't have to face the everyday problems you and I face.

Jason (Tx.) viewed D.C. as "a poor example" and said:

> If they want to become a state, I think they ought to clean up their act, get drugs and stuff out of there, get crime off the streets, and get the property taken care of. They got the power to do that, and why they don't do it, I don't know.

D.C. was also viewed as "the murder capital of the United States" (Sue, Pa.).

When discussing their conceptions of D.C., panelists would usually start by saying something nice about this "treasured city" (Mia, Md.), as if demonstrating proper manners. These statements would usually refer to what Dell (Ca.) termed D.C.'s "postcard image." However, it would not take long for many to warm to their task, as in Des Moines:

> CHRIS ONE: "Big cesspool."
>
> LYNN: "Lots of welfare recipients."
>
> SUSAN: "Very black."
>
> DAVE: "Many crooks and welfare recipients."

CHRIS TWO: "Wheeling and dealing."

CHRIS ONE: "Lobbyists, and expensive."

This recitation captures the duality of D.C.: "You have the affluent and the poor" (Sid, Ia.), "a grandeur and decadence, side by side" (George, Md.). The Maryland group saw three D.C.'s: the area west of Rock Creek Park (where most of the whites live), "the other part of town where the black sections are" (Herb, Md.), and the Federal Triangle (the federal offices) where "people come in every day, complain, and then leave [in the evening]" (Barb, Md.).

Panelists' conceptual problems with D.C. extended beyond a lack of diversity in its resources; its purpose was sometimes called into question. As Tim (Ia.) said:

> I don't want to sound negative, but Washington, D.C. just gives service to the federal government. Letting the government exist is its main goal. From the guy at the 7-Eleven to the lobbyist, they are just fueling the federal government and not contributing to the overall good. Vermont and Wyoming [small population states] contribute something to the good of all.

To some, this part of a D.C. schema gave an artificial quality to D.C.

The panelists' images of the D.C. government also contributed to the largely negative schema. "The most corrupt government in the country," asserted Mia (Md.). Dell (Ca.) believed, "You get the type of government that represents the kind of people that you have," drawing a parallel between D.C. and Africa, where "every black nation over there is not doing very much." In contrast, the United States "is the greatest nation on earth because of the great people who designed our government," Dell said. Invariably, blatantly racist statements, such as the one above, were challenged by some other panelists, usually by "true believers" or "empathizers." In this case, Cheryl (Ca.) responded to Dell by saying, "If people are not allowed to better themselves, I don't think the government does represent the kind of people they have."

It is clear that many of the negative images, in addition to being racially driven, were media-primed, as the Austin group openly discussed. Willie Bob said, "I have two images of D.C.: I have the one we learned in school with all the monuments, and then I have the television news reality." And Mary commented, "The media let us know about things we never realized before, Marion Barry and all that, that it's an embarrassment as the capital of our country." Willie Bob said, "I'm assuming there's a lot of good, too, that Washington, D.C. just has normal urban problems." Willie Bob asked, "It sounds terrible to me from what I've heard, but it can't be that bad, can it?" However, his comment was greeted with derision, prompting him to say, "It sounds like there's no hope from the way you talk. Maybe [someone should] just blow the whole thing up." It is clear that several panelists employed the availability heuristic (appendix G); that is, they had been provided with so much negative news coverage of D.C. and of cities in general that it was easy for many to write D.C. off as a lost cause. However, Buster (Pa.), who was generally quiet during the session, spoke up about D.C.'s image: "It doesn't recognize the positives that the city has, the individuals that live inside, the success stories of the people."

Christine (Md.) summed up the views of most panelists by saying, "D.C. is in a very sorry state. It's a place of suffering and great social illness. . . . Maybe it's time for something new to be considered." As children, many panelists were taught that the nation's capital was a "model for the whole country," but now D.C. "shows the bad side of America, which, I guess in a way, it still is a model" (Ivana, Tx.). On average, the comments about D.C. were generally either harshly and profoundly negative, or negative in an ostensibly liberal, understanding, condescending, or commiserating way.

The Jackson and Barry Subtheme

Jesse Jackson and Marion Barry comprised a subtheme to the negative D.C. schema. In contrast to Martin Luther King, Jr., who was warmly regarded in the pre-session questionnaires (averaging 73 out of 100 on the feeling thermometer), Jackson (scoring 40) was regarded much more icily. Jackson and Barry were both seen as political symbols of D.C. and its leaders, with their negative characteristics emphasized to an extreme. (The two are also political symbols to their supporters, who view their positive traits in the extreme.)

The Bethesda panelists, as inside-the-Beltway residents (although outside D.C. and "safely inside" the Maryland line, as George put it), were political analysts. Jackson was regarded as a very big factor against other state residents' acceptance of D.C. into the Union. It would be better for D.C. if a Colin Powell or "someone like the late Arthur Ashe" were instead discussed as a U.S. senator from D.C. (El and Herb, respectively, Md.).

Some of the comments about Jackson and Barry were vitriolic, with the racially troubled leading the way. For example, Danny (Ia.) said:

> When you already know ahead of time that they are going to elect people that you don't want in, that definitely affects my views, because

> Jesse Jackson and Marion Barry would be senators for life if Washington, D.C. becomes a state. I don't want either one. I don't want to see them on TV ever again. I can't stand them.

Some panelists analyzed Jackson and Barry from the perspective of white D.C. residents. George (Md.) "could not see how people who live in Spring Valley, who are largely white, although there are some blacks there, could feel like they were really represented" with Jackson and Barry as their senators. He added, "I mean, how would their lives be made better by having a majority black city with a majority black congressional district?" Or, putting it more simply, Pete (Ca.), an Hispanic, said, "I am a minority, but I don't feel Jesse represents me very well. I just feel he will sway too much in one direction." Others regarded Jackson as a "rabble rouser" with "too much mouth" who attracts followers "like a bunch of cattle" (Francine, Ca.), and as a "very prejudiced" person who "pushes religion too much" (Frances, Ca.).

D.C. analyst Jamin Raskin (Ragland 1993, 24) observed that Jesse Jackson symbolizes the potential of New Columbia as well as conservatives' "worst nightmare." In the focus groups, the negative comments on Jackson outnumbered the positive comments seven to one. Some thought Jackson would be "fun to watch" in debates with right-wingers, and one (Sherry, Pa.) said simply, "I would love to see Jackson put in." However, over half of the comments on Jackson were neither negative nor positive. Most panelists disciplined themselves to stay neutral. For example, Willie Bob (Tx.) epitomized this view by saying, "If that's who they want to vote for, that will be great." The majority felt that voters' choices for senators should have no bearing on whether D.C. should have voting rights. In fact, Lynn (Ia.) said discussion of whether Jackson would be a senator "is rather insulting to the issue as a whole." The Jackson-Barry subtheme ultimately was no match for the powerful democracy schema. Frequently, when Jesse Jackson would be mentioned, someone would mention "the other Jesse," namely Jesse Helms, the arch-conservative senator from North Carolina. "I can't believe people elect Helms, but they do. That's how the country works," said Tony (Md.).

One panelist—Tim in Des Moines—asked, "Is there a problem of race here? I don't like Barry and I don't like Jackson either, but I think the black vote would probably elect both of them." He shrugged, as if to say, "That's democracy for you." Lynn (Ia.) responded to Tim's point by asserting that if D.C. were "more of a white urban problem" that "fewer people would be against statehood. It's not necessarily fair, but it would probably help the issue if Washington, D.C. was less black. It would probably help it a lot."

A Lack of Identity in the D.C. Schema

If D.C. political leaders are troubled by a negative D.C. schema, they should perhaps be as concerned about the aschematic tendencies of panelists toward D.C. Aside from the negative images, the overwhelming majority of panelists demonstrated little awareness of D.C. and its people.

D.C. has an identity problem, some of which can be traced to its role as capital of the nation. As then-House Minority Whip Newt Gingrich (R–Ga.) said (Jenkins 1993, 22), "People from all over America consider Washington their city. They want to keep it that way." Several panelists also felt that D.C. is everyone's city and does not just belong to the residents. To achieve this result several panelists argued for keeping D.C. "neutral," an oft-repeated term.

Gary (Ia.) told the moderator, "I think you are the first person I've ever met that said they are from the District of Columbia." He was one of two Des Moines panelists who had lived in D.C. for awhile, but he had not met people *from* D.C., he said. In the fifty states, Gary said, there is "a common social or cultural identity that, in at least some point in its history, has made the area an entity that you can identify as a state." Gary thought that D.C. lacks this identity, unlike Hawaii or Alaska (even though the latter state could well have a greater ratio of transients and newcomers to long-term residents than does D.C.).

This lack-of-identity theme surfaced in various forms. Barb (Md.), raised in Virginia, said, "I'm often astounded because someone will come up to me and say, 'You are from Virginia—I can tell; you are a Virginia person.'" However, she wondered, "What makes you a D.C. person? Is it because you are black? I don't think so. There's lots of white people living in D.C." To Barb, D.C. people lack identity, even to each other. Similarly, Danny (Ia.) said:

> I hate to be this cold or blunt about it, but there is nothing that tags you a Washington, D.C. resident and says you can't move to Maryland [and become a part of the federal political system]. You are not there for life.

Danny, a farmer the first thirty-five years of his life, implied that perhaps D.C. residents are not tagged or branded with an identity to the extent that Iowans and others are, and may feel more free to roam. In another group, Glenn (Pa.) echoed this theme, saying, "From my standpoint, the people who live in northwest Washington are really citizens of Maryland and ought to be a part of the Maryland government." The northwest quadrant of D.C. is one where most of the whites live (although many blacks live there as well), and Glenn associated the people of this quadrant more with Maryland than with the black-controlled D.C. government. And Mary, a panelist in Austin, said, "I always thought D.C. was part of Virginia or something."

Policy Implications of D.C. Schema

The policy implications of the negative themes in the D.C. schema are not difficult to comprehend. As discussed in appendix G, people often adopt the affective heuristic in determining their opinions on political objects. They know whether they like or dislike a group and assess whether a particular policy is intended for the group's benefit. For many, this affective or emotionally ladened response determines their policy position (Sniderman et al. 1986, 408–26). D.C.'s negative images feed the affective heuristic.

The lack-of-identity theme in the D.C. schema has enormous policy implications. Many of the panelists felt that D.C. and its people either "belong" to another entity—to Maryland, Virginia, Congress—or should be "given" to them. Perhaps control of D.C. by Congress, Maryland, or some other entity may relate to a dominant ideology (Kluegel and Smith, 1986, 183–84) which holds that "white Americans see blacks as a major disruptive force in society" and view blacks' demands for change as "illegitimate." When views are considered illegitimate, they may be dismissed altogether.

While one cannot chalk up giving D.C. away to Maryland as consistent with a dominant ideology, it may be a context worth considering. Decades ago, Ralph Ellison (1952, 3), in *Invisible Man*, offered insight into the lack-of-identity theme. The novel's protagonist said:

> I am invisible, understand, simply because people refuse to see me. . . . When they approach me they see only my surroundings, themselves, or figments of their imagination—indeed, everything and anything except me.

In the Austin group, Molly asked what the new state would be called if D.C. were made part of Maryland: "Would they be called Maryland/D.C.?" she asked. When informed that the state's name would simply be "Maryland," the group erupted into spontaneous laughter, at ease with discarding D.C.'s cultural identity.

By about a six-to-one margin, giving D.C. to another state was viewed not so much as a problem for D.C. residents as it was a problem for the other state. Ivana (Tx.) observed that "D.C. is a cesspool of poverty, drugs, and racial tension. It's not the Hawaiian Islands. If it was the Hawaiian Islands, someone would have already snatched it up." Ivana assumed that D.C. should be given away because she thought it lacks the legitimacy or substance to stand on its own, but she could not imagine another state taking D.C.

Giving D.C. to Maryland was viewed as problematic. In the Bethesda group, Tony said, "I lost my job from state budget cuts already. I don't think we can afford the District of Columbia." Panelists in all the groups mentioned the tax burden and crime problems that taking D.C. would impose on Maryland.

At this point, in each of the five groups, the same clever quip was concocted. In Van Nuys, Cheryl exclaimed, "Put D.C. up for adoption! Maybe South Dakota wants them." In Austin, Ben et al. said, "Let's set up a bidding war and see which state would want it. . . . West Virginia would probably take it. . . . Rhode Island could double in size." In Bethesda, El said, "Maybe bid it out. Put out an RFP [a request for proposals]: 'beautiful piece of property, nice views.'" Glenn (Pa.) also spoke of "offering D.C. up to the highest bidder" after the panelists reasoned that D.C. residents could vote in or be taken over by Virginia as easily as Maryland, or even by New York or Rhode Island. After all, Scott (Pa.) said, "telephones work pretty well nowadays." Glenn (Pa.) added, "I have less of a problem with Pennsylvania claiming Washington than I do with D.C. as a state." Des Moines completed the circuit with the following exchange:

> PETE: I guess if Maryland doesn't want it—this is tongue in cheek—why don't you approach any of the other states?
>
> JEANIE: Auction it off!
>
> CHRIS ONE: Highest bidder!
>
> MARGARET: That's not bad. But what if nobody bid on it?
>
> DANNY: Well, Nevada does not have real estate taxes, and they have gambling in there [to support D.C.'s resource needs].
>
> CHRIS ONE: Give D.C. to Montana, and they will have their urban and their rural!

The negative image of D.C. that would make a state reluctant to "take" D.C., coupled with a lack-of-identity that would imply D.C. could be "given away" without thwarting the aspirations of D.C. residents, produced the preceding satirical resolutions. Of course, the view that D.C. should "belong" to some other entity is interpreted by some D.C. residents as having pernicious racial connotations with roots in slavery; alternatively, the view could simply arise from D.C.'s limited physical and financial stature.

Another approach would go even further than giving D.C. to Maryland or another state; it would politically atomize D.C. by, as Margaret (Ia.) explained, "enabling the District to choose whatever state they wanted to vote in. Like a registered Democrat, they might say 'I'm a registered Alabaman.'" She added:

> You could let the computers keep track, so that people could change their registration and be able to say, "This year I can vote as an Alabaman, and next year I might want to vote as a Texan."

An approach with broader appeal, accepted by about one-fourth of panelists, would be to give D.C. one senator because D.C. is a "special case" (Ben, Tx.). Jason (Tx.) pointed out that "[i]f you are a good senator, you can have just as much push as two senators." This subtheme was overridden by the democracy and founding fathers schemata. As Laura (Pa.) said, "You can't compromise. It's in the Constitution." Moreover, one senator for D.C. could upset the current balance. As Al (Tx.) said, the next step would be to look to Wyoming, Vermont, and others to see if they should have one senator also, and Pete (Ca.) thought it would open the door for his state to claim three.

Other Subthemes of the D.C. Schema

Some subthemes provided a way to counteract the D.C. schema; namely, they encouraged panelists to shift to other schemata. Chief among these subthemes was the view that D.C. residents may not be ready for full democratic participation (voting rights, self-rule, statehood, etc.) This lack of readiness falls within the negative theme in the D.C. schema. This subtheme struck a responsive chord among a small minority of panelists, and especially among the racially troubled, whose counterparts everywhere have been voicing the they-are-not-ready argument for decades with respect to civil and human rights issues. The "not ready" argument was viewed by Lynn (Tx.) as "a real poor excuse for denying them the rights that everybody else in the country has." In Harrisburg, Tom said, "There are no standards of behavior or conduct that are a condition for citizenship." Each group pointed out that crime or corruption could be found everywhere, and an example of a home state's fallible politician jumped to mind in each group. The "not ready" subtheme was no match for the democracy schema. In Austin, Ben frankly asserted that D.C. citizens are not the ones who are unready for the more advanced forms of D.C. political rights: "I think *we* are the ones who are not ready for D.C. statehood. It doesn't matter what the District is all about."

A "they-can-always-move" subtheme fits into the lack-of-identity theme and the D.C. schema. This subtheme also served as a catalyst to a schema shift. The idea of this subtheme is that if people want full democratic rights so badly, all they have to do is pack up and leave D.C. This subtheme was advocated by a rather small minority, and it was always effectively countered. George (Md.) pointed out, "People come to D.C. and live there voluntarily but they can also move. They don't have to live in the nation's capital." Tony (Md.) could not make much sense of George's statement: "But of course everybody lives everywhere voluntarily." Molly (Tx.) noted that "[y]ou have all your traditions and roots, and chances are you are not going to uproot yourself and charge off to Virginia just because you can vote there." Christine (Md.) thought that many people are "stuck" in D.C., while Cheryl (Ca.) said, "Look at the people in south-central [Los Angeles], all they have to do is take a ten-minute ride into Beverly Hills, but that doesn't mean they are going to be able to live there." This subtheme allowed people to (a) call upon their democracy schema to override what was termed a "ridiculous" point of view, and (b) identify with D.C. residents as people much like themselves.

The other themes and subthemes of the D.C. schema were more difficult for D.C. advocates to counter. Sherrie (Ia.) pointed out that D.C. is "two separate cities, one by day and one by night." The spokespeople during the day are the world's most influential politicians, and it was Sherrie's view that "there are too many voices in the daytime," so much so that the voices of the six hundred thousand D.C. residents are overwhelmed. Such thoughts lend support to the lack-of-identity theme and fail to recognize that D.C. residents have normal lives apart from questions about who is able to speak out most effectively on the issues of the day. To some extent, both the negative and the aschematic components of the D.C. schema could be countered by a campaign that brings visibility to D.C.'s people, their daily lives, neighborhoods, history, traditions, occupations, aspirations, and diversity. D.C. advocates could also encourage Americans to shift their thoughts to schemata that are more favorable to D.C.'s democratic participation by initiating the "they-can-always-move," the "they-only-deserve-one-senator," and the "they-are-not-ready" subthemes of the D.C. schema—perhaps by quoting unpopular national leaders who employ such subthemes, since these arguments can be countered rather easily. On the whole, however, these focus groups indicate that D.C. leaders would gain more by emphasizing the democracy schema and the anti-big-government schema (described below) than they would by attempting to reshape the D.C. schema.

4. The Special Treatment Schema

Often indistinguishable from the D.C. schema is the special treatment schema. So many of the descriptions of D.C., as summarized above, could just as easily serve as many Americans' stereotypical descriptions of blacks or urban areas in general, signifying that the D.C. schema serves as a proxy for many panelists' schemata of blacks or cities. Nonetheless, to whatever extent there is a distinct D.C. schema, there is also a residual special treatment schema. This schema holds that D.C.'s efforts for greater political rights would enable blacks or liberals in general to reach certain goals of unfair advantage that they cannot obtain through more legitimate means at their disposal. Voting rights, statehood, and self-rule are ways to "work the system," according to this schema. After listening to such candid exchanges, George (Md.) was correct in stating, "This aspect is not debated in the press this way, because nobody wants to say what we are saying." The exchanges also demonstrated the advantages, stressed in focus group literature, of keeping the groups racially homogeneous so that people would feel comfortable to express their innermost beliefs.

D.C. Residents Are Already Advantaged

As discussed in chapter 4, many whites feel that blacks and other minorities have overcome most or all long-standing inequitable treatment to the point that blacks are now said to be favored in many ways over whites. This view surfaced as a theme in the special treatment schema with respect to D.C. as a political entity. Dell (Ca.) epitomized the views in this theme by saying, with respect to the statehood option, "They are asking for reverse racism. Let's be colorblind and forget the whole idea."

Those speaking for this subtheme were in the minority among the panelists, since it was a difficult task to demonstrate that D.C. is advantaged when it is excluded from Congress. Much of this thinking emanated from the economic benefits D.C. residents already receive from the federal system—namely, federal government jobs and welfare. Sid (Ia.) noted that the members of the House and Senate who live in and around D.C. have become "sympathetic" with D.C. and protect D.C.'s interests. Pete (Ia.) also noted that D.C. residents' proximity to the national government gives them a "louder voice" than residents of distant states have.

The alleged advantages D.C. residents now have would be exacerbated under full voting rights, where D.C.'s congresspeople would be "super-reps" and "super-senators," because they would be added to the 535 already looking out for D.C.'s interests. They would also be "super" because they represent such a small land area. Furthermore, Ben (Tx.) thought that full voting rights would make D.C. "more equal than the others" because D.C.'s inside-the-beltway supercilious attitude, where it is thought that those on the outside "really don't know what's going on," would become "institutionalized." D.C. would then become like some of the European capitals where the *cognoscenti* count more than the provincials, who are "out to lunch" (Ben, Tx). David (Tx.) agreed that D.C. would have "preferential" treatment, offering the additional point that with self-rule D.C. residents "would have a market on the capital." David questioned the fairness of allowing the people of D.C. to "sell the capital and make all the revenues off it," although he did not say how a monopolistic franchise would be acquired. And to Glenn (Pa.), statehood is "a gimmick to give people more political power." When Americans "see something that is artificially created," their "cynicism would be fueled toward the federal government and Congress"—all because "somebody has a political agenda."

Whites' Political Power Would Be Diminished

A minority of the panelists expressed a concern that the middle and upper classes in general, and whites in particular, would lose power under D.C. self-rule. This concern provided the other major theme under the special treatment schema.

Dell (Ca.) was concerned that "[w]hites could not get what they want if they don't have a voice," or as Mia (Md.) expressed, "White middle-income families are not going to support a city that cannot provide the services they want." Tony (Md.) added, "And they are not going to feel better just because there will be two black senators supposedly representing them."

No panelist was as openly hostile to blacks as Dell, who said, "I don't want blacks to rule over me." Yet several panelists were concerned about the implications of self-rule or statehood on the white minority who would no longer have the entire Congress to protect their interests. Mary (Md.) said, "The white population is going to carry a disproportionate percentage of footing the bills" under self-rule or statehood. Herb agreed that "whites' property taxes are going to go higher because they are the ones that have the money to pay the taxes," adding that "[t]he white population is afraid of black rule. It has nothing to do with fairness." Herb said that without Congress, the perception is that the D.C. government would "fix the potholes in the other part of town rather than take care of [predominantly white] Georgetown." To Jason in Austin, it was also clear that "blacks would have more benefits by being a state, while the whites might be losing some of their benefits." David (Tx.) felt that lower income blacks "are always going to vote for change, because they have nothing to lose, whereas if you are white upper or upper middle class, you could go down." As Mia (Md.) put it, white D.C. residents will always feel that those in control will vote against whites' welfare "and for the welfare of this other group."

The special treatment schema was strongly held by a vocal minority and was often overwhelmed by the democracy schema. For example, Scott (Pa.) was effective in his response:

> I thought we talked at the outset that one of Congress' criteria for statehood was that the people should be desirous of becoming a state. If a majority of the people in D.C., whatever the color, decided that's what they want, then that carries more weight with me than the feeling that whites need to be protected by Congress.

Or as Cheryl (Ca.) simply stated, "If blacks have a majority, then that's too bad." And Mary (Tx.): "If the minorities feel more power from statehood, I don't see anything wrong with it."

Unsuccessful Subthemes

Two subthemes in the special treatment schema, falling under the diminished white power theme, deserve mention because they surfaced in the focus groups, and because one hears them in various debates over D.C.'s options. Both subthemes were unconvincing when deployed by panelists. A few panelists—usually true believers—liked the idea that D.C. voting rights would add diversity to Congress, especially to the Senate, which has one black and more typically has had none among its membership. Regardless of the merits of this argument, it fell flat among most of the panelists. George (Md.) was persuasive to his fellow panelists when he said, "I don't think you should engineer diversity. It ought to just happen because the underlying structures are free and open." If the five focus groups are any guide, D.C. advocates would not gain much by deploying this subtheme, although it would have appeal in enlisting some true believers from around the nation into the D.C. political rights movement.

The other side of the same coin is the statement—sometimes voiced by or attributed to ultra-conservatives—that D.C. is "too liberal, too urban, too black, and too Democratic"—that is, too unrepresentative of America to be considered for full voting rights. Even to the racially troubled, this was an uninspiring comment, triggering the democracy schema.

5. The Anti-Big-Government Schema

In an earlier study of public opinion and political cognition, Sears and Citrin (1982, 176) found mistrust of government to have an impressive record in generating support for tax revolt in California. In this study, an anti-big-government schema also significantly influenced opinion on D.C. self-rule. As the nation's bureaucratic capital—the home of red tape—D.C. suffers to a degree from this schema, as many panelists were skeptical of D.C. politicians' motives. These panelists viewed expanded D.C. self-rule as a means by which politicians could retain and build upon an already enormous bureaucracy.

Overall, this schema works to the benefit of the D.C. political rights movement. The nation as a whole has an anti-big-government schema (ibid., 174–76), and many panelists were passionate in their feelings that the federal government is already too big and too interfering. Panelists were appalled to learn that Congress has the power to control the daily lives of D.C. citizens. By the end of the sessions, over two-thirds of panelists favored reduced congressional control over D.C., and twenty-five of the sixty-one favored a total hands-off policy. This schema is a powerful ally of the democracy schema, and the two schemata together can overcome otherwise negative sentiments toward D.C., at least in an era—unlike recent years—in which the District itself is exercising financial responsibility.

Two major themes emerged in the anti-big-government schema.

An Excessive, Wasteful, Interfering Federal Government

When the subject of the federal government arose, nearly all categories of panelists became united, from empathizers to the racially troubled. Frances (Ca.) advocated a "grassroots movement" where "people get together and deal with the local politicians." In the absence of citizen involvement, the federal government is able to step into the void. An originalist, Dawn (Ca.) said that "the way government was originally set up was to have more state control, and now everything is federal." Dawn did not agree with a federal government role "to deal with all the little, tiny details" of D.C. business. Generally, "Congress is everywhere" (Lynn, Tx) and "wants their fingers in the pie" (Chris One, Ia.). Panelists were skeptical that Congress could guide D.C. better than Congress is able to guide itself. Lynn (Tx.) thought it ironic that "one government [D.C.] doesn't do what we want it to, so we have another government to make sure it does." Lynn viewed this arrangement as signifying that "democracy is not working, and that D.C. needs a father figure to take care of [it]." A Des Moines panelist (Pete) wondered "why [we] would . . . want government monitoring government," implying that we have enough waste as it is without adding a layer. When asked whether Congress was needed to protect D.C. against itself, Ben (Tx.) drew laughter by saying, "Are you sure we couldn't work that the other way around?" Ben said, "There's nothing in the way Congress works which would indicate that that body is protecting anything." In Des Moines, Chris One repeated the old joke, "We're the federal government and we're here to help you." These remarks are particularly ironic in light of increased congressional control imposed upon D.C. during its financial crisis of the mid-1990s. Many D.C. residents have wondered whether the District is truly being helped or merely disciplined by Congress.

Ben (Tx.), who lived in the D.C. area for a while, asked, "How effective or how much energy would you, if you were a congressman from Austin, spend if you were assigned to the District of Columbia Committee?" He assured the group that it is a "bottom of the barrel committee. . . so, realistically, there's no incentive for Congress to take care of the District at all."

Listening to the discussion, Pete (Ca.) said, "This is all news to me. Having the federal government run my city would be a disaster, just like not having representation would be a disaster." Rick (Ca.) didn't like "the idea of the federal government coming in and saying Los Angeles can or cannot do this in exchange for some money. I don't even like Sacramento telling Los Angeles what to do." Dawn (Ca.) shook her head and said:

> You've got a senator from Idaho making a decision on whether you need a bridge over a river. He goes back to Idaho. He doesn't hang out and deal with the local problems. It's like someone from Maine driving through south-central L.A. and making decisions about the number of cops in that area. They have no reality on it.

Dawn "anchored" on her home town of Los Angeles and "adjusted" to considering what congressional oversight must be like in D.C. (see heuristics, appendix G).

Few topics raised the decibel level as did this theme. Scott (Pa.) found it "outrageous that 400-something congressmen vote on D.C. budgets," and Sherry wondered how all these "outsiders" could know "what is good for

D.C. people." As Jeannie (Ia.) remarked, Congress is essentially saying, "You guys aren't grown up enough, you guys aren't smart enough, so we're going to set criteria for you that don't apply to anybody else." Jeannie's comment was effective, since a government that makes decisions for people contributes to citizens' dependency on government, a condition which the Iowa panelists regarded as prevalent among D.C. citizens in view of D.C.'s high levels of welfare dependency. Unfortunately, as Ben (Tx.) observed, "D.C. has no representation in the very entity that they would have to appeal to" in seeking a change. "It's the ultimate minority state," he said.

These remarks reflected a national mood where 56 percent of liberals and 72 percent of conservatives thought that power should be shifted from the federal government to states (*Washington Post*, April 19, 1995, A21). On the first day of Republican control of the Senate, majority leader Robert Dole (*Congressional Record*, January 4, 1995) reminded his colleagues, "Federalism has given way to paternalism, with disastrous results."

A Bloated D.C. Bureaucracy

A second theme in the anti-big-government schema is the match between excessive government in general and D.C. in particular. At least one person in every group—and nearly everyone in the Maryland group—was able to offer the information that D.C.'s government was among the nation's most bloated. Those who were suspicious of D.C.'s motives were given an added reason to be skeptical. Greater autonomy would fulfill the bureaucracy-building blueprints of D.C. leaders.

Many panelists—about a quarter—voiced the concern that the ultimate in autonomy—statehood—would add "another layer of bureaucracy." Panelists initiated this phrase in each session. When informed that the current government, already city-county-state in form, would simply become the new state government, most panelists remained unconvinced. As George (Md.) said:

> The political class in the District that wants statehood wants to maintain all these agencies. That's what it's all about. They don't want to trim it back. They want statehood because they want another layer of bureaucracy and to keep what they have.

George relied here on an availability heuristic; the theme of D.C.'s bureaucratic expansionism was so strong in George's experience that he attributed D.C.'s statehood drive to this same phenomenon.

Undoubtedly, the tax revolt movements over the past two decades have placed citizens on guard against schemes to pad the number of government employees. While U.S. taxpayers are wary of all governments, D.C. has an additional hurdle to overcome—namely, its link to the federal government in the minds of those outside D.C. Dawn (Ca.) said, "I don't want that little federal government concentrate looking after the whole country's interests."

Subthemes

Two subthemes diametrically opposed to one another also emerged in the anti-big-government schema. First, most panelists felt that there was still a legitimate role for Congress with respect to the District, even though more than two-thirds thought this role should be reduced from the current arrangement. This "money talks" subtheme, named after Chris One's comment in Des Moines, condones a level of congressional power over D.C. because Congress gives D.C. a federal payment. As Jeanie (Ia.), a D.C. supporter through most of the session, put it, "If someone paid 20 percent of my family's budget, am I going to listen to what they want me to do? Yes! I may decide to suffer [rather] than do it their way, but I'm going to listen." Mia (Md.) said, "If D.C. is taking money from Congress, I think Congress would demand that it have a voice on how that money is spent."

David (Tx.) reminded the group that "D.C. is the nation's capital, so we should all have a say in it." The Texas group envisioned all the problems that could ensue without congressional control: billboards around the monuments, toll booths to gain entry into D.C., speed traps, and gambling casinos. In Harrisburg, Scott warned of placing the federal government "at the mercy" of D.C. and wondered whether "you could get the president to work or assure that he could take the helicopter all the time."

However, these thoughts about a powerless federal government held hostage by a more autonomous D.C. never gathered much credibility. George (Md.), an originalist, informed his group that D.C., once a wilderness area located near the two small cities of Alexandria and Georgetown, was established as the nation's capital because the early Americans were distrustful of the existing large cities of New York, Boston, Philadelphia, and Charleston. Christine (Md.) responded that the fear of excessive urban power is "not pertinent anymore." Most cities, she said, are suffering so much that they lack the power to contend with the federal government.

The other subtheme of the excessive federal government theme is that Congress already has sufficient means of control over all the states, including D.C. if it should achieve self-rule or statehood. Laura (Pa.), an attorney, said, "Congress would not be forbidden from passing any act that would prevent toll booths at the edge of the District. You would still have that check on the

District." George (Pa.) also noted Congress' ability to "yank money." He said, "The weight of the federal government's wallet is going to protect it. You don't need some kind of federal sanctuary or tabernacle. I just don't buy it." The consensus in Austin, Des Moines, and Van Nuys, with support elsewhere, is "there's enough control" (Molly, Tx.) without resorting to an explicit veto. The veto "will happen naturally" because of the powers Congress already has at its disposal. Moreover, local people are "just like a veto" (Jason, Tx.), since they would have no reason to destroy the tourist industry and employment base that nourish them.

6. The Founding Fathers Schema

This schema is unidimensional, with its central element an enduring faith in the transcendent wisdom of the Constitution's framers. Under this schema, it is iconoclastic to meddle with the Constitution, and if one does, the future of democracy could be threatened. Nearly all Americans hold this schema to some degree, and originalists especially do so—not on blind faith, but based on a lifetime of careful consideration.

This schema works against changes in the District's political structure, since the District's status is preserved in the Constitution. Dawn (Ca.) was wary of all the "subtle methods" people employ to change the Constitution, and she warned of dire consequences:

> Suddenly we don't have the freedom of speech anymore. We don't have freedom of religion. It starts on small levels, and each change in the Constitution is another chipping away of our freedom.

Displaying a good understanding of American history, panelists referred to what the framers had in mind. Gary (Ia.) observed that "D.C. was set aside to be a neutral seat of government. I don't know what's changed to eliminate that." Rick (Ca.) noted that "[t]he capital wasn't in a particular state, so that state would not have undue influence over the other states." He ironically added: "That might not be valid now. It might even be valid in reverse, since I don't know of any state that would want to inherit D.C.'s problems." Others, however, thought it was still valid; hence their references to D.C.'s "double representation" (Mary, Tx.). The federal government "already represents other parts of the nation," and D.C.'s population is engaged in the federal government as its "primary business." Therefore, it would "twist things" if D.C. received representation in Congress on top of D.C.'s representation through federal government employment (Mary, Tx.). To Dawn (Ca.), the "unbiased federal center . . . should not have its own specific voice." Dawn thought that federal employees are already "ruling the whole country," and she did not want D.C.'s "special interest trying to grab the whole." Dawn elaborated that statehood would be the ultimate power grab:

> If Atlantis resurfaces out of the ocean and it was only sixty-nine square miles, and everyone went there and made it prosperous, and they met all the qualifications of a state, then, sure, go for it. But I don't want my capital city where my federal government runs to have a [way to exercise] self-interest.

In contrast to many of the other schemata, where lively point-counterpoint exchanges ensued, thoughts emanating from this schema rarely provoked opposition. When Francine (Ca.) asked, "What is different now than from the original concept?" Pete (Ca.) replied, "D.C. had fewer people back then. Now there are six hundred thousand." One panelist (Howard, Md.) said, "The founding fathers screwed up by not giving the District representation," but that was a rare aspersion.

SCHEMA CHANGE BY PANELIST TYPOLOGY

Individuals vary in the ways they are affected by new information. Chapter 5 categorized the focus group panelists into six major types. "Followers" are basically aschematic. They lack strongly held schemata on political issues. They hold the democracy schema, but most of their schemata are thinly textured. Followers did not experience much schema change—since evolving their schemata was of little interest to them—but they joined in a consensus.

"True believers" were hopeless cases for advocates of the status quo to attempt to reach. A true believer will be angry that Americans are shut out of Congress, or that Congress is overseeing the daily lives of six hundred thousand D.C. residents. Any argument used against full democratic rights was subject to scorn or bewilderment among true believers. True believers were not compromisers. Their democracy schema was strong. Their D.C. schema was richly textured. Their view of D.C. was not altogether positive, but they usually attributed D.C.'s social and economic problems to outside forces, including abusive treatment by congressional "overseers." Rhetoric that pleased true believers often repelled others. For example, if it was said that two senators from D.C. would add diversity to the segregated club of the U.S. Senate and provide national leaders for America's troubled cities, such rhetoric fed the already deeply held ideology of true believers. However, such rhetoric elicited charges of "caving in to special interests" and "engineering diversity."

Together true believers and empathizers totaled over a quarter (seventeen of the sixty-one) of the panelists. These two types of individuals would provide the foundation for a successful effort to improve D.C.'s political rights once the District achieves stability in its finances. True believers exhibited virtually no schema change, while empathizers experienced some. Most of their changes were of the "bookkeeping" or gradual variety; they incorporated information that strengthened their existing schemata. There was one "conversion." Willie Bob (Tx.), after listening to the discussion about D.C.'s political inequities, thought that D.C.'s political situation was ripe for riots among the D.C. population. Willie Bob converted to a pro-statehood stance. Most empathizers experienced some dilution of previously held extreme positions as new information was received. For example, Abby (Md.) withdrew her position of giving D.C. to Maryland after listening to the practical difficulties posed by her fellow panelists. Notwithstanding these few examples of schema change, empathizers in these sessions were egalitarian enlighteners. They did not force their views on others, and few changed their views.

"Pragmatists" (fifteen of the sixty-one panelists) constituted the second largest type and tended to be group leaders. Pragmatists outside of the Bethesda group engaged in "subtyping"; that is, they consistently found places in their schemata to hold special information pertaining to D.C. They led the groups in urging that D.C. residents vote in Maryland elections, or that D.C. be given outright to Maryland. However, pragmatists in the Bethesda group found many cold, hard reasons not to engage in such subtyping. If D.C. residents were to vote in Maryland elections, the Maryland voters' power would be diluted, and the Maryland pragmatists felt that nontraditional candidates would win. If Maryland took D.C. over, then Maryland would have to contend with and fund D.C.'s numerous social problems. If D.C. gained statehood, it would also automatically gain the authority to tax the income of Marylanders who work in D.C. Therefore, nominal statehood tended to be favored in Maryland, giving D.C. some voting representation in Congress, more D.C. citizen control over their daily affairs, but not statehood (and therefore no nonresident income taxing authority).

"Anti-big-government" types comprised the third largest group in the sessions (nine of the sixty-one). This group was subject to conversion more than any of the others. A conservative ideology or negative affect toward D.C. may have initially predisposed this type against D.C. voting rights or self-rule. However, members of this type for years had grown skeptical about government, which they perceived as self-interested, greedy, wasteful, overbearing, and generally worthless. Once they envisioned congressional scrutiny over D.C. citizens' daily lives, many rebelled against their earlier predispositions. Two such panelists illustrate deployment of the anti-big-government schema. Paul (Pa.), a Reagan Republican, resented remarks that D.C. residents may not be ready for full democratic participation and thought that gradual improvement of D.C. citizens' democratic rights was a "band-aid approach." Paul supported D.C. statehood for these reasons. Natasha (Md.) was an independent tepid to Clinton (65 on the feeling thermometer) and rather cold to Martin Luther King, Jr. (40) and Jesse Jackson (20). Natasha gave some credibility (30) to the notion that whites are better than blacks at running things and should be allowed to do so, and she thought that 70 percent of D.C. residents were receiving welfare. Natasha favored D.C. statehood throughout the session on the grounds that anything short of statehood would be paternalistic.

Racially troubled types constituted a small proportion (six of the sixty-one) of the panelists. Improvement in D.C.'s status was a difficult policy to sell to racially troubled types because the negative affect served as a heuristic that facilitated opposition. This type slipped rather easily into a negative D.C. schema and a special treatment schema. Some dilution of extremist views took place as panelists learned more about D.C. residents, and the residents were viewed less unidimensionally. However, this type was concerned about losses of white political power under D.C. self-rule. The racially troubled saw a continued need for congressional control over residents whom they viewed as not ready for full democratic rights. This type also pointed to Marion Barry and Jesse Jackson as symbols of the deficiency of D.C.'s political leadership.

At one point, Jason (Tx.) said, "Why doesn't the federal government just take over D.C.? Just make the whole thing belong to the federal government." However, as panelists discussed the need for congressional oversight to prevent billboards, speed traps, and gambling casinos, Jason converted: "You'll have a check with the local government there. Not the federal government, but the local people." Jason even liked the idea of gambling to ease D.C.'s financial woes and resented federal intrusion into what he regarded a D.C. decision. By the session's end, Jason advocated two U.S. senators for D.C. as well as a voting representative, and he opposed congressional control over D.C. budgets and bills.

There were just four originalists, and they were all well-informed educators in the focus groups who exhibited little schema change. However,

Dawn (Ca.) accepted her group's consensus (of allowing D.C. residents to vote in Maryland elections), perhaps because she was repelled by the racially oriented language of opponents of improved political standing for D.C.

SUMMARY

This chapter has presented one way out of an infinite variety in which the massive amount of raw focus group data could be organized. One could make a case for more or fewer schemata and for a different typology of panelists. Recognizing that there is no one correct way to organize the information, the organizational plan above was developed for analytical purposes. Once the plan was developed and refined, the sorting decisions became routine, which is an indication that the plan was as internally consistent and rational as feasible for a qualitative research project.

The research results seem to have a degree of face validity; that is, when presented with similar open-ended questions, other focus groups discussing this issue could offer their in-depth perceptions along rather similar paths as did these sixty-one panelists. As indicated in appendix F, we cannot extrapolate much further than that. We cannot say that the proportions favoring one option or another would be the same, or even roughly the same, if other focus groups at other times were to wrestle with this issue. What we have gained is a greater understanding of how several dozen Americans have focused on this topic, sought and processed information, exchanged viewpoints in a way that approximates "real-life" social interaction, and arrived at well-reasoned opinions. We now have some clues on how the debate on this little-known issue could proceed were it to enter into public dialogue.

7

Strategies for the Future of Washington, D.C.

> *"In a society under the forms of which the stronger faction can readily unite and oppress the weaker, anarchy may as truly be said to reign as in a state of nature, where the weaker individual is not secured against the violence of the stronger. . . ."*
>
> James Madison, *Federalist* number 51, 1788

D.C. is stuck in a time warp, the last of the segregated political lunch counters. To D.C. citizens, their lowly political status is a daily reality. They can contribute to other states' senatorial campaigns, write letters to the editor, or march on the Capitol, but the essence of their American citizenship is missing.

PROSPECTS FOR REFORM

The votes that sustain presidents and most national leaders are largely housed in the suburbs, where there is not much outcry on issues related to civil rights, urban betterment, and political equality. Kevin Phillips (1969, 37) observed a difference in emphasis between the overwhelmingly successful New Deal era and dwindling public support for the Great Society of the Lyndon Johnson years. The New Deal took from the few (i.e., the affluent) to benefit the many, while the Great Society attempted to redistribute the wealth of the many to benefit the relatively few—namely, low-income Americans. Nixon was able to win by evoking the "forgotten Americans," the average, struggling, middle-class families who had been asked to sacrifice during the Great Society years to pay for the needs of the poor and racial minorities. The strategy generated an extended period of Republican executive branch control. In much of the 1960s, liberals dismissed opposition to poverty programs as racial backlash. But by 1968, such opposition was legitimized in the form of pro-American pride in a strong economy and national defense. It no longer became urgent to help Washington, D.C. and other older, high density urban centers with their multitude of costly problems, and the poverty programs soon became discredited as wasteful by liberals and conservatives alike.

Not only did Republicans learn from this political lesson, but successful Democrats did as well. President Clinton's health care plan and budgetary reforms were well suited to Phillips's formula. Technical flaws aside, Clinton's health reform plan was designed to help millions of middle-income Americans who were not adequately insured or who were fearful that their job insecurity jeopardized their level of health insurance. Clinton's 1993 tax plan also explicitly targeted the few (the affluent) so that many millions of middle-class Americans could avoid making a heavy payment toward reducing the federal deficit.

D.C.'s political status is not a New Deal issue. In fact, it sounds suspiciously like a Great Society issue. It explicitly helps the few at what could be considered the expense of the many. If six hundred thousand or so D.C. residents gained full representation in Congress, the votes in Congress of all other Americans would be diluted. D.C. senators and a D.C. representative would provide a voice in Congress not for just D.C.'s but for America's urban interests, and the issue thus evokes the Great Society days that middle-income, mostly suburban-residing Americans had thought were safely behind them. Americans could view D.C. voting rights as a scheme to give special treatment to federal bureaucrats and urban residents on welfare—two of the least loved groups among us—when the District does not even appear on a national map without graphic enhancement. Moreover, if Congress is called upon to compensate Maryland and Virginia state treasuries over a period of time for the costs of providing a tax credit to citizens of those states who would begin paying income taxes to the District when they earned income there, then such a policy would be highlighted in all the budget debates. It would be another source of resentment among tax-paying Americans.

D.C. leaders are often cautioned against expecting voting rights, political autonomy, or statehood at a time when the jurisdiction's socioeconomic momentum is virtually collapsing. Many D.C. residents have a low opinion of the public schools and can no longer tolerate excessive crime levels. As Ned Sloan (1993), the chair of the D.C. Statehood Commission said, "Middle-class citizens of both major races are abandoning the District. The central city is becoming uninhabitable, not just in D.C., but all over America."

Despite the never-ending stream of terrible news from the District, Sloan has remained committed to statehood. Sloan pointed out that D.C. is in a "Catch-22" situation. D.C.'s declining socioeconomic conditions are damaging D.C.'s chances for equal political standing, as national leaders (as well as focus group panelists in this research) question D.C.'s ability to sustain itself economically. Yet, Sloan pointed out, "D.C.'s lack of statehood means we cannot have all the resources we need to turn our urban conditions around." Sloan observed that D.C.'s task is a daunting one under any circumstances, but added:

> With statehood's infusion of resources, we would at least have a shot at it. As it now stands, our congressional overseers micromanage us, withhold resources from us, and then turn around and criticize us for the way we manage our resources. We don't really have home rule. We have been handed a hybrid government that is completely foreign to the American form of representative democracy our children read about in their civics textbooks.

Regardless of how one views the District's plight, the District has been soundly denounced by some national leader nearly every day for decades. Many D.C. residents seem dispirited by the urban conditions and the nation's long-standing negative judgments about them and their government. This research indicates that even focus group panelists who were empathetic to D.C.'s cause experienced considerable difficulty in translating their belief in the principle of political equality into a workable policy that would actually implement political equality for D.C. residents.

The research also demonstrates that the way District residents have been treated in American federalism clashes with panelists' ideals. A clear majority of the panelists demonstrated little tolerance for excessive congressional oversight of D.C., and nearly all panelists opposed the exclusion of these Americans from congressional representation.

Samuel Huntington (1981) wrote of the ways Americans cope with cognitive dissonance between their ideals and the ways that institutions such as Congress implement the ideals. Americans cannot abandon their ideals, he wrote, and still be Americans, because their creed—in liberty, equality, individualism—forms the basis of their identity, whereas in other countries identity lies in the characteristics of the people, their arts, or the landscape. Americans cope with gaps between ideals and institutions through four behavioral models (ibid.). Through moralism, they work to eliminate the gaps. Through cynicism, they tolerate the gaps but feel bitter or helpless against institutional power. However, even tolerance and cynicism require some political effort; thus, through complacency, they disregard the gaps for an extended time. Finally, through hypocrisy, Americans deny the gaps. Huntington wrote that infrequently (the American Revolution, the Jacksonian era of the 1830s, the Progressive era earlier in this century, and the turmoil of the 1960s and 1970s), the existing power hierarchy is successfully challenged in "creedal passion periods." Here the coping model of moralism prevails, and Americans feel empowered to alter their political institutions.

Complacency has ruled the D.C. rights issue simply because the U.S. Constitution, Americans' most revered political document, establishes and condones D.C.'s unequal status. In recent decades, two attempts to break through the complacency—the D.C. voting representation amendment to the Constitution and the D.C. statehood vote in the House—failed by rather wide margins. The District's financial collapse of the mid-1990s has suspended revival of these efforts. It could take a creedal passion period, or at least a demonstration by the District that it is capable of survival outside the federal womb, to break through the inertia.

SUMMARY OF RESEARCH CONCLUSIONS

In addition to panelists' support for the principle of political equality for D.C. residents, this research has five overarching conclusions:

1. *Economic and financial stability is a prerequisite to political reform.* Theoretically a resident's democratic rights should not be contingent upon a level of financial activity in the resident's jurisdiction. However, focus group discussions among average Americans as well as Congressional demands signify that greater confidence in the District as a viable entity must precede thorough political reform. The control board's first year was characterized by squabbling between it and the District's executive branch, and by a lack of full acceptance of the board's views in Congress. The chaos can be settled through agreement among all the key players on a long-term plan that includes the following elements:

a. black ink in D.C. budgets by 1999;

b. tax rates in D.C. that are comparable to rates in surrounding jurisdictions;

c. D.C. government service levels that are on par with service levels found elsewhere in the region (which involves trimming and transferring some services and supplementing other services);

d. eligibility and benefit levels for D.C. entitlements that are on par with those found in surrounding jurisdictions;

e. D.C. government employee levels trimmed to the levels mandated by an objective analysis but sufficient enough to meet service needs; and

f. a federal payment level (including recognition for past federally accrued pension liabilities) that compensates for any resource gaps once criteria (a) through (e) above are satisfied.

2. *Presidential and congressional leadership is essential.* The focus groups have demonstrated, at least for these sixty-one panelists, that the means of implementing the principles of political equality are fluid, with frequent shifts in position taking. Given restoration of financial stability to the District, and presidential, congressional, and local leadership, Americans should be able to accept remedies for the District's political inequality, its lack of full self-government, and its socioeconomic conditions. Without this leadership, most Americans will remain content with the status quo.

3. *The democracy and anti-big-government schemata should be emphasized by those who favor a change in the District's status.* As chapter 6 demonstrated, the democracy and anti-big-government schemata are the only ones that are likely to produce favorable results when deployed if the goal is to achieve political equality for D.C. residents. Counterarguments to D.C.'s political equality should be deflected back to these two schemata. If, on the other hand, a politician's goal is to retain the status quo for the District, he or she should emphasize the founding fathers' schema, the negative D.C. image schema, the special treatment schema, and, if the argument is against statehood, the voters' state schema.

4. *When political options are discussed, pragmatic means of implementing the principle of political equality should be sought.* Most Americans lack the time, knowledge base, and ideological structure to consider fully the issue of D.C.'s political future. The focus groups have demonstrated that, at least for these panelists, the problem can be solved by a variety of means. However, upon examination, several of the options are not pragmatic. For example, retrocession of D.C. to Maryland is not likely to surmount the practical difficulties—chiefly, approval by the Maryland state legislature. This option will not satisfy the search for a "real" answer. Another frequently mentioned solution, that of giving D.C. residents voting representation in Congress, also presents pragmatic problems. Such an option would require ratification by three-fourths of the states per article 5 of the Constitution. The states in the

seven-year interval following such a constitutional amendment in 1978 did not ratify the congressional action. Nothing has changed that would lead one to think that the states would do so now. Policy discussions offering impractical options tend to breed voter cynicism.

If national leaders approach the District's political rights issue honestly, the District's options are few: statehood, which provides political equality, or some status improvement that still leaves D.C. residents sitting at their segregated political lunch counter, wondering if they will ever be served along with their fellow Americans.

5. *Some policy may be needed to gain the concurrence of D.C.'s neighboring states.* D.C. is applying for equal political rights to a body—the U.S. Congress—in which it lacks voting membership. Meanwhile, states which stand to lose financially under some options—Maryland and Virginia—have each had two senators and a full share of voting representatives in that body since 1788. It is not a fair fight. The Maryland focus group panelists were clearly unwilling to pay the tax increases necessary to compensate for the dollar drain that would ensue if D.C. were to have the standing of a state for tax purposes.

To gain Maryland and Virginia as allies, Congress (including members in those two states) and D.C. may have to (a) agree on an acceptable rate of nonresident taxation, and (b) provide for a subsidy to Maryland and Virginia for an extended time that would compensate those states for their treasury drain once the state treasuries provide a tax credit to their residents for taxes they pay on income earned in D.C. One might argue that the nonresident income tax is a typical state and municipal taxing mechanism, and that for many decades the District has in fact been subsidizing these two states because of the congressional restriction against the tax's imposition. But as a political reality, some congressional payment may have to be made to these two states. Similarly, if the District were to be retroceded into Maryland, there is no way that Maryland (or any other jurisdiction) would take the District without substantial compensation to its state treasury.

THE POLITICAL PROS SPEAK

We have heard from average Americans. Now let us see what the political pros have to say about the future of the nation's capital. The interviews were conducted from 1993 to 1995 and trace an evolution from the euphoric promise of statehood to the stark reality of the District's financial calamity, and then to a new era of Republican leadership in devising a structure for financial and political stability. The leaders' views were more than reactions to dynamic upheavals in the District. The views reflect well-reasoned philosophies years in the making and represent various types of thinkers on this issue. There were prototypical true believers, originalists, and pragmatists among the leaders, just as there were among panelists. The leaders' views were more sophisticated, since they had analyzed the issue more extensively than had panelists. Moreover, a politician's views (e.g., on a commuter tax) are necessarily constrained by constituent expectations.

A MENTALITY OF FEDERAL DEPENDENCY THWARTS D.C.'S DRIVE TO POLITICAL AUTONOMY

Mayor Sharon Pratt Kelly met with this writer in her office in July 1993 as she was in the midst of her budget battles with the D.C. Council. Though she and the former chairman of the D.C. Council, John Wilson, often battled publicly, Wilson was able to guide the Council to fiscal restraint. Since Wilson's suicide, both branches of government seemed unable to agree on fiscal targets. While that extended drama was unfolding, the crisis *du jour* was marshaling her troops to provide air-conditioned space for the homeless on the ground floor of the Mayor's building during a stretch of near-100-degree days.

A true believer in the District's cause, Kelly wanted statehood as her legacy to D.C. citizens. Ironically, huge deficits from her election year budgets gave the District a federally appointed financial control board, reducing further the District's autonomy. At the time her goal was independence, and she addressed the difficulty in achieving support for this notion, even among the local citizenry:

> Many [D.C.] people are afraid to cut the umbilical cord. They have a sense of stability and certainty about their unique relationship with the federal government. There is a misperception that this is the only way we can support ourselves. So to break away from that paternalistic relationship is unsettling to a great many citizens. This is not a very positive way to see ourselves.

In addition to fighting the dependency of D.C. citizens on their federal "parents," Kelly faced the task of adjusting the nation's perceptions about this "unique entity that is responsive only to the federal interest." The nation needs "to consider the implications of the nation's capital falling into financial ruin," pointing out that Congress restricted her from raising the funds not only to respond to D.C.'s urgent needs but, ultimately, to remain solvent. Given all the federal tax restrictions, revenues are flowing beyond the District's borders into Maryland, Virginia, and across the nation, producing a "tenuous, precarious situation."

Kelly's said that her efforts locally and nationally were made more difficult by "our difficulty in getting good stories out," adding:

> If you are a second-class citizen, you are going to be treated in a second-class status. The good news is relegated to the *District Weekly* and the bad news is on the front page.

For decades *The Washington Post* has been regarded inside the D.C. government as a limousine liberal who fights for the right national causes but often ignores, scolds, or is repulsed by a struggling family across town. The *District Weekly*, sometimes referred to by D.C. employees as "the weakly" (or, by some, even more disparagingly as the "colored pages," a satiric comment on alleged journalistic segregation of good news stories about D.C. to this obscure section of the daily newspaper) is only published inside city limits. Aside from a hard-hitting political column, it mostly covers neighborhood, D.C. agency, and school issues. A major theme in the *Post*'s daily front page and metropolitan section coverage is D.C. government mismanagement. Kelly acknowledged the *Post*'s national leadership on the statehood issue, but wanted the *Post* to focus more on structural, systemic problems of the nation's capital as underlying reasons for the barrage of news stories about the District's social and economic difficulties. While Kelly's remarks may seem paranoid to some, the *Post's* ombudsman, Joann Byrd (*Washington Post*, November 13, 1994, C6), felt a need to say:

> For the *Post* to be a facilitator in mending this torn city, it will need to figure out how to become credible with those African Americans who think the paper is the voice of and for the city's white population.

Mayor Barry echoed this theme, placing the *Post* atop his "enemies of the people" list (*Derek McGinty Show*, WAMU, December 1, 1995).

In May 1993, an interview was held with Council Chairman John Wilson, just six days before he took his own life. Wilson was in an upbeat, candid, and typically mercurial mood. He was alternately pensive and playful in our ninety-minute talk, breaking only for a television interview about his testimony that morning before the Senate Appropriations Committee on the District's 1994 budget. Many of his friends reported that Wilson was in an unusually warm, expansive mood those last few days. They concluded that he was saying goodbye to them.

Like Kelly, Wilson thought that "local people may not want the responsibility of full political independence," but he was not placing the blame on outside enemies:

> Look, we were told there was a Master Plan to get blacks out of the District so whites could take over. Well, that's only partly true, but it's not the whites who are doing the damage. The District [government] is itself forcing out the middle class, black and white. They seem to only want the poor here. The poor can't get services out there in the suburbs, but we've got any service the low-income people want right here. Meanwhile we are taxing everyone else out of the city.

Wilson said that he woke up every day at 4:00 a.m. thinking about D.C. problems and acknowledged that D.C.'s struggling economy and budget woes can only hurt its drive for political autonomy:

> There are always going to be questions about D.C.'s economic self-sufficiency. But statehood is a moral issue, not an economic issue. I've been looking at D.C. finances for twenty years. I do believe that the numbers can work under statehood—if we don't split up into nineteen municipalities, each with its own budget and workforce, and if we receive a reasonable federal payment.

In her stately office in the historic Old Executive Office building next door to the White House, Alice Rivlin, then deputy director of the U.S. Office of Management and Budget, former director of the Congressional Budget Office, former chair of the prestigious committee on D.C. finances that bears her name, and a chief architect of President Clinton's 1993 economic plan, spoke with this writer in May 1993. This was the day the House passed her plan by a 219–to–213 vote, but Rivlin said that she always had time to talk about D.C.'s efforts, which at the time featured statehood.

Rivlin pointed to the District's small geographic size and its lack of historical tradition of self-government as reasons why Americans do not fully support D.C. statehood. She seemed a little surprised that so many of the focus group panelists advocated voting representation for the District in the House and Senate, adding:

> I would have said, had you not shown me the data, that the reason for Americans' statehood opposition was a perceived inability of D.C. residents to govern themselves, or racism, but that does not explain [the panelists'] receptivity to representation.

Rivlin noted that D.C. is viewed "partly rightly and partly wrongly," like any other typical, declining central city such as Philadelphia, Detroit, and Chicago, where the core areas are beset with crime, drugs, and heavy concentrations of single-parent, minority families. She then stated:

> On the positive side, we have to fix these problems. We have grown accustomed to seeing these urban problems in the shadows of our federal buildings, but it doesn't have to be this way. The cleanest way for the District to get the revenues it needs to address its problems is through the taxing powers it would automatically receive with statehood. Anything short of statehood would require the District to get permission from Congress, Maryland, and Virginia to engage in reciprocal income taxation, and what are the odds of that ever happening? You could just forget it. And the problems would continue to fester.

The Rivlin Commission (D.C. Commission on Budget and Financial Priorities 1990, 6.1–6.14) was a year-long, well-funded, bipartisan examination by forty-five national and local leaders. Along with a variety of recommendations directed at improving D.C. government management and policies, it pointed to federal government policies as a primary reason for D.C. structural difficulties.

In June 1993, Representative Eleanor Holmes Norton met with this writer in her Longworth Building office. This writer was quite distracted, having just left memorial services for the son of a best friend. The nineteen-year-old had lost his life in urban violence. In more placid places in America, urban problems are more abstract, often relating to some spending program the nation cannot afford. In D.C., they are tragically an all too real part of daily life.

In person, Norton's power has a way of breaking through whatever mindset one may have about the District. As historian Roger Wilkins (*Washington Post*, January 23, 1995, C4) observed, "She gives home rule a fig leaf of credibility, which it desperately needs right now." Norton enjoys support from Congress, D.C. voters of all races, and the media, a rare hat trick for a D.C. leader.

Norton pointed to what is known in this research as the state schema as a main reason why the focus group panelists supported congressional representation for D.C. more than they did statehood:

> D.C. has no cows or factories. People don't see D.C. as a state. But it is all a matter of education. People need to see that D.C. has the economy that most states are trying to get. Around the nation farms are strug-

> gling, and factories are either shutting down and abandoning towns or they are destroying the air quality. In D.C. we have upscale, nonpolluting, white-collar jobs. We are the wave of the future.

Norton added other factors that may have accounted for panelists' resistance to statehood:

> There is no such thing as a city-state in this country. Furthermore, U.S. citizens do not want to lose their sense of a capital that belongs to them. But they wouldn't lose it. They would still own, through the federal government, the Mall and everything else in the federal enclave. And D.C. would have jurisdiction over the neighborhoods, as it should have.

Norton took exception to allegations that D.C. may not be ready for self-rule, saying that "Congress as D.C.'s overseer all these years must share responsibility for the District's social and economic conditions. Congress is not exactly an innocent bystander." Norton found it ironic that Congress helped create the very conditions that it uses as reasons to oppose the District's reforms. She believed that instead of merely criticizing, Congress can help solve the problems by supporting statehood and by helping to gain agreement for "a regional tax where everyone [D.C., Maryland, and Virginia] can share in the proceeds." Norton dismissed past congressional attempts to improve D.C.'s political status—including passage of the congressional amendment in 1978 to give D.C. full representation—as insincere. "Congress assumed the states wouldn't ratify it. That's why they passed it in the first place," she said.

Sam Smith, D.C. political analyst and cofounder of the D.C. Statehood Party in 1970, also spoke of the state schema in an April 1993 interview in his graceful Cleveland Park home:

> A state is something you draw on a map and has a shape. But acres don't vote, cows don't vote, factories don't vote—people vote!

Smith noted that people often point to all the federal employees in D.C., and he commented, "If you want to deny D.C. statehood on that basis, then you had better take away statehood in some other places, because federal employees are all over." John Wilson observed, "If Alaska can be a state, D.C. can. Everybody up there is a park ranger or something."

The D.C. leaders interviewed were fully attuned to how their fellow Americans felt about D.C. statehood and were frustrated that more people would not think the issue through to what they considered the issue's logical conclusion. As usual, Wilson put the whole matter of American public opinion on the issue into perspective by saying, "It doesn't matter what the American people think about D.C. statehood. Forget the American people. They don't care about D.C. Let's focus on Congress."

STRATEGIES TOWARD AUTONOMY

In 1993, D.C. leaders were either unaware of or concealing D.C.'s impending financial doom, and the push was for statehood, as these interviews trace. The comments assume an era of financial stability that would produce a climate for D.C. political autonomy. The comments also reflect a pro-statehood viewpoint shared by a majority of D.C.'s African American residents, even in the worst of times. Wilson, a pragmatist, favored a gradual approach to achieve self-rule:

> I would first go for budget and legislative autonomy. Congress would not be giving up that much. They have really only overturned a handful of D.C. legislation in the past eighteen years [since the start of limited home rule for the District]. We need judicial autonomy, too—the right to pick our own judges and prosecute our own crimes. That's reasonable, too. After all, we're not children. After that I would try for full representation in the House and Senate. We're Americans. We can get that. You keep getting all these things, then pretty soon you're a state. You don't need to scare anybody in the process. This is America's second home town. So you have to sneak up on Congress. I would be like a thief in the night.

Wilson prided himself on his legislative record in the D.C. Council—where he indicated the success rate of his bills was 85 percent—and with Congress. He said, "You play the game to win. With Congress, that means you play the game the way Congress wants it played." To make sure he got his point across, Wilson added, "What you do is you kiss Congress' ass. You kiss their ass and Congress will kiss your ass."

Wilson said that Daniel P. Moynihan, now a U.S. senator, had the right idea when he worked in the Nixon White House:

> Moynihan was for benign neglect [in solving the problems of America's minority citizens]. Well I am for treating Congress with benign neglect. Right now we blame Congress for everything that is wrong in D.C. Publicly, I would pretend that Congress doesn't even exist. Quietly and per-

> sonally, I would treat Congress with kid gloves. They would get no parking tickets ever as long as they don't block a fire hydrant. They can have a police escort to work every day if they want it.
>
> If we do our job right, balance our budgets, and do everything Congress wants, after a while it would be insulting to deny D.C. statehood. At the right time, I would appear before Congress and say, "What else can we possibly do? It is time for D.C. to be a state. We have done everything you have asked." Like the Bible says, you've got to knock on the door, and it will be opened. You don't just look at the door.

Wilson claimed that "D.C. doesn't have a strategy to get statehood." All he saw were counterproductive demonstrations and impassioned speeches, observing:

> If you've got gonorrhea, what do you do? You don't just bitch about it. You get a shot of penicillin. You need a plan. If you block the bridges coming in from Virginia [with a sit-in], and all those people complain to their senators, Congress will never vote for statehood.

It was ironic to hear this advice from Wilson about working within and trusting the system. Wilson, a former civil rights activist, once told this writer that he walked and sat stiffly because a cop jumped on his back during a civil rights demonstration in his younger days back on Maryland's eastern shore. After listening to a standard recitation of how the civil rights battles were won, Wilson reacted by pointing to *Brown v. Board of Education*, the 1954 Supreme Court case that desegregated public schools: "That was the first and biggest change, and it was an orderly process, working through the system. It was before Rosa Parks and all that."

Wilson then recounted a story about how to play the political game. While chair of the Council's Finance and Revenue Committee a few years ago, Wilson placed a tax on candy and soft drinks in the D.C. budget plan. Tip O'Neill, then House Speaker, called him and said, "John, I've got candy manufacturers in my district. Fix it. Bye." Wilson said he was puzzled by the abrupt call. After a few days, Wilson could not resist calling O'Neill back, and said, "Mr. Speaker, I know you told me to fix it. But this tax means a couple million dollars to us. I need it." O'Neill shot back: "John, don't you understand? You just hit the lottery! Now, fix it. Bye." Although the situation was no clearer to him, Wilson withdrew the candy tax. A couple days later, Wilson said, the District received an extra $17 million in federal payment. Wilson asked rhetorically what good he would have done if he had instead publicly protested the Speaker's interference.

In many respects, Alice Rivlin, also a pragmatist, adopted a similar point of view to Wilson's. She said that the first thing D.C. needs to do is convince Congress and the president that it has "a viable and responsible government." She said, "There will be no progress toward statehood until Congress and the American people feel the District has its house in order." The second part, she said, is for D.C. to explain its case for self-rule better than it is now doing. In essence, she suggested focusing on the anti-big-government schema by saying, "Self-determination is a good theme. You will have a more responsible D.C. government when people are placed in charge of their own affairs."

"A long-term strategy is needed," Rivlin said, suggesting a three-step process. First, she would reduce what she termed "congressional second-guessing of the District" by allowing the District to adopt its own laws and budgets. Second, she would "move toward" taxation of nonresident income in the District. The third step would be statehood.

Rivlin then advanced the notion of a federal-D.C. compact based on her concern that D.C. may lack a political infrastructure in Congress for the foreseeable future to support a successful statehood vote. She proposed that a timetable be agreed upon between D.C. and the federal government. D.C. would agree to meet certain conditions; for example, it would agree to balance its budgets, meet certain levels of workforce reduction, improve the school system to meet certain specified standards, renovate a certain number of public housing units over a specified time, and improve its health care system. As the District met its commitments, the federal government would gradually phase in more autonomy according to the timetable until such time as all commitments were met; then statehood would be approved.

Statehood would require an act of Congress, but given a scenario in which the president and bipartisan congressional leaders were signatories along with the leaders of the District to an explicit, well-publicized compact, the odds of the act's adoption should be enhanced. Rivlin acknowledged that a compact may not be the most rational and fair approach, since the District would be agreeing to certain requirements that no other state had to meet to gain admittance into the Union. Nonetheless, she was searching for a way to move beyond political limbo and lock the District into a process through which statehood would be the ultimate outcome.

Jesse Jackson called this writer from his car in July of 1993 en route to Baltimore to plan a picket line before the upcoming All-Star game there to protest major league baseball's unwillingness to develop an affirmative action plan for its ownership and front office management. A week before this interview, Jackson and thirty-one others were arrested as they applied what Jackson called "street heat," blocking a major intersection near the Capitol, and in a gesture that to them recalled the Boston Tea Party, pouring tea onto the streets. Jackson, a true believer, resisted Rivlin's pragmatic suggestion of the compact, saying:

> We have people enough. We pay taxes enough. We meet all the historical prerequisites. No other state had to meet internal behavioral requirements. If the people of Puerto Rico vote in favor of statehood, I think they will be admitted into the Union. I don't think they will have to meet standards of good behavior.

Jackson pointed out that

> D.C. does not have any leverage to negotiate our interests with Congress. D.C. cannot even offer benefits to keep companies in town or attract new companies because D.C. is under occupation.

Jackson also disagreed with Wilson's benign neglect advice:

> If you look at the legislative history of the public accommodations acts, the voting rights acts, and open housing, you will see that Congress responds to pressure. Congress never initiates anything. Everything is a reaction. Congress has no respect for D.C., and it manipulates D.C. people and issues without shame. Since D.C. lacks the power to negotiate, we must keep up the pressure through demonstrations as well as education and hearings. Change won't happen by itself. The end of slavery is always inspired by the enslaved, not the slaveholders.

Sam Smith saw Congress as an insensitive institution, intransigent when it was not inert, and he commented on its composition: "If the Senate were a private club, you would want to resign from it before you ran for office. It's one of the most segregated institutions in the United States. Statehood for D.C. would help correct that." He noted that a persuasive president like Lyndon Johnson could convince the American people and Congress of the injustice of having a colony, which Smith defined as a non-self-governing territory, right here in our midst. "You can't run a federal government out of a colony," he said. Smith recalled "all the sob stories Johnson used to tell to break down racial barriers and help towns avoid riots," adding:

> The same could be done today. Clinton probably got screwed up at Oxford, so he doesn't know that the way you argue is by anecdote. But Clinton should talk about the basic political rights that Americans routinely have but that D.C. people lack. Tell stories that get people upset. Hey, we're Americans. How about it?

Rivlin had grown accustomed to hearing an endless list of issues to which President Clinton should attend, and she cautioned:

> Presidents have to think about the politics of issues. President Clinton is on record as favoring statehood, but it is hard for a president to make statehood a major cause because D.C.'s image is so negative in the rest of the country. It would be easier if the president moved for Puerto Rico's statehood at the same time he moved for D.C.'s. People would then say, "How can we support statehood for a place so far away, where the people don't even speak English, and deny it to D.C.?" That's not how I would regard it, but many would.

In a plebiscite on statehood of November 14, 1993, Puerto Rico voted to retain its commonwealth status by a two percentage point margin. Unlike the residents of the District, Puerto Ricans pay no federal income taxes, and manufacturing plants receive special tax breaks to locate there. A reluctance to relinquish these tax advantages was thought to be a primary reason behind the Puerto Rican voters' rejection of statehood (*New York Times*, Nov. 15, 1993, A1, B8). The District lost a potential partner with which to join and seek statehood.

Jesse Jackson commented that "[i]t is in the president's practical self-interest to follow through on his commitment to D.C. statehood. He will gain two senators—votes he can use." Senator Paul Simon (1993) added:

> This is just a wild guess, but if D.C. had two senators, I believe Lani Guinier would have had an opportunity to defend her nomination [as the chief enforcer of civil rights in the Justice Department], and she would have made it through.

Kelly agreed with Jackson about the need, in her words, to embarrass Congress.

> I'm not sure we even can behave according to the compact standards [of Rivlin] when Congress does not give us the freedom and tax base to do so. We are running out of time. You cannot have so much of your personal income placed beyond your reach, and stay in the throes of what to us is still a deep recession, and not soon have a day of reckoning.
>
> Ultimately, you have to take power from somebody. We have to pull the covers off this arrangement. The civil rights legislation would not have happened if television was not there to cause America to be ashamed by what was happening. That is what moved Congress. I don't

> think we are going to find any liberators in Congress. The American people are the liberators. But so far we have been too timid to take our case to Congress.

In August 1993, Mayor Kelly led a group of thirty-seven statehood protesters in blocking a Capitol Hill intersection. She and the others were arrested for civil disobedience as Capitol Hill police frisked her rudely. In the ensuing years, she witnessed her day of reckoning as the District's finances tumbled and hopes of statehood were dashed. In Kelly's last State of the District address in early 1994, she admitted that she "didn't have a clue" about the struggles and obstacles faced by D.C. youth. D.C. voters agreed with her assessment, and gave her just 13 percent of the primary vote several months later.

THE SEARCH FOR NEW POLICY OPTIONS

Despite the margin of defeat in the 1993 congressional vote on D.C. statehood, D.C. leaders were heartened by the support of House Speaker Thomas S. Foley, Majority Leader Richard Gephardt, and other Democratic luminaries. They were also encouraged by the relatively mild rhetoric of D.C. opponents during the House debate on the issue, with the exception of Representative Tom DeLay (R–Tex.), who called the District "a liberal bastion of corruption and crime." DeLay, who later became House majority whip, urged Congress to "take it back" and end limited home rule for the District. DeLay scolded the District for its "hug-a-thug" attitude on violent crime, opining that recent D.C. police recruits were "illiterate" and "borderline retarded" (*Washington Times*, November 22, 1993, A8). Despite DeLay's comments, Norton was able to observe (*Washington Post*, November 23, 1993, E3) that even many congresspersons who voted against the District indicated in their testimony that they were not against forms of democracy for the District other than statehood. Norton stated that her proposals for greater political autonomy for the District would have improved chances for support (ibid).

Retrocession (that is, giving D.C. and its people "back" to Maryland) is sometimes advanced as a way of including D.C. residents in the democratic process. However, as Norton said, "Over the course of two hundred years, each jurisdiction has built its own culture, character, and demography." Rivlin thought that the proposal to give D.C. to Maryland emanated from "a combination of racism and the thinking that D.C. should be bigger." Rivlin asserted:

> Retrocession is unrealistic. Obviously, Maryland doesn't want the District of Columbia. And those of us who do feel that the District is a strong entity, and potentially a strong government, feel negatively about being absorbed into some other entity.

Reform-minded D.C. Councilmember Kevin Chavous, a true believer in the District's self-rule goals, thought that it was understandable that people who did not know the area would think retrocession was a logical solution. He joked that he had no idea why there should be a North and a South Dakota:

> They seem pretty similar to me. Why not just combine them? But to the Dakotans, of course, there are probably plenty of historical and cultural reasons why there should be a North and a South.

Chavous likened D.C.'s situation to that in South Africa, where the white Afrikaners knew they were wrong, but they just could not share. He viewed giving D.C. away to another jurisdiction as a lack of willingness of America's majority race to share political power. However, Chavous added:

> Looking on the positive side of it, when people offer retrocession, at least they know there's a problem. Over the last thirty years, Congress has demonstrated that they know something is wrong. That's why Congress gave D.C. citizens the vote in presidential elections in 1961, gave us a delegate in 1971, gave us something that resembles home rule in 1975, and passed the constitutional amendment [that went unratified by the states] to give us full representation. They are still searching.

Chavous and Wilson thought that instead of giving D.C. away to another entity, D.C. could take parts of other states. Chavous thought that D.C. should annex Prince George's County in Maryland. He said, "Most people from P.G. came from D.C., so the county residents have more roots in D.C. than they do in Maryland." Wilson went even further than Chavous:

> I'm going to commit heresy and say this. Northern Virginia has nothing in common with the rest of Virginia. Prince George's has nothing in common with Maryland, and yes, Montgomery County, too. Instead of guessing whether the District could support itself as a state, let's make it the richest state in the United States by combining all those places. It would help the stability of our region. White people would not be scared to death. The new state would have a realistic ethnic, economic, social, and political mix. We ought to be more imaginative about it.

Lurking around all of the policy options is the resource and tax question. Annexation of other states' wealthy counties would mean a tax drain from those states, which lengthens the odds against what already would be a longshot. Article 4, section 3 of the Constitution provides that

> no new State shall be formed or erected within the Jurisdiction of any other State; nor any State be formed by the Junction of two or more States, or Parts of States, without the Consent of Legislatures of the States concerned as well as of the Congress.

It is virtually impossible to imagine Virginia and Maryland voluntarily giving some of their most economically productive counties over to the state of New Columbia.

A NEW ERA OF STRENGTHENED FEDERAL CONTROL OVER D.C.

The final interviews reflect a new era of federal control in which nearly everyone agreed that financial stability is a prerequisite to any consideration of political reform.

It took a nine-hour vigil stretching over two days to see Marion Barry. It was understandable, though, for Barry was basking in his incredible comeback victory in the November 1994 general election. Job seekers, old friends, hangers-on, media hounds, business bit players, and occasional power brokers like Jack Valenti (head of the Motion Picture Association, who sought Barry's help in ridding D.C.'s streets of pirated cassette movies) craved Barry's attention. Valenti aside, most wanted a little shot at redemption themselves.

Barry pulled himself together during his prison term, relying on a religious reconversion and his supporters' faith in him. Barry's words, "Amazing grace, how sweet it is, that saved a wretch like me" resounded to a stunned D.C. and nation as he accepted the victorious primary vote. During the election, Barry linked his own fall from grace to the city's, and tied his salvation to the District's. To Representative Tom Davis (R–Va.) (1995), the association was not far-fetched: "The thing is that Marion Barry in a unique way can help bring that dream back in a way that I can't and Newt can't and other members can't." Davis recognized that D.C. leaders must renew D.C.'s spirit, while Congress decides how much to drop in the collection plate.

Barry's philosophy about the District's future was in some ways in tune with that of the Republican leadership when he said, "We have to make Washington livable again. We have to make our government effective and efficient again, and we have to restore confidence. . . ." Barry believed that "we were all gung ho for home rule," but "should have negotiated a better deal" in 1973. He wishes the District had identified "nine or ten functions the federal government ought to continue to pay for." For example, the District should have said, "Let us run the jail and let [the federal government] run our state prison." In Barry's view, this deal should have been struck not because the feds are better managers, but because the District lacks state resources: "Look at the various programs the federal government operates. They don't do very well."

In addition to downsizing, Barry advocated budget autonomy and prosecutorial authority, both incremental improvements in the District's status. Barry was pessimistic about achieving more in the near term, saying, "Right now we are at an all time low, so the question is how can we get the Walshes of the world to see us in a more positive light." James Walsh, the Republican representative who controlled the District's budget, expressed fear upon Barry's election that any possibility of progress had vanished.

A constitutional amendment giving D.C. residents partial or full representation in Congress would be doomed to failure, Barry said. The Constitution has only been amended seventeen times in U.S. history (counting the Bill of Rights as one time), and Barry considered the two-thirds vote of both houses to initiate an amendment, and especially the three-fourths vote of the states to ratify one, as insurmountable obstacles for D.C. to overcome. Representative Tom Davis (1995) agreed, noting that "half the states did not even want to hold a hearing on it" when it was attempted earlier. Barry thought that Americans "don't want to be bothered with those people [D.C. residents], whoever they are." He felt, "We are considered welfare recipients, and everyone in the country hates welfare recipients." Every day Barry saw a different citizenry than the stereotype, and they, in turn, saw a different mayor than the notorious political symbol.

Barry understood the popularity of D.C.'s retrocession to Maryland, which is a "great idea" to many people "because they never thought about it and they don't know the history of our city." Barry said retrocession has never been a real option.

Barry thought that statehood will be dormant for years to come, even though it is the only option that has a "real chance" of delivering self-government and representation for D.C. residents in Congress that are on a par with those experienced by all other Americans. Barry, a pragmatist, advocated "temporarily abandoning" statehood in exchange for "another status where the District residents do not pay federal income taxes," a proposal to revive

D.C.'s population level and the local economy. But, he said, "Congress would not give up all this," noting that Congress is "fighting its own budget deficits."

Even budget autonomy, a lame reform on the scale of U.S. political rights, must clear high hurdles. First, Barry said, Congress is cutting D.C. budgets, not supporting them. Second, he thought there was little popular support for D.C. budget autonomy, saying, "Most people believe that our budget is approved by Congress because Congress supplies us with our money, and because people think that D.C. residents are just wards of the state—that the federal government takes care of us." Barry knew that the mid-nineties was not a reform era for liberal urban governments, and Barry viewed his task as working for D.C. government respectability with a Republican Congress. During his new term as mayor, Barry has advocated the needs of the jobless, the elderly, and public housing residents before a control board and congressional subcommittees whose main mission has been to restrain spending and balance D.C. budgets.

Some segments of D.C. thought that a change in congressional philosophy was long overdue. This writer talked with members of the D.C. business community who are lifelong Democrats but who said that they were glad to see the arrogant Democrats lose power in Congress. One said, "They were rude, they didn't call you back, they didn't follow through, and they lied to you." The Republicans, in contrast, were friendly and responsive to D.C. business needs, especially in facilitating the downtown arena and convention center.

True to this image, Representative James Walsh (R–N.Y.), chair of the House D.C. Appropriations Subcommittee and Representative Tom Davis (R–Va.), chair of the House Subcommittee on D.C., were affable and candid in 1995 interviews. Walsh emerged from his office to greet this writer personally (not via a chain of staff) at precisely the appointed hour, while Davis, seeing that his interviewer had arrived early, suggested a "let's get to know one another" stroll to the House floor where he would vote. Neither set any time limit for the interview. Both frequently asked questions, seeking an open exchange of views, and they appeared as eager to learn as to teach. Both had prepared themselves for the interviews with their own handwritten notes. This was all unusual and refreshing to this writer.

Walsh gave an honest account of how the District arrived on his doorstep impoverished and undernourished:

> We have a city government elected by the people that can only take legislation so far. Then Congress has to review it. And then you have the

> Maryland and Virginia legislators who . . . are going to take action in their own parochial interests that might not be positive for the District of Columbia. . . . Then you have people like myself and other members of the authorizing and appropriations subcommittees in the Congress who have a constitutional obligation to the District but who at the same time realize that our responsibilities are to our home districts. But we have to balance that because we have a legal responsibility to oversee the District of Columbia, and our view is not necessarily the same as the people who live here. And I am not really responsible to the people that live here. So it's a very complex relationship.
>
> Then, within this city, the department heads don't see anyone make hard decisions at the upper levels of the city government. They are always passing the buck to Congress or someone else, so they don't make the hard decisions. So everybody walks. Nobody is accountable. It's just a fundamental problem, I think, and that's why it will never really be resolved.

For all these reasons, Walsh said, he received strong support from Congress and the D.C. business community for the financial control board, "with emphasis on the word 'control'."

He noted that while Barry and Norton claimed that the local government would still be running the D.C. government, Walsh saw it quite differently. Walsh sought strong control board members "to resolve the issue of accountability." The buck stops with the board. Walsh was happy to discuss all the District's options, but noted that "the status quo with the asterisk" (i.e., the current form of government controlled by a federally appointed board) was "what we are going to have for the next five years."

Beyond that, retrocession of D.C. to Maryland appealed to Walsh because he felt that "after a period of thorough debate," and "not on a first time vote," Maryland would accept the city. Walsh noted that Maryland is a Democratic state and the governor and legislators should prefer this option because it strengthens the Democratic party in Maryland. Walsh thought that "D.C. residents would probably prefer this option to having no representation, plus they would be getting a lot better services than they have now."

Walsh recognized that Maryland Republicans "would certainly not support" retrocession. However, Walsh viewed retrocession as a vastly preferable option for Republicans across America than full voting rights for D.C. residents or statehood. Davis, however, was less sanguine about retrocession, saying that it solves one problem (of representation for D.C. residents in Congress), but "it creates a tremendous financial problem for Maryland having to pay for D.C. and Baltimore."

Walsh turned frankly political upon considering other options to provide D.C. residents with congressional representation. He said Republicans would never swallow giving D.C. two Democratic senators. Walsh said that an additional Democratic House member, whether achieved through retrocession or D.C. voting rights, "would not be a big deal."

Walsh also thought that D.C. statehood has a practical problem because D.C. is too small. Walsh compared D.C. to Alaska, which is larger than many countries. "Alaska has cultural differences and enormous management and transportation problems, while D.C. is not even a big city. Rather, D.C. is a "small, presumably manageable city." Walsh observed that ancient Greece had city-states, "but that was because they were so self-reliant. The District of Columbia is anything but self-reliant," he said.

Davis, like Walsh, was opposed to statehood on political grounds. First, exemplifying the Walsh notion that D.C. overseers in Congress act parochially, Davis opposed D.C. statehood because it would bring a nonresident income tax to the region—and to Davis's affluent home district. Davis argued that D.C. is not the center of its region but the center of the nation. Because its main business is government and there is no tax base without the federal government, the District should be supported with a properly sized federal payment, Davis said.

Davis thought the D.C. government should be restructured "in addition to just firing people and cutting benefits." This probably means that "they [should] get out of the Medicaid business, which is the fastest growing part of their government. It's deteriorating the city." Other state-type functions, such as welfare, should be examined to see what the District's proper size should be. Davis thought that the original home rule plan, giving D.C. excessive responsibilities in comparison to its resources, was "exacerbated by the city's antibusiness policies, [and] set the city up for failure." However, once the city is properly downsized, with scaled-back tax rates that fit the new functions, the federal payment and not suburban taxes should provide the residual. "The whole relationship needs to be reworked," Davis said, based on "a dialogue between the city and Congress."

A city that has shed its state and county functions would have a reduced possibility of ever becoming a state, which is a coincidental or planned outcome of the Walsh and Davis policies. Davis stated that he "is not going to sit here and say anything on the record but opposition" to D.C. statehood, although he did allow that if the District would "start doing things well" over the long term, "funny things happen sometimes." But to Davis, full voting rights for D.C. in Congress seemed rather ludicrous given that his home district of Fairfax County is more populous than is D.C. "Fairfax has to share two senators with eleven other [Virginia] counties," David observed.

An idea intriguing to Walsh was complete removal of federal income tax liability to D.C. residents, which could be enacted on the grounds that D.C. residents cannot vote in congressional elections. Walsh said that the issue of taxation without representation "resonates" among Americans: "We fought a Revolutionary War over it." Walsh viewed this proposal as an explicit exchange for disallowing D.C. representation in Congress. Davis again found Walsh's idea to be unrealistic, saying that federal tax forgiveness for D.C. "has a huge budgetary impact. The budget rules. That is actually taking money out of the Treasury. And that is why it ain't going to happen."

Walsh and Davis were in full agreement over the nonresident income tax for D.C., with Walsh calling it "just another way to get more money." The District would need far fewer resources if it could "get rid" of its state functions, Walsh observed. The federal government could take some D.C. prisoners, and D.C. could contract out to Maryland and Virginia prison systems for the rest. D.C. could also contract out to Maryland and Virginia for Medicaid, welfare, motor vehicle registration, and possibly the libraries and health system "if [it] can't manage them." Regardless of the form of government ultimately chosen for D.C., Walsh thought the keys to making the nation's capital "a healthy city forever" were the basics: making the streets safe, providing a good education to students, and keeping spending and taxes in check. Davis thought that the Republicans could "go—like Nixon to China—where the Democrats couldn't" and design a financial structure that would permit the District to succeed. But Davis, the pragmatist in these discussions, warned of "different elements in our party who are not willing to give the city a fair shake, who want to treat it like their fiefdom. . . . They just don't understand the city." Davis concluded that there is a potential in the Republican party to help or to hurt D.C., and "that chapter is unwritten."

As in the focus groups, the true believers (Jesse Jackson, Sharon Pratt Kelly, Kevin Chavous, and Sam Smith) were perplexed. To them, no separate but unequal option short of political parity with all other Americans made any sense for D.C. citizens. They wanted a fair deal from Congress that brought financial stability, and they wanted statehood. Eleanor Holmes Norton, who thought like a true believer, but fought for D.C. rights like a pragmatist, joined Alice Rivlin, John Wilson, Marion Barry, James Walsh, and the many focus group pragmatists in fashioning improvements that for now fall short of political equality. Norton, Rivlin, and Wilson would put D.C. on a route toward statehood, while Walsh and Barry were focused solely on lifting the District from its immediate crisis. As in the focus groups, virtually none of the leaders interviewed thought that the status quo for the District was palatable or workable except Tom Davis, who grasped too well Congress' propensities for punitive, rather than positive, reform.

THE ONUS PROBANDI

In his *Nicomachean Ethics,* Aristotle expressed three precepts about equality that have profoundly influenced Western philosophy (Westin 1990, 185):

1. It is just to treat people who are equal equally.
2. It is also just to treat people who are unequal unequally.
3. The foregoing propositions are self-evident, being universally accepted even without the support of argument.

Over the centuries a presumption of equality has evolved in Western thought from Aristotle's precepts (ibid., 185–256). Around the turn of this century, Henry Sidgwick wrote that an *onus probandi,* or burden of proof, is upon those who wish to treat people unequally (ibid., 230, n. 2). Moreover, Isaiah Berlin (1961, 137) wrote, "The assumption is that equality needs no reasons, only inequality does so." That is, if one were to treat people in a uniform, regular, similar, and symmetrical manner, then one's actions need not be explained. In contrast, differences in treatment and unsystematic behavior do require an explanation and, as a rule, justification. Berlin wrote that if he had a cake and there were ten people who desired a piece of it, he would give each person one-tenth of the cake, and such an action would require no justification. However, if he departed from this principle of equal division, he would be "expected to produce a special reason" (ibid.).

Most of the panelists in this research, when presented with the District's political status, could not accept the unequal division of America's cake. Philosophically, one could argue that Congress has the *onus probandi* to prove that it is just to treat D.C. people unequally compared to all other Americans. Politically, however, D.C. residents seem to have the burden of legitimizing themselves in the eyes of a legislative body that has refused to admit them for over two centuries.

APPENDIX A

The Players

SNAPSHOTS OF FOCUS GROUP PARTICIPANTS

Participants did not use their real first names for focus group sessions. All scores noted in parentheses are based on the feeling thermometer, with 0 = coldest and 100 = warmest.

Van Nuys, California
November 14, 1992

1. *Bruce*: Empathizer, strong (90) Democrat, always votes, aged fifty-two, single. B.S. degree and graduate work, freelance location manager for motion picture studios, earns over $100,000. Supported Clinton (98), felt warmly toward Martin Luther King (90), Jesse Jackson (80), and Ron Brown, but not toward Bush (0) or Reagan (0). Thought that D.C. residents were out of touch with the rest of America (70). Favored (100) equal treatment of blacks. PE Points: 25. Joined consensus in favoring combination of options two and five—namely, increased self-rule and minimization of congressional control of D.C. along with D.C. residents voting in Maryland elections.

2. *Cheryl*: Empathizer, claimed to be strong (85) Independent but only sometimes votes, age thirty-four, single. High school diploma, writer, earns under $20,000. Gave high score for M.L. King (80), was cold toward Jackson and all the politicians listed (10 or less). Thought that D.C. residents were out of touch with the rest of America (70) and felt (70) that blacks should be treated equally. Gave some credibility (40) to the notion that whites were better than blacks at running things and should be allowed to do so. Did not know whether D.C. had voting representation in the Senate. PE Points: 25. Joined consensus for greater self-rule coupled with D.C. residents voting in Maryland elections.

3. *Dawn*: Originalist, fairly strong (65) Independent, always intends to vote, aged twenty-four, single. High school diploma, sells art and music, earns over $60,000. Highest marks went to Reagan (50), Bush (40), M. L. King (40). Was cold toward Clinton (0), Jackson (0), and the sentiment that we would have fewer prob-

lems if we treated people more equally. Thought that D.C. residents already had voting representation in the Senate and that 70 percent of D.C. residents worked for the federal government. PE Points: 25. Joined consensus of focus group (see Bruce).

4. *Debbi*: Anti-big-government, lukewarm (50) Republican, always votes, aged thirty, married. A.A. degree, homemaker and student, family earns over $60,000. Felt warmly toward Clinton (95), Reagan (90), Oliver North (85); coldest toward Jackson (10). Strongly (90) supported treating blacks more equally. Thought that only 15 percent of D.C. residents were black and that 75 percent work for the federal government. PE Points: 25. Joined the consensus.

5. *Dell*: Racially troubled, strong (80) Republican, always votes. Aged sixty-one, single. B.A. degree, former computer compositor, now an investor; did not provide income data. Strongest support was for Reagan (90) and Bush (75); lowest for Ron Brown (30). Gave a (75) to the notion that whites were better at running things than blacks and should be allowed to do so. Thought that half the people in Washington worked for the federal government and that only 20 percent of D.C. residents were black. PE Points: 0. Was the only California panelist that favored the status quo for D.C.

6. *Frances*: Anti-big-government, lukewarm (50) Libertarian, always votes, aged forty-five, married, lives in a more urban area. Some college, runs a gift shop and also lists herself as a "counselor and mother," family earns over $100,000. Gave high scores to no one but was coldest toward Bush (0) and Reagan (0). Thought that people who live in Washington were out of touch with the rest of the United States (80). Gave (80) to the sentiment that blacks should be treated more equally and gave some credibility (30) to notion that whites are better than blacks at running things and should be allowed to do so. PE Points: 25. Joined consensus.

7. *Francine*: Racially troubled, solid (100) Democrat, always votes, aged seventy-one, married. High school diploma, homemaker, family earns $30,000–40,000. Strongly supported Clinton (100) and Oliver North (100). Had weak feelings about M. L. King (10), Jackson (10), Ron Brown (10), Bush (10), and Reagan (10). Was rather warm (75) to the thought that blacks should be treated more equally. Thought that D.C. already had voting representation in the U.S. Senate. Thought that 50 percent of D.C. residents were receiving welfare and that 50 percent were black as well. PE Points: 15. Joined consensus for more self-rule for residents of D.C. but did not favor voting representation in Congress.

8. *Greg*: Follower, strong (65) Independent, usually votes, aged thirty, single, lives in urban area. Some college, operations director, earns over $50,000. Gave low feeling scores to those listed, especially Clinton (10) and Reagan (10); gave Bush a score of (35). Thought (90) that D.C. residents were out of touch with the rest of America. Thought to some degree (50) that blacks should be treated more equally. Thought that 91 percent of D.C. residents were receiving welfare and that only 35 percent of D.C. residents were black. PE Points: 25. Joined the consensus.

9. *Jann*: Follower, lukewarm (50) Independent, always votes, aged twenty-eight, single. B.A. degree, production assistant for TV commercials; did not provide income data. Responded warmly to M. L. King (90), coolly to Clinton (0), Bush (25), Jackson (25). Reagan (50) and Oliver North (50) were in the middle. Felt strongly (100) that blacks should be treated more equally. Thought that 75 percent of D.C. resi-

dents worked for the federal government and that only 25 percent were black. PE Points: 25. Joined the consensus.

10. *Madelyn*: Follower, strong (80) Independent, always votes, aged thirty-five, married. High school degree, computer documentation specialist and technical writer, family earns over $50,000. Strongly supported only M. L. King (80); weakest sentiments were for Jackson (20). Clinton, Bush, Reagan all (40). Did not agree (0) that D.C. residents were out of touch. Thought (80) that blacks should be treated more equally. Thought that D.C. residents already had voting representation in the Senate. PE Points: 25. Joined the consensus.

11. *Pete*: Anti-big-government, strong (90) Republican, always votes, aged forty-two, married. High school diploma, president of a sales agency, earns over $60,000. Strongly supported Reagan (90), M. L. King (90), Bush (80), and Oliver North (80). Weakest sentiments were for Jackson (20). Thought (80) that whites were better than blacks at running things and should be allowed to do so. Thought that 10 percent of D.C. residents were black. PE Points: 25. Led in urging that D.C. residents vote in Maryland elections. Also joined consensus for greater self-rule for D.C.

12. *Rick*: Pragmatist, rather strong (70) Democrat, usually votes, aged forty-one, married. B.A., lives in Hollywood, writer, family earns over $100,000. Strongest support was for M. L. King (70); gave a score of 30 to Clinton, 0 to Reagan, 0 to Bush, 0 to Ron Brown, 5 to Jesse Jackson. Thought (90) that Washington residents were out of touch. Favored (80) blacks being treated more equally. Thought that 60 percent of D.C. residents were on welfare. PE Points: 25. Led in favoring a combination of two options that brought consensus: greater self-rule and allowing D.C. residents to vote in Maryland.

13. *Ross*: Pragmatist, strong (95) Independent, only sometimes votes, aged thirty-nine, married. High school diploma, manufacturer's sales representative, family earns over $50,000. Favored only M. L. King (70), giving (0) to all others listed except Oliver North (25). Did not agree (0) that D.C. residents were out of touch with America. Had fully accurate knowledge of D.C. facts and demographics. Was lukewarm (50) in thinking that blacks should be treated more equally. PE Points: 25. Supported the consensus.

Austin, Texas
November 19, 1992

1. *Al*: Empathizer, weak (25) Independent, usually votes, aged forty-one, married, two children. B.S. degree, marketing manager, family earns over $100,000. Supported Perot (80). Gave low marks to Reagan (10) and Jesse Jackson (20). Others: Gore (70), M. L. King (70), Ron Brown (60), Bush (50), Clinton (50). Did not feel (0) that D.C. people were out of touch with America. Supported (75) treating blacks more equally. Thought that D.C. already had voting representation in the House. PE Points: 90. Wanted a "voting district," not a state. Thought that because D.C. is taxed, it should have representation. Wanted to end congressional control over D.C. Was willing to give D.C. the "job and salary" (the rights of statehood such as representation, the end of congressional veto over D.C.) but not the "title" (statehood).

2. *Andrew*: Follower, weak (20) Independent, sometimes votes, aged thirty, single. B.S. degree, manager of furniture plant, earns $30,000–40,000. Supported Bush (80). Gave lowest score (40) to Jesse Jackson; gave a score of 50 to all others. Thought that 20 percent of D.C. residents were black and that D.C. already had voting representation in the House and Senate. Gave some credibility (30) to the notion that whites were better than blacks at running things and should be allowed to do so. Thought that only 5 percent of D.C. residents were on welfare and that only 5 percent worked for federal government. PE Points: 0. Opposed to statehood. Thought that D.C. should join with Maryland. Otherwise, supported one senator, one voting representative, and no veto by Congress over D.C. laws and budgets.

3. *Ben*: Empathizer, strong (80) Democrat, always votes, aged thirty-one, married. M.A. degree, architect, family earns $30,000–40,000. High regard for M. L. King (100), Clinton (80), Ron Brown (80). Gave low marks to Bush (20), Reagan (20), Perot (20). Favored more equal treatment of blacks. Thought that only 10 percent of D.C. people worked for federal government and that 10 percent received welfare. PE Points: 60. Supported one senator, one voting representative, no congressional control over D.C. affairs.

4. *Chico*: Follower, stated that he was strong (100) Republican but only "sometimes" votes, aged forty-three, married, Latino. Foreman of furniture plant, earns under $20,000. Strongly supported Perot (100). Had little regard for Jackson (30), M. L. King (20), Clinton (20), Ron Brown (20), Al Gore (20). Thought that only 10 percent of D.C. residents were black and that D.C. had voting representation in the House and Senate. Gave some credibility (50) to the notion that whites were better at running things than blacks. PE Points: 100. Supported statehood. Thought that maybe one of two senators could be reserved for whites if whites were concerned about Jesse Jackson being elected senator.

5. *David*: Pragmatist, rather strong (75) Republican, always votes, aged twenty-eight, marital status unspecified. B.A. degree, insurance agent, earns $30,000–40,000. Liked M. L. King (70) and somewhat favored Perot (60), Reagan (60). Others: Bush (50), Clinton (50), Oliver North (50), Ron Brown (40), Gore (30). PE Points: 50. Supported representation but not statehood. Supported one or two senators, one voting representative.

6. *Ivana*: Racially troubled, lukewarm (55) Republican, always votes, aged forty-one, married, two children. B.A. degree, kindergarten teacher, family earns $50–60,000. Rated Perot highest (60). Gave low marks to Clinton (0), Ron Brown (10), Reagan (15). Gave low rating (15) to the feeling that blacks should be treated more equally, with a high (80) rating for treating "people" more equally in this country. Thought that 85 percent of D.C. residents were on welfare, the same percentage that she thought were black. Thought that 45 percent of D.C. residents worked for the federal government. PE Points: 60. Favored one senator, one voting representative, and no Congressional veto of D.C. bills and budgets. Thought that Jesse Jackson was a big factor in why D.C. does not have political equality.

7. *Joe Bob*: Follower, fairly strong (75) Democrat, usually votes, aged forty-two, married. One year of college, custodial supervisor, family earns $30,000–40,000. Strongest support was for Clinton (80) and M. L. King (75), weakest for Reagan (2) and Bush (10). Rather high score for Jackson (60); low score for Oliver North (1). Rather strongly supported (75) the equal treatment of blacks and gave some support

(25) to the notion that whites were better at running things than blacks and should be allowed to do so. Thought that 50 percent of D.C. residents worked for federal government. PE Points: 100. Thought that D.C. should be a state and believed that D.C. people paid taxes and died for their country like other Americans.

8. *Jason*: Racially troubled, strong (80) Republican, always votes, aged fifty-five, married. High school diploma, pawnbroker, family earns $30,000–40,000. Strong supporter of Perot (80), Bush (75), Clinton (75). Had some positive feeling for M. L. King (60), less for Jackson (40). Scored rather highly (60) for the idea that whites were better at running things than blacks and should be allowed to do so. Thought that D.C. already had voting representation in House and Senate. Felt (60) to a degree that D.C. residents were out of touch with America. Thought that 60 percent of D.C. residents worked for federal government. PE Points: 90. Supported full representation (two senators, one voting representative), opposed allowing Congress to keep veto power over D.C. bills and budgets. Admitted that the "title" of statehood was all that was lacking in what he was willing to give D.C.

9. *Lynn* (male): Anti-big-government, strong (85) Independent, always votes, aged twenty-five, single. B.S. degree, works on the technical support staff of an insurance company, earns $20,000–30,000. Supported Ross Perot supporter (90), liked Bush (70), had little regard for Jesse Jackson (10). Others: M. L. King (60), Reagan (50), Clinton (50), Ron Brown (50), Oliver North (0). Gave little (10) credibility to notion that whites were better than blacks at running things. Thought that 80 percent of people in D.C. worked for the federal government. PE Points: 60. Supported one senator, one voting representative, and the end of congressional control over D.C. Would not give D.C. "title" of statehood.

10. *Marlene*: True believer, strong (90) Democrat, always votes, aged sixty, married, resides in downtown Austin. M.S. degree, interior designer, family earns $30,000–40,000. Strong supporter of Clinton (90), Ron Brown (90), M. L. King (90) and Jackson (80). Weak supporter of Bush (40) and Reagan (20). Believed strongly in the equal treatment of blacks. Others: Perot (60), Oliver North (0). PE Points: 100. Advocated statehood; like other participants, wanted full representation (two senators, one voting representative) and full self-government; reasoned that she was for statehood since nothing is left that would keep D.C. from being a state.

11. *Mary*: Pragmatist, strong (85) Democrat, always votes, aged thirty-two, single. B.A. degree, teacher, earns $20,000–30,000. Highly regarded M. L. King (100), Clinton (95), Ron Brown (95), Jackson (95). Gave low marks to Bush (0), Reagan (0), Oliver North (0). Strongly favored (100) equal treatment of blacks. Thought that D.C. already had voting representation in the House and Senate. PE Points: 0. Supported joining D.C. to Maryland.

12. *Molly*: Empathizer, still an Irish citizen, has lived in the United States for fifteen years, aged forty, married. B.A. degree, social services coordinator, family earns $30,000–40,000. Highest regard was for M. L. King (100), lowest for Reagan (0), Bush (15), Oliver North (15). Others: Clinton, (50), Ron Brown (25), Gore (50), Jackson (40). Strongly favored (90) more equal treatment for blacks. Thought that D.C. people were somewhat (50) out of touch. PE Points: 100. Favored statehood.

13. *Willie Bob*: Empathizer, lukewarm (50) Independent, always votes, aged thirty-seven, married. B.S. degree, architect, family earns $60,000–100,000. Liked Bush (80), Perot (80), M. L. King (80). Lowest regard was for Gore (40) and Jackson

(40). Favored more equal treatment of blacks. Thought that D.C. people were somewhat (50) out of touch. PE Points: 100. Favored statehood.

Bethesda, Maryland
February 13, 1993

1. *Abby*: Empathizer, for "right now" a strong (100) Democrat, usually votes, aged thirty-seven, nearing divorce. M.A., college English lecturer, earns over $20,000. Supported Clinton, with warm feelings for M. L. King (100) and Gore (95), but not Bush (0) or Reagan. Gave a score of 65 to Ron Brown, 50 to Ross Perot and 25 to Jesse Jackson. Did not think D.C. residents were particularly out of touch (25). Favored equal treatment of blacks (100). PE Points: 50. Did not find it practical to give D.C. to another state because D.C. lacks the resources to be a state. Favored one senator, one representative, and a move toward ending congressional control. Believed that what we have is not working.

2. *Barb*: Pragmatist, rather strong (80) Democrat, usually votes, aged thirty-two, married. M.S. degree, occupational therapist, family earns over $60,000. Gave highest scores to Gore (85), M. L. King (85), Clinton (80); gave a score of 60 to Ron Brown and 50 to Jackson. Assigned low scores to Bush (30), Perot (30), Reagan (10), North (10). Did not think (15) that D.C. residents were out of touch. Felt rather strongly (70) about treating blacks more equally. Thought that most of D.C. residents (60 percent) worked for federal government. Thought that D.C. should be joined with Maryland even if residents of the two jurisdictions didn't want that. PE Points: 0. Would make D.C. part of a neighboring state and provide federal dollars as an incentive.

3. *Christine*: True believer, strong (100) Independent, always votes, early thirties, single. B.A. degree, plans to enter graduate school, unemployed. Strongly supported M. L. King (100) and Clinton (93). Was the only one in group to feel somewhat warmly (81) toward Jesse Jackson. Others: Perot (50), Brown (50), Gore (50), North (9), Bush (4), Reagan (3). Strongly favored (100) treating blacks more equally. Thought that D.C. already had voting representation in the House. Thought that 50 percent of D.C. residents worked for federal government and that only 30–40 percent are black. PE Points: 100. Favored full statehood, with some financial help at the outset from the federal government. Believed that a coterie of governors could serve as powerless consultants to the fledgling state.

4. *El*: Pragmatist, strong (99) Independent, usually votes, aged thirty-eight, married. J.D., communications lawyer, family earns over $100,000. Gave highest scores to Gore (90) and M. L. King (90). Clinton and Ron Brown received scores of 70. Had weak sentiments for Bush (0), Perot (30), Reagan (30), North (0), Jesse Jackson (0). Only gave a 50 to treating blacks more equally and gave some credence (20) to notion that whites were better than blacks at running things and should be allowed to do so. Thought that D.C. was already represented in the House and that 60 percent of D.C. residents were black. PE Points: 50. Favored one representative, one or two senators. Thought that Congress should continue to decide D.C. issues because it gives D.C. funds.

5. *George*: Originalist, Republican, always votes, aged forty-five, married. J.D., attorney in D.C. law firm, family earns over $100,000. Gave highest score to Reagan (90); however, Clinton (80) outscored Bush (75). Gore and Perot received scores of 50. Others: Ron Brown (20), M. L. King (20), North (20), Jackson (10). Gave M.L. King the lowest score in this group. Thought that D.C. residents were out of touch (70). Only gave a score of 50 to treating blacks more equally, and gave a 50 to the notion that whites were better than blacks at running things and should be allowed to do so. Was knowledgeable about D.C. facts. PE Points: 0. Believed that status quo was "not all that bad" and that voting status for the D.C. delegate in the Committee of the Whole (since repealed) should be tried before making further changes. However, would "not be against" a constitutional amendment to make the delegate a voting representative because D.C. lacks resources to be a state. "Not be against" could be interpreted as support for the voting representative, which would indeed take a constitutional amendment to attain, but preference was for the status quo.

6. *Herb*: Pragmatist, strong (90) Democrat, always votes, aged sixty-two, married. J.D., lobbyist, family earns over $60,000. Gave high marks to M. L. King (100), Gore (90), Clinton (90). Ron Brown received a 70; Bush, Reagan, and Perot each received a 50. Responded coolly to North (0) and Jesse Jackson (20). Thought that D.C. residents were out of touch (60). Strongly supported (100) treating blacks more equally. Was knowledgeable about D.C. Thought that it was okay for D.C. not to have voting representation in Congress. PE Points: 80. Favored two senators, one representative, a greater degree of self-rule with some congressional oversight; was unsure about statehood.

7. *Howard*: Pragmatist, mild (50) Independent, always votes, aged fifty-nine, married. M.A. degree, highly successful artist, family earns over $250,000. Responded warmly to M. L. King (90). Others: Gore (60), Clinton (51), Bush (50), Reagan (50), Perot (0). Thought that D.C. residents were somewhat out of touch (50). Strongly favored treating blacks more equally. Thought that D.C. was already represented in the House; otherwise knew D.C. statistics. PE Points: 35. Viewed statehood as superfluous. Gave up on Maryland taking D.C. as being too impractical. Advocated one senator, one representative, and full home rule.

8. *Jeff*: Empathizer, Independent, usually votes, aged forty-three, single. Ph.D., computer programmer, earns over $50,000. Responded warmly to M. L. King (90). Clinton received a score of 70, Gore a 65, Perot a 50, Ron Brown a 50, Jackson a 50, Bush a 10, Reagan a 1, North a 0. Thought that D.C. people were rather out of touch (50). Knew D.C. statistics. PE Points: 100. Favored statehood. Thought that the paternalistic relationship between the federal government and D.C. had to end.

9. *Mia*: Racially troubled, strong (80) Democrat, always votes, aged forty-eight, married, M.A. degree, high school English teacher, family earns over $60,000. Gave high scores to Clinton (90), Gore (80), M. L. King (80). Others: Bush (70), Perot (60), Ron Brown (50), North (40), Jackson (40), Reagan (0). Thought that D.C. people were out of touch (80). Gave credibility (60) to the notion that whites were better than blacks at running things and should be allowed to do so, assigning the highest score to this notion in this group. Thought that 80 percent of D.C. residents were black. PE Points: 15. Believed that if D.C. gets funds from Congress, then Congress should have control over D.C. Favored a voting representative for D.C., nothing else.

10. *Natasha*: Anti-big-government, Independent, usually votes, former D.C. resident, aged forty-one, divorced. B.A. degree, technical writer, earns over $60,000. Responded warmly to Gore (85); tepidly to Perot (75), Bush (75), Clinton (65); coldly to M. L. King (40), Reagan (30), Jackson (20), North (50). Was one of just two in this group to give a low score to M. L. King. Gave some credibility (30) to the notion that whites were better than blacks at running things and should be allowed to do so. Thought that 70 percent of D.C. residents were on welfare and that 50 percent worked for D.C. government. PE Points: 100. Favored statehood. Believed that if we let D.C. residents rise to challenge, good leaders would emerge.

11. *Tony*: Pragmatist, Democrat, usually votes, aged forty, single. Some college, folk singer and substitute teacher, earns under $20,000. Strongly supported Clinton (100), Ron Brown (100), M. L. King (100), Gore (98). Responded coldly to Jackson (40), Perot (20), Bush (0), Reagan (0), North (0). Strongly favored (100) treating blacks more equally. Knew D.C. statistics but thought that only 50 percent of D.C. residents were black. PE Points: 65. Would give D.C. home rule, a voting representative, and one or two senators. Would not give D.C. to a neighboring state, since it could not afford D.C.; said, however, that D.C. could be given to Connecticut, since it could afford D.C.

Harrisburg, Pennsylvania
February 18, 1993

1. *Ashley*: Empathizer, strong (90) Democrat, always votes, aged forty-six, divorced, one child. Master's degree, medical librarian, earns over $30,000. Felt strongly about M. L. King (100, the only person in the Pennsylvania group to give this rating), Clinton (90), Gore (90). Others: Perot (70), Jesse Jackson (20), Oliver North (10), Reagan (10), Bush (10). Thought (50) that D.C. residents were somewhat out of touch with America. Felt strongly (95) about treating blacks more equally. Thought that 75 percent of D.C. residents were on welfare and that 75 percent of D.C. residents were black. Thought that only 5 percent of D.C. people worked for the federal government. Had no opinion about whether Maryland and D.C. should be forced to join together even if they didn't want to join. PE Points: 100. Favored statehood. Felt that it was not fair to force Maryland to take D.C. and that D.C.'s wishes should be respected.

2. *Buster*: Follower, moderately strong (50) Independent, recently of voting age, aged twenty-one, single. High school diploma, student and owner of clothing business, earns less than $20,000. Responded warmly to M. L. King (90), Clinton (90), Bush (80), Gore (80). Others: Reagan (70), Perot (70), Oliver North (40), Jesse Jackson (20). Gave highest rating (75) of this focus group to the notion that whites were better than blacks at running things and should be allowed to do so. Thought that 50 percent of D.C. residents worked for federal government. PE Points: 100. Favored D.C. statehood because Maryland does not want D.C. and because D.C. residents desire statehood.

3. *George*: Pragmatist, moderately strong (60) Democrat, always votes, aged forty, divorced. B.A. degree, administrative assistant, earns over $30,000. Gave highest scores to Clinton (75), M. L. King (75), Oliver North (70). Others: Gore (60), Bush

(50), Jackson (50), Ron Brown (25), Reagan (25), Perot (25). Thought (80) that D.C. people were out of touch with America. Gave high score (100) to treating blacks more equally. Thought that D.C. already had voting representation in the House. PE Points: 0. Drew an analogy between a state being forced to take a nuclear waste dump and Maryland being forced to take D.C.—they don't want it but have to take it anyway for the common good. Thought that Maryland and D.C. should "eat their vegetables, eat their broccoli," and join together.

4. *Glenn*: Pragmatist, strong (90) Democrat, always votes, aged forty, married. B.S. degree, writer and association manager, family earns over $50,000. Gave highest scores to M. L. King (95), Clinton (85), Gore (80); lowest to Reagan (0) and Oliver North (0). Others: Jackson (60), Ron Brown (30), Bush (20). Thought (90) that D.C. people were out of touch with America. Thought (75) that blacks should be treated more equally. Thought that 10 percent of D.C. people were receiving welfare. PE Points: 0. Favored a "friendly takeover" of D.C. by Maryland. Advocated statehood if takeover did not work. Believed that the current situation was "totally unacceptable." Added no points for statehood if Maryland takeover did not work because of his strong advocacy in the group for takeover.

5. *Laura*: Empathizer, strong (90) Democrat, usually votes, aged twenty-nine, single. J.D., attorney and consumer advocate for Pennsylvania state government, earns over $30,000. Gave unusually high marks to Oliver North (81) and Jesse Jackson (80). Also responded warmly to Gore (95), M. L. King (94), Clinton (92), Perot (90), Bush (85), Ron Brown (85), Reagan (80). Thought to some degree (65) that blacks should be treated more equally and gave a little (10) credibility to the notion that whites were better than blacks at running things. Thought that only 28 percent of D.C. residents were black and that only 10 percent of residents received welfare. PE Points: 100. Would give D.C. to Maryland only if Maryland wants it.

6. *Mary*: Pragmatist, moderately strong (73) Republican, sometimes votes, aged thirty-three, single. Some college, financial analyst, earns over $20,000. Gave a score of 50 to everyone from Reagan to Jackson. Thought (75) that D.C. people were out of touch and that blacks should be treated more equally (100). Thought that 47 percent of D.C. residents received welfare. Thought that 72 percent worked for the federal government. PE Points: 0. Advocated "force feeding" D.C. to Maryland, arguing that people would forget about their opposition to this in the long run.

7. *Paul*: Anti-big-government, moderately strong (75) Republican, always votes, aged forty-eight, married, two children, B.A. degree, a finishing engineer, family earns over $60,000. Responded warmly only to Reagan (80) and Bush (75). Others: Perot (65), Oliver North (50), Ron Brown (50), Jackson (15). Gave unusually low score to M. L. King (25). Gave a score of 0 to Clinton and Gore. Was lukewarm (50) to the notions that blacks should be treated more equally and (50) that D.C. residents were out of touch. Thought that 90 percent of people in D.C. worked for federal government and that only 10 percent received welfare. PE Points: 100. Favored statehood, even though he "leaned to the right" on most issues.

8. *Scott*: Anti-big-government, moderately strong (75) Republican, always votes, aged twenty-six, B.A. degree, law student and law clerk in Pennsylvania government, earns over $20,000. Strongest support was for Reagan (100) and Bush (100); was unusually warm to Oliver North (95). Others: M. L. King (70), Perot (60), Clinton (50), Ron Brown (50), Jackson (45), Gore (40). Thought (60) that D.C. people

were somewhat out of touch. Did not think that if blacks (0) or people in general (0) were treated more equally that we would have fewer problems in America. Thought that 70 percent of D.C. people worked for federal government. PE Points: 100. Favored statehood, saying it was easier to accomplish than forcing D.C. into Maryland. Wanted political rights for the residents of D.C.

9. *Sherry*: True believer, strong (90) Democrat, usually votes, aged forty-seven, married, four children. Master's degree, legal secretary, earns over $20,000. Had warmest sentiments toward M. L. King (99), Clinton (98), Gore (95), and an unusually high score for Jesse Jackson (95). Also gave high score to Bush (85), but not to Reagan (40), Perot (40), or Oliver North (10). Strongly favored (100) treating blacks more equally and did not think (0) that D.C. residents were out of touch with America. PE Points: 100. Supported statehood. Did not want to force D.C. into Maryland.

10. *Sue*: Empathizer, lukewarm (50) Independent, always votes, aged twenty-eight, single, Asian American. J.D., attorney, earns over $20,000. Responded warmly to M. L. King (89), Clinton (95), Gore (90), Jackson (85). Others: Perot (60), Ron Brown (50), and a score of 20 each to Reagan, Bush, and Oliver North. Thought (80) that blacks should be treated more equally. Thought that 50 percent of D.C. residents worked for federal government. PE Points: 100. Favored statehood. Believed that a majority of Maryland residents do not want D.C. and that majority of people in D.C. want statehood, so the decision was obvious to her.

11. *Tom*: True believer, strong (85) Democrat, always votes, aged thirty-five, married. B.A. degree, legislative aide to a Pennsylvania state senator. Responded warmly to M. L. King (90), Clinton (85), Gore (85), Jackson (80). Others: Ron Brown (75), Bush (35), Perot (25), Reagan (10), North (5). Felt strongly (90) about treating blacks more equally. Thought that 40 percent of D.C. residents were receiving welfare. PE Points: 100. Thought that D.C. people wanted statehood and that it would work as well as being the quickest route. Would consider giving D.C. to Maryland if Maryland showed any "semblance of interest." (No points subtracted for Maryland's "semblance of interest," since he regarded it as so unlikely.)

Des Moines, Iowa
March 13, 1993

1. *Angie*: Pragmatist, Democrat, not a strong (50) Independent, aged twenty-seven, married. B.A. degree, research analyst with State of Iowa. Responded warmly to M. L. King (75), Clinton (75), Gore (70). Others: Bush (50), Perot (50), Ron Brown (40), Reagan (35), Oliver North (25), Jackson (25). Felt (75) that blacks should be treated more equally. Thought that 40 percent of D.C. residents received welfare and that 45 percent worked for the federal government. Thought that it was okay for D.C. residents not to be represented in Congress, and favored a forced merger with Maryland. PE Points: 45. Supported nominal statehood. Thought that Congress could retain control over D.C.if D.C. could have representation; favored one voting representative, one senator.

2. *Chris One*: Follower, rather strong (80) Democrat, always votes, aged thirty-eight, married. B.A. degree, waitress at truck plaza, family income over $50,000. Responded warmly to M. L. King, Clinton, Gore (all 80). Others: Perot (70), Ron

Brown (70), Jesse Jackson (70). Responded coolly to Bush (30), Reagan (20), Oliver North (20). Thought (90) that blacks should be treated more equally. Thought that 50 percent of D.C. residents worked for the federal government. PE Points: 45. Would prefer that Maryland take D.C. but thought that nominal statehood (one representative, one senator) would be more practical. Would retain congressional control over D.C., although thought it "would be nice" if Congress concerned itself only with federal interests pertaining to D.C.

3. *Chris Two*: Follower, Independent, usually votes, aged forty-three, single. M.B.A., supervisor in consumer advocate office, State of Iowa, earns over $50,000. Supported Perot (80). Others: Clinton (75), Jackson (75), Gore (70), Bush (70), Reagan (60), M. L. King (60), North (50). Thought (90) that blacks should be treated more equally. Thought that D.C. residents already had senators and a voting representative. Thought that 75 percent of D.C. residents worked for the federal government and that only 20 percent were black. PE Points: 75. Believed that D.C. was a city, not a state, and that D.C. was set up to be the seat of federal government. Favored nominal statehood, one elected representative and two senators, with federal control over D.C. affairs.

4. *Danny*: Racially troubled, Republican (75), always votes, aged forty-five, divorced. Farmed for thirty-five years, now an insurance agent, earns over $30,000. Responded warmly to Bush (100) and Oliver North (95), coolly to others: Reagan (40), Ron Brown (15), Perot (10). Gave a 0 each to M. L. King, Jesse Jackson, Gore, Clinton. Thought (90) that D.C. people were out of touch with other Americans. Was indifferent (1) to treating blacks more equally. Gave highest score (50) in this group to the notion that whites were better than blacks at running things and should be allowed to do so. Thought that 75 percent of D.C. residents were on welfare and that 75 percent were black. Thought that it was okay for D.C. not to have representation in Congress. PE Points: 45. Could live with one senator and one representative for D.C. Thought that D.C. could not be a state because "it has nothing to offer this country." Advocated a degree of congressional control over D.C. because the federal government takes care of it.

5. *Gary*: Originalist, strong (85) Democrat, always votes, aged thirty-eight, married. J.D., attorney for the State of Iowa, earns over $60,000. Responded warmly to Clinton (90), Gore (90), coolly to Bush (50), Jackson (50), Perot (30), North (10), Reagan (0). Thought (75) that D.C. residents were out of touch. Strongly supported (90) treating blacks more equally. PE Points: 20. Believed that D.C. was a federal enclave, so the federal government should still have control. Favored representation of one representative and maybe a senator.

6. *Jeanie*: Empathizer, strong (85) Democrat, always votes, aged forty-five, married. B.A. degree, reimbursement specialist for home health care company, family earns over $60,000. Responded warmly to Gore (90) and Clinton (80). Others: M. L. King (75), Jackson (65), Ron Brown (50), Perot (20), Bush (15), North (15), Reagan (0). Thought (60) that D.C. residents were out of touch. Thought (75) that blacks should be treated more equally. Thought that 40 percent of D.C. residents were on welfare. Said that maybe D.C. should be forced into Maryland. PE Points: 60. Believed that Congress could still have voice in D.C. affairs, but that no extraordinary control was necessary—just the same pursestring control as it has with other states. Favored some kind of representation (e.g., one representative, one senator).

7. *Lynn (female)*: Pragmatist, Independent, usually votes, aged twenty-seven, single. B.A. degree, provides human resources training support for a tractor company, earns under $20,000. Gave warmest support (70) to Clinton. Others: M. L. King (65), Gore (60), Brown (55), Perot (50), Jackson (50), Reagan (30), Bush (20). Thought (60) that blacks should be treated somewhat more equally. Thought that 70 percent of D.C. residents were on welfare and that 85 percent of residents were black. PE Points: 55. Favored "nominal statehood": representation in Congress (one representative, one or two senators), with the federal government retaining a lessened degree of control.

8. *Margaret*: Empathizer, moderately strong (75) Democrat, always votes, aged forty-one, married, children. B.A. degree, teacher and day care provider, family earns over $50,000. Responded warmly to M. L. King (90), Clinton (80), Gore (80), Jackson (80). Others: Ron Brown (50), Bush (45), Perot (45), North (12), Reagan (0). Strongly supported (100) treating blacks more equally. Thought that 40 percent of D.C. residents worked for federal government. PE Points: 25. Favored nominal statehood (one representative, unsure about senator) with "a little more" self-rule.

9. *Pete*: Anti-big-government, Republican (65), always votes, aged forty, divorced, children. B.A. degree, manager at building services store and freelance photographer, earns under $20,000. Responded warmly only to Bush (75). Others: M. L. King (50), Reagan (45), Gore (30), Clinton (25), Jackson (25), North (25), Perot (10), Ron Brown (10). Thought (80) that D.C. people were out of touch. Did not respond warmly (20) to treating blacks more equally. PE Points: 60. Favored representation of one representative and one senator. Thought that D.C. could not be a state because it lacks the combination of people and natural resources of a "normal" state. Did not want the federal government to oversee local affairs.

10. *Sherrie*: Follower, Republican (60), usually votes, aged forty-seven, married. Some college, secretary in state adoption agency, family earns over $100,000. Supported Bush (90). Others: Reagan (85), M. L. King (80), Clinton (75), Gore (75), North (60), Perot (30), Jackson (30). Thought (60) that D.C. people were somewhat out of touch. Thought (75) that "people" should be treated more equally, blacks less so (50). Thought that D.C. already had senators and voting representation. PE Points: 45. Favored representation of one representative and one senator, same level congressional control. Thought that D.C. was a city, not a state, and that it lacked resources and has been historically neutral.

11. *Sid*: Originalist, strong (80) Democrat, always votes, aged early forties, married. Ph.D., college professor and consultant. Responded warmly to M. L. King (90), coolly to Reagan (50), Jackson (40), North (10); gave all others a score of 70. Did not think that D.C. residents were out of touch. Favored (80) treating blacks more equally. PE Points: 0. Believed that federal government had obligation to provide services. Might be in favor of a national private charitable fund to help D.C.

12. *Susan*: Pragmatist, Democrat (strength: 60), always votes, aged thirty-six, single. Master's degree, research analyst with large health insurance company, earns over $30,000. Responded warmly to Gore (90), M. L. King (90). Others: Clinton (70); Brown, Jackson, Perot (all 40); Bush (20); Reagan (10); North (10). Thought (60) that D.C. people were somewhat out of touch. Responded warmly (90) to treating blacks more equally. Thought that 40 percent of D.C. residents worked for federal government and that 80 percent were black. PE Points: 45. Favored nominal statehood: one

representative, one senator. Thought that D.C. could not survive on its own and that no other state would want D.C. because it is a liability. Thought that D.C. was set up as a neutral seat and that Congressional control over D.C. affairs would be more palatable if D.C. had representation.

13. *Tim*: Anti-big-government, Republican (50), always votes, aged forty-nine, married, children. B.S. degree, sales manager with a nuts and bolts manufacturing company, family earns over $60,000. Responded warmly to Oliver North (80), Bush (80), Reagan; more coolly to M. L. King (50), Clinton (60), Gore (60). Was less favorable toward Perot, Ron Brown, Jackson (all 20). Did not think (0) that D.C. people were out of touch, and favored (80) treating blacks more equally. PE Points: 5. Supported representation only if Maryland and Virginia would absorb D.C. Believed that D.C. should rule itself as much as possible.

APPENDIX B

Summary of Panelists' Responses

Summary of Panelists' Responses to Pre-session Questionnaire

	Ca.	*Ia.*	*Md.*	*Pa.*	*Tx.*	*Total /Avg.*
Number in Focus Group	13	13	11	11	13[1]	61[1]
Party:						
Democrat	3	7	5	6	4	25
Republican	3	4	1	3	4	15
Independent or Third Party	7	2	5	2	4	20
Strength of Party Identity	75	70	86	75	65	74
Women/Men	7/6	8/5	6/5	5/6	4/9	30/31
Average Age	41	40	44	36	39	40
Married	7	8	6	5	8	34
Suburban	10	7	11	7	2	37
College Graduate	4	10	10	9	10	43
Graduate Degree	0	4	8	4	2	18
Income $50,000+	7	8	7	3	3	28
Feeling Thermometer (warmest = 100):						
George Bush	27	53	28	55	46	42
Bill Clinton	39	65	87	74	57	64
Ross Perot	[2]	40	43	55	63	50
Ronald Reagan	33	36	24	44	32	34
Ron Brown	29	45	59	52	54	48
Al Gore	39	67	77	70	62	63
M. L. King, Jr.	64	68	81	81	73	73
Oliver North	38	34	9	39	26	29
Jesse Jackson	22	44	34	55	45	40
Take a Guess: What percentage of people who live in Washington, D.C. work for the fed. gov't?	38	37	34	50	37	39

Summary of Panelists' Responses to Pre-session Questionnaire, *continued*

	Ca.	*Ia.*	*Md.*	*Pa.*	*Tx.*	*Total /Avg.*
What percentage of people in D.C. are black?	40	62	66	57	58	57
Opinion: Residents of D.C. are U.S. citizens but not represented in the U.S. House or Senate. Is this okay with you?						
Yes	2	2	2	1	0	7
No	6	5	7	9	8	35
No Opinion	5	6	2	1	5	19
What if the residents of Md. and D.C agreed that it was not a good idea for Md. and D.C. to be joined together as one state. Should it be done anyway?						
Yes	2	1	1	0	0	4
No	7	3	9	10	9	38
No Opinion	4	9	1	1	4	19
Feeling Thermometer (warmest = 100):						
The people who live in D.C. are out of touch with the rest of America.	48	50	45	41	42	45
If people were treated equally in this country, we would have fewer problems.	69	73	88	73	81	77
If blacks were treated equally in this country, we would have fewer problems.	71	69	85	76	78	76
Whites are better at running things than blacks and should be allowed to do so: number who gave a score of 20 or greater.	4	1	4	1	4	14

Summary of Panelists' Responses to Pre-session Questionnaire, *continued*

	Ca.	*Ia.*	*Md.*	*Pa.*	*Tx.*	*Total /Avg.*
Take a Guess: Does D.C. already have voting representation in the U.S. House?						
Yes	4	1	4	1	5	15
No	5	11	11	10	7	44
Don't Know	5	1	0	1	2	9
What percentage of D.C. residents are on welfare?	30	36	24	29	28	29

1. One panelist was not a U.S. citizen but a citizen of Ireland, here for 15 years.
2. Not measured in California.

APPENDIX C

Focus Group Stances

Stances of Focus Group Panelists

	Ca.	*Ia.*	*Md.*	*Pa.*	*Tx.*	*All*
Number in Focus Group	13	13	11	11	13	61
Presession Questionnaire:						
For D.C. statehood	4	1[1]	2[1]	6	5	18
Opposed	2	3	7	0	6	18
No opinion	7	9	2	5	2	25
Opening Round of Session:						
For statehood	1	2	2	6	4	15
For representation, not statehood	2	1	1	0	6	10
Opposed to statehood	6	8	5	1	3	23
No opinion	4	2	3	4	0	13
End of Session:						
For statehood	0	0	3	8	5	16
For greater self-gov't.	12	5	7	8	10	42
For full self-gov't.	0	2	5	8	10	25
For any sort of voting representation in Congress[2]	11	12	10	11	13	57
For D.C. voting representation (at a minimum)	0	11	9	8	11	39
For at least one senator for D.C	0	9	7	8	11	35

Stances of Focus Group Panelists, *continued*

	Ca.	*Ia.*	*Md.*	*Pa.*	*Tx.*	*All*
End of Session (continued):						
For full D.C. voting representation (two senators)	0	1	4	8	7	20
For achieving representation through Md. elections	11	–	–	–	–	11
For representation through absorption by Md.	0	1	1	3	2	7
For status quo	1	1	1	0	0	3
Political Equality Points:						
(See explanation in Appendix E)	22	40	54	73	70	52

1. Includes one "qualified yes."
2. By any means (own elections, Md. elections, through absorption by Md.).

APPENDIX D

Political Equality Points

Explanation of Assignment of Political Equality Points

100 = panelist is for full political equality, including D.C. statehood

30 = for each senator that panelist would grant to D.C.

15 = panelist would grant voting representative to D.C. without requiring D.C. to join Maryland elections.

10 = panelist would grant voting representative for D.C., to be achieved by voting in Maryland elections. Under this option D.C. residents would have the advantage of voting for Maryland senators, but the option may not be conducive to D.C. statehood or to retaining control over D.C. cultural identity.

5 = for each additional senator that panelist would "consider" for D.C. (e.g., "D.C. should have one *or* two senators" = 30 points + 5 points for the second senator = 35 points).

5 = panelist advocates end to congressional control over D.C. laws and budgets.

0 = panelist would give D.C. to Maryland or another state.

0 = panelist favors status quo (keep nonvoting delegate to Congress; keep congressional control over D.C. laws and budgets).

Note: The criteria in assigning points were a function of what best achieves full political equality, not what best achieves representation. Political equality with other Americans assumes control over one's cultural identity without sacrificing it to some other culture. Otherwise, voting in Maryland elections would have been assigned higher points and absorption by Maryland would have equaled 100 points. Should D.C. residents express a desire to vote in Maryland or be subsumed into Maryland, then the point designation would increase.

APPENDIX E

Political Equality Point Averages

Number/Average Political Equality Points for Categories of Focus Groups Participants

	Ca.	*Ia.*	*Md.*	*Pa.*	*Tx.*	*All*
True Believers	–	–	1 / 100	2 / 100	1 / 100	4 / 100
Empathizers	2 / 25	2 / 43	2 / 75	3 / 100	4 / 88	13 / 72
Pragmatists	2 / 25	3 / 48	5 / 46	3 / 0	2 / 25	15 / 32
Anti-Big-Gov't	3 / 25	2 / 33	1 / 100	2 / 100	1 / 60	9 / 56
Originalists	1 / 25	2 / 10	1 / 0	–	–	4 / 11
Racially Troubled	2 / 8	1 / 45	1 / 15	–	2 / 75	6 / 38
Followers	3 / 25	3 / 55	0	1 / 100	3 / 67	10 / 54
Totals	**13 / 22**	**13 / 40**	**11 / 54**	**11 / 73**	**13 / 70**	**61 / 52**

APPENDIX F

Qualitative Research Methodology

As Theodore Noyes (1951, 161), editor of the *Washington Star*, said in 1938:

> The fact remains that relatively few living Americans living outside the District know that taxation without representation continues to exist under the American flag.

The District's political future exemplifies countless issues that receive little attention from most Americans. Most do not feel responsibility for developing an opinion on unformed issues, especially when they do not believe their views to be of value to policymakers. Most Americans hold widely defined moral, ethical, and democracy-based principles, but lack a well structured, overarching ideology to accommodate and assess most of the new information and issues they encounter. Unless people have a personal experience with an issue, or the issue ensues from a dramatic, widely covered event, receipt of new information will usually lead, at most, to a snap judgment, but not to a public opinion of any quality.

This appendix explores the use of qualitative research to assess public opinion on unformed issues such as D.C.'s political status. Qualitative research involves an in-depth exploration of a person's views without attempting to direct and compartmentalize those views at the outset via forced-choice questions. Those whose qualitative views are sought are active participants in producing information. The potential uses as well as the advantages and disadvantages of qualitative research will be presented in this appendix, with an emphasis on focus group applications. Focus groups add an interactive element; they allow panelists to be influenced by the views of their fellow group members, a characteristic lacking in quantitative opinion surveys but found in everyday life.

The Uncertainty of Public Views on D.C.'s Political Status

Then-Governor Bill Clinton (1991, 550) observed at hearings into D.C. statehood that he once lived in the District, and that he had

> seen firsthand how the residents of the District share the same concerns, fears, and hopes as Americans everywhere else. . . . I can't imagine the men and women of Arkansas waking up a single day of their life without the right to call their representatives in Washington and tell them exactly what they think ought to be done.

Clinton went on to state several of the standard arguments of statehood proponents. President Clinton reiterated his support for D.C. statehood in 1993 at a national town meeting at the White House, stating that once he "saw the facts about the size, the taxes, and the contribution to the national interest," he thought that D.C. should be an independent state (press release of Representative Eleanor Holmes Norton, May 27, 1993). One of the panelists of the Bethesda, Maryland focus group observed, in true inside-the-Beltway style, that he would expect President Clinton to remain an outspoken D.C. statehood advocate only as long as his political capital had not been expended on other left-leaning issues. The panelist commented that the president's support early in his administration for gays in the military may have lowered his ability to speak out on similar controversial, symbolically explosive issues. Since then, the Republican electoral victories and D.C.'s financial crisis have made attempts to achieve D.C. statehood seem foolish in the near term and have revived discussions among policymakers on a variety of other options.

D.C.'s political options are largely irrelevant to an American public that is concerned about its own rights and needs. Yankelovich (1991, 77) observed that it is a "truism that people pay more attention to issues relevant to their lives than those that are not." D.C.'s political status is a nonissue to the vast majority of Americans who have not considered the matter. As then-Governor Clinton (1991, 556) described in House testimony:

> I will be honest with you, on a daily basis, this is not an issue most Americans wake up thinking about. Most of them probably never gave it five minutes thought. No one ever really lobbied me about it, no one ever really talked to me about it. I admit I took no initiative on it.

Development of Higher Quality Public Opinion

Herbert Asher (1992, 21) pointed out that people will respond to questions about which they have no genuine attitudes or opinions, and the analyst often treats such "nonattitude" responses "as if they represented actual public opinions." As a consequence, a "misleading portrait of public opinion" emerges if no distinction is drawn between real opinions and a desire to cooperate in an interview situation. For example, Asher cited Bishop, Oldendick, and Tuchfarber (1980), where fully a third of respondents offered an opinion regarding the repeal of a nonexistent "Public Affairs Act of 1975." Asher (1992, 36) noted further that if people were asked whether they favored selling military equipment to Saudi Arabia, they might answer the question based on predispositions toward the weapons industry and not on the basis of any information pertaining to our nation's diplomatic situation with Saudi Arabia. Similarly, when asked about cooperative space exploration between America and Russia, many respondents would give views based on their view of Russia rather than the best way to explore space (ibid.). Negative predispositions toward the District similarly affect respondents' views on potential political structures for that entity.

Asher (ibid.) observed that "the whole of public opinion may be less important than the opinion of a particular subset of people." He explained that on certain issues, the views of people with "genuine attitudes" will "have the greatest impact on government policy and policymakers." The focus groups in this research into D.C.'s political status produced a subset of a few people with genuine attitudes, offering policymakers greater insight into public opinion on this topic than quantitative surveys would likely yield at this early state of opinion evolution. Decades ago, George Gallup (1947, 386) urged development of research methods to distinguish between people's "snap judgments" and higher quality, more thoughtful opinions. Since it would be unusual for Gallup's survey respondents to have given careful consideration to the District's political options, one is intuitively safe in categorizing the responses as snap judgments and therefore lower in quality than reasoned opinion.

Eleanor Singer (1988, 416–26) noted a host of problems with public opinion surveys, among them "the failure to do justice to the richness of people's experience." She also observed "the tendency of people to give an opinion even when they do not have a real point of view on the subject." Yankelovich (1991, 22) added that "[f]or subtle and complex human responses, one needs subtle and complex opinion surveys." However, he stated that the trend is moving in the opposite direction, toward "oversimplified, cheap, and crude public opinion polls" that satisfy the appetites of the mass media but often offer little revealing insight.

Yankelovich detailed wide swings and blatant contradictions in survey responses to questions in different polls on the same issues. Survey results are most volatile, he noted, when the issue is new to the public (ibid., 33). He wrote (ibid., 6) that a respondent's "first impulses" are often "strikingly different from their considered judgments." With the exception of a few dramatic, emotional issues, the public often does not assert "ownership" of issues. Its consciousness has not been raised, and it has not "worked through" the various stages of forming a thoughtful opinion that either conforms to its values or resolves conflicts among its values (ibid., 59–81). This working-through process is necessary for the public to reach a stage in which it has resolved "where it stands cognitively, emotionally, and morally." It often takes a dramatic event (e.g., Vietnam, race-related upheavals, Three Mile Island, Chernobyl, the Persian Gulf) or at least some personal experience with the issues at hand—for example, crime, abortion, and inflation—to initiate the working-through process (Yankelovich 1991, 59–137). Short of an attention-riveting event, it can take decades to raise the public's consciousness sufficiently so that a stage of considered judgment can be reached. Yankelovich offered slavery as an example of an extended working-through process: while the Civil War resolved the slavery issue, an "enduring heritage of racial tension" still persists (ibid., 116).

Balance of trade is still an unresolved issue for most Americans. Most people have no incentive to grapple with the issue. Moreover, political leaders generally have not presented trade-offs and policy choices to the public to facilitate an intelligent public debate on the balance of trade issue (ibid., 101). If the balance of trade issue is not adequately considered by the public, then the District's political status is an issue that is even further down the priority scale. D.C.'s future epitomizes thousands of issues which are new to most people, where no dramatic event relating to the issue has captured their attention, and where most people have almost no personal experience to enable them to assert ownership of the issue and begin a working-through process.

The Public's Difficulty in Forming Opinions

It is not just the pollsters who bear responsibility for not tapping into the complex thought patterns of American citizens. Citizens themselves have not prepared themselves for many survey questions. In *The American Voter*, Campbell et al. (1960) found that only 2.5 percent of the American electorate held a coherent political ideology, while only 9 percent more could be categorized as "near ideologues." The remainder could not be expected to develop high-quality opinions on the major issues of the day. Writing around the same time, V.O. Key, Jr. (1961, 546) observed that the "highly attentive and active public . . . constitutes normally no more than 10 to 15 percent of the adult population, although at times of crisis far higher proportions may focus their attention on particular actions of government." As Key predicted, after a period of political upheaval in the 1960s and early 1970s, Nie, Verba, and Petrocik (1976, 116) were able to revise upwards the proportion of the electorate who thought in ideologically structured ways to about 22 percent.

Nonetheless, the conclusion of Campbell et al. (1960, 543) regarding a "general impoverishment of political thought" remains accurate today. Americans do not approach issues conceptually, abstractly, intellectually, or ideologically (Yankelovich 1991, 19). Responses to an opinion survey about D.C.'s political future would likely not be based on carefully refined views on congressional representation, democratic trends, or the ten or so available options. A more in-depth approach to explore citizen views is necessary.

Media and Political Leaders' Influences on Public Opinion

The media play a central role in influencing how much importance the public will give an issue. The media select the stories to be covered, determine how prominently and for how long an issue will be given media attention, and judge how the controversies surrounding the issue are to be interpreted (McCombs and Shaw 1976).

Moreover, politicians have become adept at using the media to select those issues to which they wish to draw the public's attention. By means of televised addresses, staged public appearances, photo sessions, and political advertisements, the public's field of critical issues is narrowed and cultivated, albeit shallowly. Successful presidents influence the content of the nightly network news shows to their benefit and negotiate with Congress by means of televised appeals to the public (Kernell 1986).

The technical side of policy issues is often explored thoroughly among political insiders and analysts in conferences, workshops, think tanks, political leadership forums, and the like. By comparison, the level of education on political and societal issues made available to the general public is "amateurish" (Yankelovich 1991, 175–76).

Surveys often do not distinguish between respondents' opinions, attitudes, and values. All three terms comprise "public opinion" (Ladd 1989, 337). Opinions connote superficial, "less deeply rooted judgments," while attitudes suggest "more fundamental perspectives on enduring social and political questions." Values constitute the deepest levels of ideals and commitments and include moral, religious, and ethical judgments (ibid., 310–11).

Ladd (1989, 345–77) stated that "the further one probes, the more one sees a public that holds firmly to core values and assessments in each area of public policy." Ladd noted a "remarkably stable and predictable pattern of responses to Gallup poll data over many years." However, on many issues, public opinion is not what polls say it is (ibid., 352). This is especially the case with respect to issues of lesser prominence that have not been carefully considered by the public. As Yankelovich stated (1991, 125–26): "Americans find themselves in a vortex of conflicting value cross pressures on many issues. Personal needs, reality demands, values derived from parents or absorbed from the larger culture or its many subcultures, lessons learned from living—all pull in different directions." While core values may remain rather stable over long periods, the time a person needs to develop an opinion in most areas is assigned a rather low priority in the vast majority of people's lives compared to the pressures of family, job, and the like.

Most people do not believe that their views carry much weight with policymakers in any event (ibid., 126). Thus, developing a responsible position on farm policy, international trade, or D.C.'s structural options is not regarded by many as a serious obligation. It is a purpose of this research to determine if qualitative research can relate views about unexplored topics such as D.C.'s political future to basic value structures of individuals.

Qualitative Research and Focus Groups

Research is often classified as qualitative or quantitative (Krueger 1988, 37). Krueger (ibid.) observed that the quantitative approach "grows out of a strong academic tradition that places considerable trust in numbers that represent opinions or concepts." However, a potential deficiency of opinion surveys and even face-to-face interviews is that "those methods assume that individuals really do know how they feel" (ibid., 23).

Focus group interviewing is a form of qualitative research designed to provide "candid portraits" of participants' perceptions (ibid., 23). Morgan (1988, 9–10) described focus groups as "basically group interviews, although not in the sense of an alternation between the researcher's questions and the research participants' responses. Instead, the reliance is on interaction within the group, based on topics that are supplied by the researcher, who typically takes the role of moderator." The "data" to be analyzed are transcripts of the group discussions.

Focus groups have been helpful in assessing needs (e.g., in evaluating a social service program), developing plans, recruiting new clientele, testing new programs and ideas, improving existing programs, and in providing a further understanding of a topic that would lead to improved research approaches, such as designing survey questionnaires in quantitative research (ibid., 34–48). The research gained from focus group interviews generates hypotheses based on participants' insights and helps orient the researcher to new research fields (Morgan 1988, 11, 24). Focus groups "are useful when it comes to investigating *what* participants think, but they excel in uncovering *why* participants think as they do" (ibid., 25, Morgan's emphases).

The use of focus groups in social science research can be traced to Merton and Kendall (1946), who examined the persuasiveness of wartime propaganda, and earlier to various forms of nondirective interviewing. In 1931 Stuart Rice questioned the value of interviewing in which the subject "plays a more or less passive role." Such research results in a situation where information and points of view "of the highest value" may not be disclosed by the subject because the interviewer has led the discussion in a "preconceived" direction (cited by Krueger 1988, 19).

Since Merton, Fiske, and Kendall's (1956) classic work in focus group research, most focus group applications have been in the field of market research (Krueger 1988, 19–20; Morgan 1988, 10). For example, soft drink companies discovered from focus groups that consumers drink beverages not because of thirst but primarily because of the "sociability features associated with the product." Slogans such as "things go better" with Coca-Cola were derived from focus group research (ibid., 20). In the early 1980s, focus groups reported VCRs as a good way for people to stay home and save money, leading VCR manufacturers to think of this product as more than just a "yuppie fad" (Langer 1991, 39). The University of Minnesota College of Agriculture found through focus groups that its recruitment campaigns which relied on the grandeur of the University, with pictures of thousands of students milling about the campus, tended to intimidate rural youth. The College's recruitment results improved by emphasizing "friendly teachers" who take a personal interest in their students (ibid., 21–22).

There is increasing attention given to focus group research in the social sciences. Morgan (1988, 15–24) and Stewart and Shamdasani (1990, 144–50) noted numerous sociological and health-related uses of focus groups research. Morgan and Spanish (1985, 404) described focus groups as a "qualitative data collection method adapted from market research" and then proceeded to apply the focus group methodology to an issue in the field of sociology of health. Morgan and Spanish stated that

> although a vast medical literature exists on the causes and prevention of heart attacks, we know surprisingly little about either the content or the development of the layperson's health beliefs about heart attacks.

Through focus group discussions, Morgan and Spanish (1985, 420) demonstrated the common existence of a health belief schema, or conceptual structure, that included various controllable factors related to smoking, drinking, being overweight, failing to exercise, and other activities that were generally known by focus group participants to be related to heart attacks. Moreover, Morgan and Spanish (ibid.) found how people developed this schema: through vicarious experiences and interactions with social networks to a much greater extent than through direct experience with a friend, family member, or self. Based on this conclusion, Spanish and Morgan were able to give initial guidance to health professionals to build laypersons' knowledge in preventing heart attacks (ibid., 420–21). In view of the lack of previous findings about how laypeople regard heart problems and their prevention, a quantitative data collection method (i.e., a survey questionnaire) may have proven difficult to design. Moreover, it would not have permitted the probing of participants' attitudes and perceptions that led to the conclusions of Morgan and Spanish.

In another example, Conover, Crewe, and Searing (1990) "employed a method seldom used in political science: focus groups" to help develop a theory of democratic citizenship. The researchers compared how U.S. and British citizens viewed the nature of their citizenry in their respective democratic societies by conducting four focus groups in each country. They found that U.S. citizens emphasized civil rights such as freedom of speech, religion, and of movement more than British citizens did. Meanwhile, British citizens emphasized social rights—that is, the right to a roof over one's head, food, clothes, an education, and other such "communitarian" themes. These differing but complementary viewpoints emerged as a result of qualitative research. It would have been more difficult to begin the research with an opinion poll simply because the starting point of what might constitute the democratic theory was unknown. The survey questions would have been nebulous and even if they were known at the start of the research, the responses from survey participants would not likely have been obtainable without the in-depth exploration afforded by the focus groups.

Similarly, little in-depth knowledge currently exists about Americans' views on D.C.'s political future. In-depth, qualitative research is appropriate at this stage.

Advantages of Focus Group Research

As McCracken observed (1988, 16), researchers must balance the "trade-off between the precision of quantitative methods and the complexity-capturing ability of qualitative ones." All research methods have their limitations, and one method should not be used as a substitute for another. In general, Stewart and Shamdasani (1990, 12) stated that in the social sciences focus groups are most often used for "exploratory research" into topics where there is little knowledge about "the ways potential respondents talk about objects and events." Therefore, qualitative research is often a starting point for identifying alternatives for subsequent closed-ended survey research (ibid.). Focus groups are useful as "confirmatory tools" as well, to help determine whether a more in-depth explanation of respondent views validates the findings of quantitative research (ibid., 12, 122–38).

One advantage of using focus groups in social science research is the opportunity to interact directly with respondents. A researcher may obtain "large and rich amounts of data in the respondents' own words" (Stewart and Shamdasani 1990, 16). The researcher may obtain "deeper levels of meaning" than she or he could by using a forced-choice questionnaire and thereby identify "subtle nuances" (ibid.).

Krueger (1988, 44–45) observed that the focus group interview is a "socially oriented research procedure." People are "social creatures who interact with others." The interview places people in "natural, real-life situations" as opposed to the more controlled, artificial, predetermined, fixed-questionnaire quantitative format. Merton, Fiske, and Kendall (1956, p. 146) found decades ago that this natural format lessened inhibitions among the participants. One result is "increased candor" (Kreuger 1988, 44–45). Individuals are also likely prompted to recall details of their experience which may not otherwise be recalled in individual interviewing (Merton, Fiske, and Kendall

1956, 146). Each person who introduces a personal comment "implicitly establishes a standard for the rest who progressively report more personalized responses" (Ibid., 143).

Disadvantages of Focus Group Research

As with all methods of gathering information, focus groups have major limitations as well. The researcher has less control in the group interview, which often results in "detours in the discussion," the raising of "irrelevant issues," and other "inefficiencies" (Kreuger 1988, 46).

A more significant limitation involves data analysis. The information cannot be readily quantified, and comments must be interpreted within the context of the group discussion. As Kreuger (ibid.) cautioned, participants may occasionally "modify or even reverse their positions after interacting with others." Whether these modified responses ensuing from social interaction are more or less accurate than initial responses to a fixed questionnaire is a matter of interpretation. As Morgan (1988, 21) stated, "The problem with relying on interaction in groups is never knowing whether or not it would mirror individual behavior." Morgan added, however, that "individual behavior is subject to group influence" (ibid.), implying that this potential research distortion has beneficial effects as well in that it replicates actual societal opinion formulation. Humans are social animals, after all.

Merton, Fiske, and Kendall (1956, 148–49) noted the "leader effect" in group interviews. Those who are the more articulate, more opinionated, or have the highest social standing may be accorded the role of leader by the group. The leader may monopolize the discussion, with others accepting the role of listeners. Moreover, even when leaders in the group do not excessively dominate the discussion, some participants will be inhibited by group situations (ibid.).

Researchers may partially compensate for leader effects by assuring, to the extent feasible, homogeneity within the group's composition. As Kreuger (1988, 25–26) stated: "Focus groups are best conducted with participants who are similar to each other. The rule for selecting focus group participants is commonality, not diversity." Social status, occupational status, educational level, and income are all determinants that equate to knowledge and "more valued opinions" (ibid.), thereby providing the potential for dominance among those considered knowledgeable and a lack of active participation among the others. Merton, Fiske, and Kendall (1956, 138–39) stated that educational homogeneity outranks all other considerations in planning effective group interviews. Educational disparities may result in near-total dissipation of interaction.

For most topics, mixed-gender groups may be more effective than same-sex groups, although some researchers conduct both mixed and same-gender groups (Stewart and Shamdasani, 1990, 43–44). Morgan (1988, 46) stated that if the issues raised by a given topic are not gender-linked, then "even real differences in styles of discussion may not affect the information that is conveyed."

Racial differences are more of a complicating factor, since "given the rather selective integration of American society, there are more topics through which racial differences may become an issue during group discussions" (ibid.). In a work on intensive interviewing, Seidman (1991, 76–77) wrote, "In our society, with its history of racism, researchers and participants of different racial backgrounds face difficulties in establishing an effective interviewing relationship." Seidman observed (ibid.) that it is "especially complex for whites and Afro-Americans to interview each other."

In her analysis of American attitudes about fairness, equality, and distributive justice, Hochschild intensively interviewed twenty-eight residents of New Haven, Connecticut, twelve of whom were wealthy participants, with the remainder low-income. Hochschild (1981, 316, n.84) stated that she "deliberately limited the study to whites, in order to minimize communication barriers between the respondents and myself and to keep the focus on economic and social, not racial, differences." Nonetheless, as Seidman stated (1991, 76–77), "Interviewers and participants of good will who are from different racial backgrounds can create a relationship that runs counter to prevailing social currents." He noted that it would be an "unfortunate methodological situation" if whites could only interview whites, blacks only blacks, Latinos only Latinos, and so forth (ibid., 77). One should weigh the ease and purported productivity of same-race interviewing against the loss of information that could ensue from racial exclusion. In America's increasingly heterogeneous society, one could also argue that monochromatic group interviews are artificial.

The topic of discussion in the focus group could also help determine the degree of heterogeneity that might be warranted. For example, Krueger (1988, 92) cautioned against mixing individuals of different life stages and styles "unless the topic clearly cuts across these life stages and styles." A market researcher, Jane Templeton (1987, 174), placed the matter in perspective: "Wholly heterogeneous panels would have nothing to talk about, wholly homogenous ones would have no need to talk." Templeton echoed the frequently expressed concerns of social scientists about excessive heterogeneity in focus groups by stating that views perceived as "foreign" will lead some participants to drop out of the discussion. Nonetheless, Templeton also observed that in a more homogeneous group responses could also be limited to "monologues with choral murmurs of assent" (ibid., 174–80).

Another limitation to the focus group research method, and all qualitative research, is the inability to generalize research results in any quantitative way to a larger population. Some "cautious generalizations" may be possible (Kreuger 1988, 44). Nonetheless, in discussing the value of research findings using intensive interviewing, Lamb (1974, viii) noted that this method "suggests" or "implies" truths about American politics, but never "proves" them. Lamb, however, questioned whether reducing human responses to numeric values, as scientific surveys purportedly attempt to do, actually produces more accurate information than does qualitative research (ibid.).

Hochschild (1981, 25) noted that qualitative research can generate findings that survey research does not, observing that "pollsters may too often be limited by either a failure of imagination or the exigencies of statistical techniques." She added: "Intensive interviews are a device for generating insights, anomalies, and paradoxes, which later may be formalized into hypotheses to be tested by quantitative social science methods" (ibid., 24). Despite these benefits of qualitative research, Hochschild stated that "obviously, one cannot safely generalize from a sample of this kind [twenty-eight intensive interviews] to a national population; it would be worthless, for example, for one to point out what percentage of my sample sought more or fewer government services for the poor" (ibid., 23).

The Research Procedure

With these benefits and limitations of qualitative research in mind, five sites were selected:

(a) *Montgomery County, Maryland.* Montgomery County, one of America's most affluent counties, is a suburb of Washington, D.C. The residents are well-informed on a variety of issues and are well-educated generally. The county is moderate to liberal in its political views and has a recent history of sending liberal Republicans to the U.S. House of Representatives. The panelists here already had views on the District's structural options, and it therefore proved instructive to compare their responses with those of others who had not previously thought about the issue.

This affluent Maryland suburb was also chosen because it is in a state that would be most affected by changes in D.C.'s political status, in that (1) if the congressional restrictions were lifted, a nonresident income tax could be imposed by the District on Maryland residents who earn income in the District; and (2) Maryland is mentioned (Raskin, 1990, 438–40) as a jurisdiction in which D.C. residents could vote for representation in the House and Senate or as the state to which D.C. could be retroceded.

(b) *Austin, Texas.* A large, powerful, often conservative sunbelt state added balance to the other sites. Texans are generally regarded as independent-minded. The Texas panelists were therefore tested to see if they were wary of big government and to determine whether the D.C. self-rule issue was associated in any way with their concerns about big government. The capital of the state was chosen to see if state capital residency provided any insight into issues faced by residents of the nation's capital.

(c) *Van Nuys, California, a populous suburb of Los Angeles.* Here a cue is taken from Judith Langer, a leading market researcher and focus group expert. Langer (1991, 38–39) advised focus group researchers to learn from the vanguard to assess a product's or issue's potential and also to hear from the mainstream to separate real trends from fads. Los Angeles was cited by Langer (*ibid.*, 39) as a place where trends start. It would be startling to find a trend in progress in Los Angeles pertaining to D.C.'s political future; nonetheless, trends in individual and minority rights, perceptions about Congress, and other topics could relate to the D.C. issue.

A suburban site was chosen to assure some distance from the emotionally charged riots that took place earlier in the year and to assure that there was no extraordinary sensitivity to the needs of the urban residents of the District, a condition which could bias participants in their evaluation of the D.C.'s structural options. On the other hand, there are many more conservative areas than Van Nuys in the Los Angeles area.

(d) *Harrisburg, Pennsylvania.* This is an example of a mid-size city that is beyond the District's orb of influence but close enough so that there is some awareness about the District, its residents, culture, problems, government, and political status. Harrisburg is also a capital city, which provided a few insights into the special status of capital residents without unnecessarily biasing participants' views about policy options.

(e) *Des Moines, Iowa.* A northern heartland state far removed from the District was chosen to see if contrasts with sunbelt and coastal sites were discernable on D.C.'s political options. Des Moines is socially as well as geographically distant from the District. Iowa's population is 97 percent non-Hispanic white, while Des Moines has an 88 percent non-Hispanic white population, unusual for a fairly large city. In contrast, D.C.'s population is 27 percent non-Hispanic white (U.S. Bureau of Census 1993, 136). In Iowa, only 44 percent of the state's residents live in metropolitan areas, compared to 78 percent for the nation as a whole (U.S. Bureau of the Census 1992, 29). Washington, D.C. is, of course, 100 percent urban.

Composition of Focus Groups

In the previous discussion (see "Disadvantages of Focus Groups"), it was stated that most focus group researchers prefer to keep the composition of the focus group as homogeneous as possible with respect to education, social standing, race, and other participant characteristics. Seidman (1991, 76–77), Kreuger (1988,92), Templeton (1987, 174–80), and others provide broad definitions of what constitutes "homogeneous," especially when the topic cuts across different lifestyles. Nonetheless, traditional focus group research cautions against the distracting and intimidating effects of heterogeneity.

A possible solution to this research dilemma would be to allow heterogeneity in a group's composition to the extent that it would likely be found in the daily lives of participants. For example, if the Los Angeles suburb selected has become accustomed to some racial and income-level heterogeneity in its population, then this degree of heterogeneity would not be assumed to stifle discussion and would therefore be accepted. On the other hand, if Des Moines, Iowa, for example, is accustomed primarily to racial and income-level homogeneity, then such composition would also be provided for in the composition of the focus group. The sites chosen for this research tend to be rather homogeneous in their compositions, as is most of America. Obviously, a large urban center such as Detroit, with its majority black population, would likely support equal political rights for D.C. residents, but not much would be learned from such a focus group (Morgan 1988, 72–73).

With these research considerations in mind, the following recruitment criteria were implemented for the five focus groups. Racial heterogeneity in the groups was limited. Most white Americans are accustomed to some diversity, and their comments would likely not be excessively stifled by the presence of other races in the focus group. Nonetheless, a minority of white Americans, as discussed in chapter 4, has strong opinions which can be described as racially troubled. These Americans in particular may feel constrained in expressing their strong viewpoints in the presence of blacks. To capture such sentiments for this research, racial heterogeneity in the focus group composition was allowed only for those groups where the social distance was relatively minor. Thus an occasional well-assimilated Hispanic or Asian American was invited.

Some homogeneity by income and education was also provided. Celinda Lake, who helped run focus groups for the Clinton campaign of 1991–92, said, "The goal is that the group ought to come in and look around and say, 'This is a group just like me; I can say anything I want'" (Carlson 1993, 29). One reporter (ibid.) thought that "focus groups only work when they contain the right mix of people . . . which is to say, not much mix at all." Since full homogeneity is rarely encountered in "real life," a mixture of ages was included to add diversity, as was a good mix of occupations.

Panelists' views on D.C.'s political status or any other topic were not asked prior to their selection. Nonetheless, groups were structured to have a reasonable mix of Democrats, Republicans, and Independents so that this mixture would serve as proxies for liberals, conservatives, and middle-of-the-roaders and assure some balance in the sessions.

Recruiters assured that focus group panelists did not know each other. When people know each other, parameters of the relationship have already been established. For example, one of the two may have higher status, causing the other to yield to him or her. Or one may already know what topics to avoid in the presence of the other; if Mary knows that John does not like to hear about politics, religion, or race, Mary could steer clear of those topics.

Planning for Group Focus Sessions

A number of practical guides are available to help plan focus group sessions (Morgan 1988; Krueger 1988; Templeton 1987; Stewart and Shamdasani 1990).

The ideal size of a focus group is about seven to twelve members. Groups of more than twelve limit each participant's opportunity to share insights, while groups of six or fewer limit the total range of experiences (Kreuger 1988, 93). Morgan (1988, 44) indicates that one must overrecruit by 20 percent to meet the targeted number of participants. An attempt was made to reach the upper limit of focus group size to gain a few of the benefits of quantitative analysis associated with the rather large number of pre-session questionnaires.

Panelists who were reasonably well educated and issue-oriented were recruited in disproportionate numbers. They were not necessarily "ideologues" or even "near-ideologues," in the terminology of Campbell et al. (1960), but most had attained at least some minimal level of political participation.

An interview guide was prepared to provide a general agenda for focus group discussions. An interview guide provides far less structure than does a survey questionnaire, and no potential responses are suggested (Stewart and Shamdasani 1990, 60–61). The interview guides generally contain a dozen or so questions (ibid., 62) to provide direction for the two-hour sessions. The interview "guide" is aptly named: the moderator should remain free to probe deeply when necessary, skip over unproductive topics, revise the order of questions, and otherwise remain flexible (Morgan 1988, 56–57), since the insights of focus group participants are of greater importance than rigidly completing a checklist of questions.

After some opening remarks by the moderator, the technique of asking each focus group participant to provide opening comments about their nation's capital and its political structure was used to convey at the outset the notion that comments from all were welcome (ibid., 58). This opening icebreaker also provided a basis upon which to gauge evolution in opinion development. As additional information was discussed, as policy options were introduced, and as participants were influenced by group interaction, their views in most cases changed during the course of the session.

Research Design Considerations

Morgan (1988, 69) wrote that the major research choices in planning focus group projects involve whether the research is exploratory or hypothesis testing, whether the level of moderator involvement intends to produce structured or unstructured discussions, and whether the analysis will rely on enthnographic or numerical summaries of the data. These decisions will be discussed in turn.

This research into D.C.'s political future is exploratory. As Stewart and Shamdasani (1990, 102) wrote, "The most common purpose of a focus group interview is for an in-depth exploration of a topic about which little is known."

The level of moderator involvement was tailored to the goals of the research project. Many focus group analysts favor highly nondirective or self-managed focus groups (Morgan 1988, 49). Nonetheless, Morgan (ibid.) advised that "researchers must decide what they want their interview materials to produce and then make decisions about moderator involvement in line with those goals." Morgan "would not hesitate to advise someone . . . to use a high moderator involvement format, *if* that was the appropriate way to produce the data that would meet their research goals" (ibid., Morgan's emphasis).

Low levels of moderator involvement are possible when the basic issues are well known and when full-scale, quantitative content analysis will be pursued (ibid.). Neither condition pertains to this research project. In this case, it was necessary for the moderator to introduce information that was new to the participants to see if this information influenced opinion formulation. Since policy options for D.C. were not self-evident, these too had to be introduced to meet the "choicework" goals of the research. Achieving these goals required an average level of moderator involvement, although the involvement was limited as much as possible to assure that participants had a full opportunity to raise their own points of view (Morgan 1988, 50; Templeton 1987, 45).

This research relies on ethnographic rather than quantitative data summaries. An ethnographic summary is qualitative, relying primarily on direct quotations from the group discussion rather than on a numerical content analysis. However, as Morgan (1988, 64) pointed out, the ethnographic approach often benefits from systematic tallying of some of the key topics, just as a more quantitative content analysis can be improved by including quotations that support the data presented.

Transcripts of the taped focus group sessions, supplemented by written notes, were typed, coded, and sorted. In this way, it was possible to use such phrases as "a prevalent view of focus group participants" or "several participants felt that" or even "most participants agreed that. . . ." (Krueger 1988, 119).

Conducting the Focus Group Sessions

After some brief getting-acquainted, non-issue-oriented small talk (Krueger 1988, 76–77), each two-hour session proceeded as follows:

> (5 min.) (a) *Introduction to the issue by moderator.* This writer served as moderator. After discussing how the session would proceed, the moderator presented to the group a brief description of D.C.'s political status.
>
> (10 min.) (b) *Opening comments by participants.* The opening question, to which all provided brief comments, asked what the strongest argument was either for or against D.C. statehood, the most controversial of D.C.'s options. This question established a barometer to see if the initial positions shifted when further information and policy options were introduced later in the session. Another opening question asked what participants' "image" was of the District to gain some understanding of how favorably people viewed this jurisdiction. As demonstrated in appendix G, "affect" or emotional reactions, often play a strong role in public opinion formulation.
>
> (60 min.) (c) *Pro and con discussion.* Given the premise that participants were not only poorly informed about D.C.'s political status but also had little interest in the issue, "pro" and "con" discussions was initiated; that is, discussions on an argument in favor of D.C. voting rights and political autonomy were followed immediately after by discussions pertaining to a contrary argument as a means of stimulating panelist involvement.
>
> (20 min.) (d) *Policy Choices.* Policy options were introduced for discussion: Should the District be retroceded to Maryland? Should District residents be allowed to vote in Maryland congressional elections? Should District residents be permitted to be represented in Congress by a voting representative and by one or two voting senators? Is statehood a good option? Should the federal government assume complete control over D.C.? Or is the status quo the best option? Participants were encouraged to give their views on each option as it was presented and were informed that they would be given a chance to modify their views once all the options were on the table.
>
> (20 min.) (e) *Concluding comments.* By this point in the session, the participants had gained familiarity with the issue. The moderator encouraged participants to discuss the issue among themselves, each arguing for their favored policy option. After this interchange, panelists were asked to give their final views on policy options.

APPENDIX G

Schema Theory

Could the focus group panelists from around the country be expected to have or to develop a point of view on D.C.'s political future during the course of the session? If so, how could the sessions be structured to stimulate such issue development? In her analysis of how Americans process the news, Doris Graber (1988, 136–38) found that "[t]he impact of prior information is profound." She stated (ibid., 239) that "[p]eople evidently learn many generalizations about political issues from the media or other sources. Subsequently, they may fit specific experiences into these learned general schemata."

This observation leads to a discussion of schema theory. Fiske and Linville (1980, 543) defined a "schema" as consisting of a network or cognitive structure of "organized prior knowledge, abstracted from experience with specific instances," that guides "the processing of new information and the retrieval of stored information." Kuklinski, Luskin, and Bolland (1991, 1342) reasoned that "we make sense of the world" through schemas. "We tend to see, understand, and remember things the way we expect them to be, that is, in conformity with our schemas." We draw "schema-consistent inferences."

Functions of Schemata

Schemata have several useful functions. According to Graber (1988, 29), "They determine what information will be noticed, processed, and stored so that it becomes available for retrieval from memory." This screening process aids efficient thinking. As Fiske and Taylor observed (1984, 12), people are "cognitive misers." People are limited in their capacity to process information as well as in their desire or perceived need to process information. Moreover, people have other priorities in life than grappling with concepts or coping with a seemingly endless flood of daily information. Schemas are time-saving and labor-saving tools that people store away for use as needed.

As Kinder (1983, 414) noted, the cognitive process enables new events to be interpreted "in terms of old knowledge." A schema therefore "provide[s] the context within which new developments are understood." Thus it becomes unnecessary for the individual "to construct new concepts wherever familiar information is presented" (Graber 1988, 29–30). Conover and Feldman (1984, 96–7) added that a schema helps fill in missing information and helps one proceed beyond the information given. Schemata also provide short cuts or "heuristics" that simplify the problem-solving process.

Sears and Citrin (1982, 76) cautioned that a schema "is less comprehensive, taking in less political territory, than an 'ideology.'" Kinder (1983, 414) agreed, stating that schemata

> serve the average person much as formal, explicit theories serve the scientist. They provide explanations. They clear up ambiguities. They furnish predictions. They supply proposals for intervention and reform. There is, of course, every reason to expect that the tacit theories of ordinary men and women will be less complete and less internally consistent than the formal theories of professional scientists.

Nonetheless, to Conover and Feldman (1984, 121), the presence of schemata serves as a clear indication that people "do organize their beliefs." Often people will resort to "generalized decision roles," slogans such as "Once a loser, always a loser," or common sense logic (Graber 1988, 177). People also have schemata that reflect generalized norms of their political culture. People often label these norms the "American way." Graber (1988, 210) found that all of the panelists in her research appeared to share cultural norms.

Conover and Feldman (1989, 936–40) provided an example of how schemata are used by citizens. When voters are confronted with sparse or ambiguous information in a campaign, they use their previously acquired information to infer where the candidates stand. The voters draw on their own issue positions, ideological cues from the candidates, and party cues. Conover and Feldman (ibid.) noted in particular the pronounced effects of party cues even as the strength of political parties is diminishing. Those party cues figured prominently in voters' assessments of candidates' issue positions. The parties therefore provided the context for ideological evaluations of a candidate "even when the candidate is not perceived in ideological terms." In consonance with such research, President Bush in the 1992 campaign attempted to paint his challenger, then-Governor Clinton, as a tax-and-spend Democrat, hoping to encourage voters to draw upon their schema of what a Democrat is and then fit Clinton into such a schema.

Graber (1988, 97–100) analyzed how citizens act on cues from the media; for example, citizens assess the prominence accorded a candidate or issue by the media. Citizens also act on cues from their social environment—for example, when conversations of friends and associates draw citizens' attention to an issue or candidate. Moreover, Graber (1988, 211) emphasized, "Good citizens also keep abreast of other important national and local political issues [beyond political election news stories]. The fact that these issues may be beyond their capacity to understand is not considered a valid excuse for ignoring them." Perhaps focus group participants can be expected to consider the political options for the District of Columbia, draw upon their schemata, and engage in a lively interchange of views on the topic—even if they had never encountered this idea prior to the focus group sessions.

Characteristics of Schemata

Fiske and Taylor (1984, 171) noted that "[s]chemata facilitate information processing, for the most part, by allowing the general case to fill in for a specific example." They added that "[i]f people changed their schemata to fit every nuance of every new example, the information-processing advantages of schemata would be substantially lost."

Schemata, once formed in the individual, remain available over time. This "perseverance effect" describes a primary characteristic of schemata: "They often persist stubbornly even in the face of evidence to the contrary" (ibid.). A person's schemata can therefore be expected to influence strongly her or his response to the new information presented in connection with D.C.'s political status. If schema theories are valid, a panelist's schemata may predispose her or him favorably or unfavorably toward a policy position, although the contextual cues and the specific information provided will influence the ultimate opinion.

Sears and Citrin (1982, 76) elaborated on this phenomenon: "Having a schema about a particular attitude object [e.g., a person, an event, a policy, or concept] implies a tendency to think about, and evaluate, that object in terms of a specific set of dimensions, but without necessarily holding any specific set of positions on those dimensions." For example, in their analysis of a tax revolt schema (i.e., a cognitive structure held by many Californians that enabled or encouraged them to revolt against tax burdens in that state), Sears and Citrin (1982, 43–72) found five dimensions of the tax revolt schema that influenced Californian's actions and responses to survey questionnaires: (a) citizens' general feelings about whether state government, or government in general, was too large; (b) how citizens felt about the value of government services in general; (c) how they felt about increases or cuts in specific services; (d) their perceptions about "government waste" and "overpaid government workers"; and (e) how they felt about the size of their tax burden. All five dimensions combined to predispose many Californians to participate in the tax revolt once the option was presented to them. This research into D.C.'s future also identifies schemata and dimensions of the schemata held by the research panelists.

Graber (1988, 221–25) listed a dozen expectations from schema theory that helped to guide her research into the ways people process media information. For example, she expected to find a limited number of dimensions "because schemata are created to cope parsimoniously with vast amounts of information" (ibid., 221). She also expected people to be "quite consistent in using their readily available schemata" (ibid., 222). Graber also expected people "to interpret dissonant information [which conflicts with schemata] so that it fits into their prevailing schemata, or to neutralize it by calling it an exception or by denying its validity." This expectation supports the perseverance effect discussed above.

Additionally, Graber expected "uniformity among people's schemata that are derived from basic cultural orientations; these schemata are part of the common heritage taught by parents, teachers, and religious and social advisors (Graber 1988, 222). Thus Sears and Citrin (1982, 185) were able to trace the origins of the five dimensions of many Californians' tax revolt schema, as summarized above, not only to Republican party identification but also to a "general political conservatism." By appealing to prevalent conservatism, tax reformers were able to bring in the Independents and conservative Democrats needed to produce success for the tax revolt forces, resulting in the two-to-one margin of victory for Proposition 13 (the "Jarvis-Gann amendment") in June 1978 (ibid., 2).

Sears and Citrin (ibid., 185) added that "symbolic racism" was as powerful, if not more so, than were Republican party identification and political conservatism in predicting support for the tax revolt. The place of race in Americans' basic cultural orientations and how it may affect public opinion on D.C.'s policy options was discussed in chapter 4.

Graber (1988, 223–24) also raised the possibility of "clashing general value schemata." For example, a person may have a schema about what a state should be, may have negative perceptions about D.C. leaders, and may be skeptical about D.C. residents' abilities to make informed political choices. On the other hand, she or he could have a schema on "taxation without representation" which, it may be believed, no American should have to withstand. These (and other) general value schemata may easily clash. Alternatively, if there is potential for clashes within an array of schemata, and if people do not routinely check for consistency, how can there also be a high potential for uniformity and consistency in political thinking? Graber (1988, 96–100, 223–24) noted that much is dependent upon "cues" or stimuli contained in the information received. The context for focusing on particular aspects of schemata and for evaluating policies will differ from one instance to another, Graber noted. General values may be stable and consistent, while individuals may be encouraged to focus on certain aspects or interpretations of the general values depending upon what cues they receive.

Finally, Graber (1988, 224) stated that some people are more experienced and have greater sophistication in schematic thinking than others, and their schemata will have greater numbers of dimensions, with greater depth of development, than will others. Graber (ibid.) also observed that in areas where information is "highly complex and unfamiliar, a total absence of schemata would not be surprising." Even though focus group panelists in the D.C. policy options research may not have encountered the issue previously, one would think that there would be sufficient schemata upon which to draw to be able to express and to evolve a viewpoint, given the presentation to them of enough information to forge links to previously processed information and inferences.

Graber (1988, 245) concluded that her expectations were largely confirmed by her research findings. "Cognitive processing does follow patterns that are best explained in terms of schema theory," she stated.

How People Form Public Opinions

The fields of social and political cognition are challenging some of the traditions of public opinion research. Iyengar and Kinder (1987, 64) advised that people do not pay attention to everything; to do so would "breed paralysis." Instead, people form impressions around a few major themes. In a similar vein, Kinder (1983, 414) advised that public opinion researchers should not treat people as if they are merely collections of discrete opinions. People do more than take positions on specific topics; "they try to understand what is going on," he wrote. The themes embedded in one's schemata assist in understanding issues.

Because people do not work out their positions on each issue in an *ad hoc* way (Sniderman 1986), researchers in social and political cognition attempt to understand how people organize their thoughts and form public opinions. One starting point is an acknowledgement that "there is no unambiguous reality in the external world—people actively construct social reality" (Fiske and Taylor 1984, 179).

Graber (1988) summarized this process of constructing one's own reality out of information and other stimuli. The process begins with physical signals that reach an individual's sensory organs (ibid., 147–48). The signals are then screened. A key step here is what Graber refers to as "attention arousal." People may respond to media cues; for example, the media may give a high degree of prominence to a story, or people may respond to certain "verbal cues" or key words of interest to them. Additionally, they may pay attention to cues from their social environment. When an issue is a topic of conversation among friends or workmates or has aroused considerable public controversy, people will generally make the effort to acquire, process, and store information. Nonetheless, generally speaking, one's motivation to be informed about the news is not as powerful as are numerous other motivations in life, although people will often give "lip service" to the importance of keeping informed (Graber 1988, 96–118).

Once new information is perceived, it is "condensed and simplified for brief storage in short-term memory." It becomes part of a "data pool" which is checked against the individual's "reservoir of 'memory schemata' to determine whether it can be appropriately integrated." If the new information can be integrated, it "becomes part of the individual's repertoire of schemata." This integration can fail to occur "if no suitable schema is available or created" as a result of perceiving the incoming information, or because "an overload of information prevents preliminary processing." When integration fails, it is dropped from temporary storage—that is, quickly forgotten (ibid., 147).

Even when people choose to integrate new information, they are "cognitive misers." That is, they are limited in their capacity to process information (Fiske and Taylor 1984, 12, 139–245). For example, people will manage the tide of information by ignoring large numbers of news stories. Additionally, they will use schematic thinking to reduce the information that needs to be stored. Individuals will "extract only those limited amounts of information from news stories [and other sources] that they consider important for incorporation into their schemata" (Graber 1988, 250).

People economize with the help of shortcuts or heuristics. One such heuristic is "representativeness." In matching new information with potential categories in her or his schemata, a person will decide how the new object's features resemble the essential features of the category (Fiske and Taylor 1984, 268–270; Graber 1988, 152–160). For example, the D.C. political rights movement could be recognized in some minds as a basic striving for control over one's destiny, the kind of motivation that drove American independence over two centuries ago. It could be matched by others with a schema of giving excessive, undeserved benefits to minorities.

Another heuristic is "availability," which involves an assessment of the likelihood of an event happening or of how frequently the event is taking place, based on how quickly a person can recall instances of such an event in the person's own experiences. Ease of retrieval and strength of association are key factors in employing this heuristic. For example, if one were to be asked if a baby boom is now taking place and she or he could easily recall several friends having children (ease of retrieval), and if this recollection is strengthened by a culture in the town that emphasizes the family and therefore encourages the topic of birth in daily conversation (strength of association), then one could conclude that a baby boom is now taking place (Fiske and Taylor 1984, 270–72).

The "simulation heuristic" makes use of availability in that one constructs hypothetical scenarios based on past experience to assess a potential outcome. For example, based on one's assessment of the District's predominantly minority population, one might conclude that with congressional voting rights, D.C. would consistently send two black Democrats to the U.S. Senate. This heuristic is useful in predicting outcomes and in determining causality (Kahneman and Tversky 1982).

Fiske and Taylor (1984, 273–74) also summarized the "anchoring and adjustment heuristic." People start with a reference point or "anchor" and make reasoned adjustments based on new information about an object. For example, when asked if D.C. citizens would exercise their democratic duties responsibly if granted voting representation in the House and Senate, residents of a Los Angeles suburb might form an opinion of how residents in urban areas of Los Angeles perform their civic duties (the "anchor") and adjust this conclusion according to varying perceptions, for better or worse, that they may have of D.C. citizens.

These forms of rapid reasoning—heuristics—help people to form judgments from complex information. They are inferential techniques. People usually do not base their judgments on everything that they remember. Rather, "[p]eople make inferences and forget the data on which they were based." Inferences, when compared to information, are "more vague, . . . less vulnerable to verification, and . . . refer back to autobiographical information." The information from which inferences were initially drawn was more accurate and less shaded by individual judgment. Yet, "inferences seem to be more easily retrieved" than raw, unprocessed information (ibid., 238). Moreover, people do not easily distinguish internally generated ideas (inferences) from externally generated information. Their memory and schemata are the results of previously processed information (ibid., 238–240).

None of the above should imply that the resulting mix of schemata is fully organized and rational. As Graber (1988, 223) reminded: "American democracy is a conglomerate of basic beliefs and values, many of them irreconcilable in practice. This mélange does not readily lend itself to a comprehensive, hierarchical organization of ideas." Moreover, political leaders and the media often make unsystematic linkages between the various aspects of political life. Average Americans therefore lack models to guide them in organizing their schemata in overarching ways (ibid.). Graber questioned whether an overarching structure of political concepts or schemata is even possible given the conglomerated nature of American democracy. As Graber (ibid.) stated, "The guiding concept is pragmatism rather than a single logic."

A person's varied and often unconnected array of schemata rests in an inactive state, waiting to be "cued" or changed to an active status (Fiske and Taylor 1984, 175–76). A schema-relevant stimulus activates the schema, and the schema then channels the way the new information is processed (Kuklinski, Luskin, and Bolland 1991, 1342). Focus group discussions on D.C.'s political future could not be expected to arouse much interest among the panelists unless the issue is framed with the help of verbal cues so that it relates to various controversies with which the participants may already be familiar. Thus, "pro and con" arguments for D.C. political autonomy were designed as stimulating verbal cues.

"Priming," in the view of Iyengar and Kinder (1987, 114), is an insidious manifestation of television power. Priming presumes that when citizens evaluate complex political issues, they do not take into consideration all they know. Rather people take into account what comes to mind, "those bits and pieces of political memory that is accessible." Television is a powerful force in determining what springs to mind. Priming refers to "the effects of prior context on the interpretation and retrieval of information" (Fiske and Taylor 1984, 231). For example, when a citizen is primed by television news stories focusing on the need for a strong national defense, she or he will likely judge a president on how well the president has provided for national defense (Iyengar and Kinder 1987, 63, 114).

When performed by television news, priming goes beyond agenda setting, which encourages viewers to focus on a political object (an issue, candidate, etc.) through prominent placement of a news story or use of certain key words. Priming involves a second step in which viewers are encouraged to realize that the problem or issue that is the subject of the coverage has implications for viewers' evaluations of the political object. In this way, "television news sets the terms by which political judgments are rendered and policy choices made" (ibid, 95–96, 114).

Iyengar and Kinder found that the strongest association in eliciting viewers' evaluations of political objects is partisanship. Moreover, they found that priming is strengthened among Democrats for problems prominent on the agenda of the Democratic party; for example, Democrats will respond to and assimilate news stories and evaluations of stories pertaining to the environment, unemployment, and civil rights, while Republicans will be more effectively primed by news about inflation, arms control, and national defense (ibid., 93–96).

Priming research has implications for focus group discussions about D.C. policy options. To the extent that focus group panelists in Des Moines or Los Angeles have heard anything at all about the District, what have they heard? Have they heard about the high homicide rates in the District and other poverty-related problems (public housing, welfare, etc.)? Did news coverage of the personal problems of Marion Barry and other problems of governing this struggling urban jurisdiction color perceptions? Or have television and other sources presented news on the vast majority of the D.C. citizenry who are law-abiding, employed, and going about their daily business? A strong possibility exists that focus group panelists may have been primed to evaluate the District negatively. Moreover, if such news stories tap into symbolic racism schemata (Sears and Citrin 1982, 214), then a possibility exists that many of the participants, Democrat and Republican, liberal and conservative alike, could potentially be predisposed toward a negative evaluation of the District.

Affects and Predispositions

Inferences may be affective rather than cognitive; that is, they may be based on feelings and emotions rather than objectively reasoned. Conover and Feldman (1986, 51–74) found that people react emotionally to personal economic conditions as well as to the state of the nation's economy. People's emotional responses were relatively independent of their cognitive assessments of the same situation. The writers found two distinguishable patterns of negative emotions: "anger and disgust" as well as "uneasiness and fear"; the former pattern has the stronger impact on political judgments. Conover and Feldman (1986, 75) concluded that emotions have a "significant and strong impact on political evaluations" even when compared to the effects of more conventional cognitive variables. Moreover, Sniderman et al. (1986, 429) concluded that "a fundamental means by which mass publics maintain a consistency in their belief systems is by adjusting their opinions and beliefs to their likes and dislikes."

Affect plays a prominent role in the development and expression of opinion because, first, people's likes and dislikes are relatively easy to remember accurately, and second, because people tend to avoid clutter. A person's likes and dislikes provide an obvious basis for achieving coherence in his or her beliefs, especially when one considers that for practical reasons, people "cannot attend to a great many factors" in arriving at positions on political issues. Sniderman et al. (ibid., 428–29) speculated that "ideological inference might itself be an example of affective calculus." Therefore, people "need to know very little about politics: only whether they like or dislike a group and whether a particular policy is intended for that group's benefit or not" (ibid., 428). Sniderman et al. (1986) drew a strong relationship between affect and race and observed a profound impact of this relationship on public opinion formulation, as discussed in chapter 4.

Other Processing Difficulties

The fields of social and political cognition alert one to several other potential difficulties that people may have in processing new information.

Unpredictable Accuracy. Because schemata are economizing tools, they can be expected to produce "misconstruction and miscollection when called upon," while at other times accuracy and insight will result (Kuklinski, Luskin, and Bolland 1991, 1347). Compromises in accuracy are often observed because "schemas are necessarily simpler than the events that evoke them" (Kinder 1983, 414). Therefore, "nuanced and textured appreciation for a particular event gets sacrificed to the economies that accrue with the event's classification as a general type" (ibid.). That is, when generalizations are constructed, accuracy in recalling the specific attributes of an individual, issue, or other political object may be sacrificed. When the object is a group, the resultant generalizing process is termed stereotyping (Hamilton 1981).

Contrary Evidence, No Evidence, and Extreme Evidence. As discussed earlier, the perseverance effect involves the stubborn persistence of schemata even in the face of contrary evidence. A variation on this effect occurs when people sometimes interpret the exception as proving the schema (Fiske and Taylor 1984, 171–72). If evidence is offered in opposition to a person's schema and the evidence is considered weak or inconclusive, then the recipient's characterization of the evidence is proof that the evidence is off-target. The schema is thought to be revalidated and even strengthened.

A schema may also be strengthened even when no new information is received. All one has to do is think about a schema and one's judgment is generally further polarized in the direction that the schema was already heading (ibid., 172). Additionally, when new information of any sort is perceived, the tendency of people is to adjust the information to fit the schema and not to modify continually the schema to fit the new information (ibid., 177). When extreme information is received that matches the expectations of one's polarized judgments, this more extreme information is incorporated more readily and recalled more easily than is relatively moderate information (ibid., 172, citing Judd and Kulik 1980).

Rejection of New Information. In Graber's (1988, 104–7) study of how people process the news, the most frequent reason given for not considering a news story (other than the fact that they inadvertently "missed" hearing it) was "no interest." According to one participant in Graber's study, "If I don't have a relation to something, if I'm not personally interested in it, I don't want to waste my time on it" (ibid., 107).

If D.C.'s political future had not been an example of symbolic politics (i.e., if it had not tapped into long-held and deeply emotional values learned at an early age), or if it had not otherwise related to focus group panelists' schemata, then the focus group sessions could have been uneventful and this research project would have been fruitless. However, most panelists connected with the issue. Graber (ibid., 241–43) found that intelligence, experience, and interest, along with higher education (and not necessarily higher education by itself), were the strongest predictors of sophistication and, therefore, more complex schemata. Those with multidimensional schemata found ways to incorporate new information pertaining to D.C. into their network of previously processed information and helped others in their matching efforts as well.

Graber's research (ibid., 130–31) gave only limited support to "cognitive balance theories" which hold that people avoid altogether information that conflicts or threatens their attitudes. A basis for these theories is that dissonant or threatening information does not satisfy a primary goal of information seeking, that of gratification. Graber found that people frequently but not consistently slight annoying or disturbing information. She also found that once opinions become entrenched, people will limit additional new information, whether supportive or contradictory. However, she found "no automatic rejection of discordant information" (ibid., 130–31, 258–59).

Thresholds and Symbols in Accepting New Policy Directions

In a study of whites' racial attitudes, Sears, Hensler, and Speer (1979, 382–83) found that more people can pass an "easy test" (e.g., acceptance of equal treatment of blacks and whites in hotel accommodations and voting rights) than the "harder tests" (e.g., friendship across racial lines and affirmative action, with the latter often regarded as preferential treatment).

Sears and Citrin (1982, 92–93) found policy thresholds in their analysis of California's tax revolt. Easy tests involved advocacy of smaller government and a belief that government was too wasteful. A harder test was to favor cutting specific services; considerably fewer people passed this latter test.

This research helps construct policy thresholds—for example, whether acceptance of full voting rights for D.C. residents requires passing a higher threshold level than other alternatives, such as having District citizens vote in Maryland elections and thereby achieve some limited degree of representation in Congress. The research also assesses the political symbols (racial or otherwise) into which the various D.C. policy options tap.

Can a Person's Schemata Change?

Much of the above paints a bleak picture of Americans' abilities to adapt their concepts—their schemata—to new information and ideas. Since much thinking is formed during an early socialization process; since these early thoughts seem to be almost self-reinforcing, thereby leading to predisposed attitudes; and since much of the new information is merely adapted to fit previously processed information networks, then how can we envision any receptivity for political equality of D.C. residents or any other new idea?

Without minimizing the strength of the perseverance effect, it should be acknowledged that schemata can and do change. When major upheavals occur, when serious new problems become obvious, and when respected opinion leaders voice their support for change, people's confidence in the continued validity of their existing schemata will often be shaken. Vietnam, Watergate, the civil rights movement, and the AIDS crisis are examples of events that produced massive change in the schemata of large numbers of Americans (Graber 1988, 256).

People's schemata can also change as a result of less dramatic events. Graber concluded that "[a]lthough our panelists were reluctant to change their well-established views, all of them did so on occasion." People feel "strong cultural pressures to be consistent and steadfast" in their positions. Yet when people felt a need to adapt a schema to changed conditions, most were able to do so (ibid., 130–31). When Graber's panelists, by their own initiative, called attention to changes in their beliefs, they did so "without expression of regret or apparent embarrassment." Discomfort seemed acute only when the interviewer pointed out errors or inconsistencies in their thinking. However, in such cases they still made and acknowledged the changes even though they suffered some "pain of dissonance" (ibid.).

When there is only a partial fit between new information and a person's schema, the individual generally does not apply the schema with complete confidence. Under certain circumstances the schema itself may be altered. Fiske and Taylor (1984, 176–78) summarized models of how schemata change on the basis of encountering discrepancies. Under the bookkeeping model, each discrepant encounter changes a schema gradually. Under the conversion model, a single intense encounter with incongruence can change a schema totally and suddenly. No less a public figure than then-candidate Bill Clinton (1991, 556) described his own conversion to supporting D.C. statehood:

> I was in Memphis a few weeks ago at the dedication of the National Civil Rights Museum. At the time I was not a declared candidate for President. I wasn't sure what I was going to do. But Reverend Jackson was there and he came up to me. I had never discussed it with him or anybody else, and he said, "Did you know we pay more taxes than ten States and had more soldiers in the Gulf war than twenty states?" I said, "No, but I will check that out, and if it is true I will be for statehood." That is exactly what happened. Just as simple as that. . . . I should have been out there trying to pass it twelve years ago.

In this case, the conversion to support was not from opposition but from a complete lack of consideration of the issue.

The subtyping model suggests that a discrepancy will cause the perceiver to form subcategories within the overall schema. The overall schema may be maintained, but it may have more texture and substance and thus accommodate a greater variety of new information. However, sometimes a schema subcategory will conveniently be established to hold all the exceptions to the overall schema that one encounters.

All of the above models have the effect either of describing schema change or at least diminishing confidence in schema application. When a schema is applied with less certainty, schema-based inferences may be less extreme than when a schema is used with full confidence (ibid.).

It is commonly held that people's views are moderated as they age; hence the view among the 1960s counterculture that "you can't trust anyone over thirty." Fiske and Taylor (1984, 173–74) hold that "mature schemata are likely to be more complex than immature ones" because more data is encountered as one progresses through life, including more discrepancies to previously constructed schemata. Therefore, "the more variety one has encountered, the more complex the issues, the less clear-cut it all seems, and the less extreme one's judgment."

The "dilution effect" helps the social perceiver make less extreme, more conservative inferences, as summarized by Fiske and Taylor (1984, 256–58). When diagnostic information is diluted with nondiagnostic information, inferences are less extreme. That is, information may initially be provided that taps into people's schemata in highly predictable ways, leading to an extreme conclusion. However, additional information may be provided on the political object that is nondiagnostic; this added information does not tap into schemata and elicit a quick judgment but merely deepens one's understanding of the object. Then the inference will be less extreme, or "diluted." For example, if a person is informed that the District is exclusively a city, without farmland or mountains, and that it is not even among American's top fifteen largest cities in population, then receptivity to full voting rights in Congress based on this diagnostic information may not be great. However, this easy conclusion could be diluted by providing additional information on occupations and education levels of District citizens, how the District's current government is structured, the jurisdiction's history, and any number of other "nondiagnostic" characteristics of the District that are ostensibly extraneous to the policy judgment.

Fiske and Taylor (ibid., 338) advised that "[t]he extremity of an affective [emotion-laden] response to something can be based on the complexity of one's knowledge about it; complexity encourages moderation of affect." It is easier to dislike a person, group, or policy when new information fits a negative stereotype. However, when new, more detailed information is produced that dilutes a previously perfect fit between object and schema, affective reactions may be moderated.

Capacity of Focus Group Panelists to Consider New Issues

Graber's research (1988, 256–57) supported earlier findings of Ladd and Lipset (1980, 2–9) that ambivalence characterized much of the thinking of contemporary Americans across income and racial lines. Such ambivalence, Graber wrote, "allows political communicators to tap selectively into contradictory schemata to evoke desired support or opposition." While this situation provides an opportunity for a politician, it signifies a responsibility for the qualitative researcher to provide a balanced array of stimuli—hence the use of pro and con discussions in the focus groups on D.C.'s policy options. Moreover, because Americans are accustomed to reconciling their conflicting schemata as political communicators prime them in one direction and another, D.C.'s political future was discussed beyond an initially expressed predisposition. Focus group panelists were asked to complete a written questionnaire about their views on D.C.'s political status prior to the start of focus group discussions, and panelists' views were monitored for change as the session continued. The reasons for any opinion change were discussed during the session.

The good news in Graber's political cognition research (1988, 252–53) is that "[a]verage Americans are capable of exacting enough meaningful political information from the flood of news to which they are exposed to perform the modest number of citizenship functions that American society expects of them." She added (ibid., 252):

> All [of her panelists] had acquired schemata into which they were able to fit incoming political information. All were able to work with an array of schema dimensions, and all frequently used multiple themes in their various schemata. All had adopted culturally sanctioned values as the schematic framework into which schemata covering more specific matters were then embedded.

Because of this level of panelist capability, and the array of schemata, dimensions, and themes at their disposal, most focus group panelists on the issue of D.C.'s political future were able to perform the function of developing responsible positions in the course of a vigorous two-hour discussion.

APPENDIX H

Outline of the Six Schemata, Their Themes and Subthemes

Schema 1: Democracy

Americans share a core belief in democracy as a means to achieve a free, fulfilling way of life.

Theme 1A: Universality
All Americans are entitled to participate in the political process.

Theme 1B: No taxation without representation
Americans should not be taxed by the federal government unless they are allowed to vote on taxation and other policies of their government.

Theme 1C: Equal political power for all
No American should have more political strength than any other American. We are all equals in the voting booth.

Theme 1D: Restorative powers of democracy
In foreign lands as well as our own, democracy can dramatically improve daily living conditions and the general well-being of the people.

Schema 2: State

People have a concept of what a "state" in the United States should look and be like.

Theme 2A: Size and shape
Many believe states should be of a certain size and have a distinctive shape on a large map of the United States. A state should not be just a dot or star.

Subtheme 2A(i): A certain kind of population
D.C.'s population may be unrepresentative of a state's population. D.C. is clearly a city and not a state.

Theme 2B: Sufficiency and diversity of resources
A state should have enough resources to support itself. Its resources should be diverse and not monolithic (mainly government and tourism).

Schema 3: D.C.

People view D.C. as a mixture of the postcard image of the nation's capital and of news reports on crime, drugs, etc., but have little specific, tangible knowledge of D.C. culture.

Theme 3A: Negative images
Many images of D.C. are similar to panelists' views of their own urban centers, with their many socioeconomic problems.

Subtheme 3A(i): Jackson and Barry
Several panelists especially pointed to Jesse Jackson and Marion Barry as reasons why their negative view of D.C. should be supported.

Subtheme 3A(ii): D.C. residents are "not ready"
Some panelists thought that D.C. residents are not ready to assume the responsibilities of self-government.

Theme 3B: Lack of identity
Many panelists had little awareness of D.C. and its culture, relying instead on television-driven stereotypes of urban life to describe D.C.

Subtheme 3B(i): They can always move
If full democratic rights are so important to people, all they have to do is move out of D.C.

Schema 4: Special Treatment

Several panelists thought that people, and especially blacks and urban residents in general, are seeking advantages through government and the political process that they could not obtain on their own.

Theme 4A: D.C. residents are already advantaged
D.C. residents receive many advantages (e.g., federal government jobs, welfare) without the additional advantage of enlarged political rights.

Theme 4B: Whites' political power would be diminished
D.C. self-government would result in a loss of political power among D.C. whites who, it is felt, would no longer have Congress to protect their interests.

Subtheme 4B(i): Greater diversity in the U.S. Senate
Voting rights would enhance the diversity of the U.S. Senate because minorities and urban interests would gain greater entry.

Subtheme 4B(ii): D.C. is "too liberal, too urban, too black, and too Democratic"
D.C.'s population may not be representative of the United States, and the issue of D.C. voting rights is viewed by some panelists as a means of engineering diversity.

Schema 5: Anti-Big-Government

Many panelists are skeptical of and even hostile to big government.

Theme 5A: An excessive, wasteful, interfering federal government
The federal government looks out for its own interests, and its actions hurt more than they help the American people.

Subtheme 5A(i): Congress can already control states and cities
Several panelists felt that Congress has many ways to assert federal control (e.g., through spending-related mandates) and does not need to exert an extra level of control over D.C.

Theme 5B: A bloated D.C. bureaucracy
D.C.'s own bureaucracy is wasteful and would grow even more cumbersome without congressional control.

Subtheme 5B(i): "Money talks"—a legitimate role for Congress
Several panelists felt that because Congress gives D.C. a federal payment, it therefore has a right to control D.C. affairs and protect federal interests.

Schema 6: Founding Fathers

In their great wisdom, the founding fathers established D.C. as a capital city apart from the states, and D.C. should remain true to their vision. Once we tamper with the Constitution, we are asking for trouble.

Bibliography

Alberts, Bette A. 1991. *D.C. statehood: Historical background and recent legislative actions of Congress.* Report prepared for Congress by Congressional Research Service. Washington, D.C.: CRS.

Albright, Madeline K. 1991. *Hearing and markup on admission of state of New Columbia into the Union.* U.S. Congress. House. Committee on the District of Columbia. Subcommittee on Judiciary and Education, 102d Cong., 1st sess. 18 Nov.

American Enterprise Institute. 1979. *A conversation with Mayor Marion Barry.* Washington, D.C.: American Enterprise Institute.

Annie E. Casey Foundation. 1994. *Kids count data book: State profiles of child well-being.* Greenwich, Conn.: Annie E. Casey Foundation.

Asher, Herbert. 1992. *Polling and the public: What every citizen should know.* 2d ed. Washington, D.C.: CQ Press.

Barrett, Laurence I. 1990. Puerto Rico, the 51st estado: Statehood gains momentum with a boost from Bush. *Time,* 26 March.

Bell, Roger. 1984. *Last among equals: Hawaiian statehood and American politics.* Honolulu: Univ. of Hawaii Press.

Berlin, Isaiah. 1961. Equality as an ideal. In *Justice and Social Policy,* ed. Frederick A. Olafson. Englewood Cliffs, N.J.: Prentice-Hall.

Bishop, George F., Robert W. Oldendick, and Alfred J. Tuchfarber. 1980. Pseudo-opinions on public affairs. *Public Opinion Quarterly* 44:198–209.

Best, Judith. 1984. *National representation for the District of Columbia.* Frederick, Md.: University Publications of America.

Black, Earl, and Merle Black. 1987. *Politics and society in the South.* Cambridge, Mass.: Harvard University Press.

Bowkett, Gerald E. 1989. *Reaching for a star: The final campaign for Alaska statehood.* Fairbanks, Alaska: Epicenter Press.

Bowling, Kenneth R. 1991. *The creation of Washington, D.C.: The idea and location of the American capital.* Fairfax, Va.: George Mason University Press.

________. 1992. *Hearing and markup on admission of state of New Columbia into the Union.* U.S. Congress. House. Committee on the District of Columbia. Subcommittee on Judiciary and Education, 102d Cong., 2d sess. 24 Mar.

Brazer, Harvey. 1957. *Some fiscal implications of metropolitanism.* Washington, D.C.: The Brookings Institution.

Brown, Ronald H. 1991. *Hearing and markup on admission of state of New Columbia into the Union.* U.S. Congress. House. Committee on the District of Columbia. Subcommittee on Judiciary and Education, 102d Cong., 1st sess. 14 Nov.

Burkholder, Richard, and Christine Gelhaus. 1991. Americans would support Puerto Ricans' choice regarding island's future status. *Gallup Poll Monthly,* no. 305:42.

Campbell, Agnus, Philip E. Converse, Warren E. Miller, & Donald Stokes. [1960] 1976. *The American voter.* Chicago: University of Chicago Press.

Carlson, Peter. 1993. Hocus focus. *The Washington Post Magazine,* 14 February, 15–17, 28–30.

Carmines, Edward G., and James A. Stimson. 1982. Racial issues and the structure of mass belief systems. *The Journal of Politics* 44: 2–20.

Clinton, Gov. Bill. 1991. *Hearing and markup on admission of state of New Columbia to the Union.* U.S. Congress. House. Committee on the District of Columbia. Subcommittee on Judiciary and Education, 102d Cong., 1st. sess. 18 Nov.

Conover, Pamela. 1985. The impact of group economic interests on political evaluations. *American Politics Quarterly* 13:139–56.

Conover, Pamela, Ivor M. Crewe, and Donald D. Searing. 1990. The nature of citizenship in the United States and Great Britain: Empirical comments on theoretical themes. *Journal of Politics* 53:800–32.

Conover, Pamela, and Stanley Feldman. 1984. Group identification, values, and the nature of political behavior. *American Politics Quarterly* 12:151–75.

———. 1984. How people organize the political world: A schematic model. *American Journal of Political Science* 28:95–126.

———. 1986. Emotional reactions to the economy: I'm mad as hell and I'm not going to take it anymore. *American Journal of Political Science* 30:50–78.

———. 1989. Candidate perception in an ambiguous world: Campaigns, cues, and inference processes. *American Journal of Political Science* 33:912–40.

Converse, Philip E. 1975. Public opinion and voting behavior. In *Handbook of political science,* vol. 4, ed. Nelson Polsby and Fred Greenstein. Reading, Mass.: Addison-Wesley.

Cooper, Timothy. 1993. Should Washington, D.C. be 51st state? *Chicago Sun-Times,* op-ed. column, 16 October.

Danzinger, Gloria. 1989. Washington, D.C.: Our 51st state? Is racism the reason D.C. is denied statehood? *Utne Reader,* no. 33: 24.

Davila-Colon, Luis R. 1981. Equal citizenship, self-determination, and thc U.S. statehood process: A constitutional and historical analysis. *Case Western Reserve Journal of International Law* 13:315–74.

D.C. Commission on Budget and Financial Priorities [the "Rivlin Commission"]. 1990. *Financing the nation's capital: The report of the Commission on Budget and Financial Priorities of the District of Columbia.* Washington, D.C.: The D.C. Commission on Budget and Financial Priorities.

———. 1994. *Four years later—the Rivlin report revisited.* Washington, D.C.: KPMG Peat Marwick.

D.C. Department of Employment Services. 1992. Labor market information: Statistical supplement, 1980 and 1990 Census, September. Computed from Census data.

D.C. Department of Finance and Revenue. 1992. *Tax rates and tax burdens in the District of Columbia: A nationwide comparison.* Washington, D.C.: The D.C. Department of Finance and Revenue.

________. 1995. Study of property, income and sales tax exemptions in the District of Columbia. Washington, D.C.: The D.C. Department of Finance and Revenue. 7 April.

D.C. Financial Responsibility and Management Assistance Authority. 1995. *Report on the District of Columbia Fiscal Year 1996 Budget.* Washington, D.C.:15 August.

D.C. Office of Policy and Program Evaluation. 1991. *Indices: A statistical index to District of Columbia services.* Washington, D.C.

Dearborn, Philip M. 1992. *Avoiding a District of Columbia financial emergency.* Washington, D.C.: Greater Washington Research Center.

Dignan, Mark B., Robert Michielutte, and Penny Sharpe. 1990. The role of focus groups in health education for cervical cancer among minority women. *Journal of Community Health* 15:369–75.

Dumas, Kitty. 1990. Fauntroy adds another twist to D.C. statehood drive. *Congressional Quarterly Weekly Report* 48:743–44.

________. 1990. Boxing with shadows. *Congressional Quarterly Weekly Report* 48:2409.

Ebel, Robert D. 1993. *Hearings, H.R. 51, to provide for the admission of the State of New Columbia into the Union.* U.S. Congress. House. Committee on the District of Columbia, Subcommittee on Judiciary and Education, 103d Congress, 1st sess. (July 28).

Edmonds, Thomas N., and Raymond J. Keating. 1995. *D.C. by the numbers: A state of failure.* Lanham, Md.: University Press of America.

Ellison, Ralph. [1952] 1990. *Invisible man.* New York: Random House, Vintage Books.

Farber, Stephen B. 1990. The budgetary impact of alternative forms of governance for the District of Columbia. Report prepared for the D.C. Commission on Budget and Financial Priorities. Washington, D.C.

Feig, Barry. 1989. How to run a focus group. *American Demographics* 11:36–37.

Fiske, Susan T., and Patricia W. Linville. 1980. What does the schema concept buy us? *Personality and Social Psychology Bulletin* 6:543–57.

Fiske, Susan T., and Shelly E. Taylor. 1984. *Social cognition.* Reading, Mass.: Addison-Wesley.

Foley, Thomas S. 1987. *Hearings, to provide for the admission of the state of New Columbia into the Union.* U.S. Congress. House. Committee on the District of Columbia. Subcommittee on Fiscal Affairs and Health, 100th Cong., 1st sess. 17 Mar.

Fortune, Connie. 1978. *Hearings, joint resolution to amend the Constitution to provide for representation of the District of Columbia in the Congress.* U.S. Congress. Senate. Committee on the Judiciary. Subcommittee on the Constitution, 95th Cong., 2d sess. 27 Apr.

Gallup, George. 1947. The quintamensional plan of question design. *Public Opinion Quarterly* 11:386.

Graber, Doris A. [1984] 1988. *Processing the news: How people tame the information tide*, 2nd ed. New York: Longman.

Greeley, Andrew M. 1974. Political participation among ethnic groups in the United States: A preliminary reconnaissance. *American Journal of Sociology* 80:174–204.

Grier, George. 1994. *Comings and goings in the Washington area.* Washington, D.C.: Greater Washington Research Center.

Gurin, Patricia. 1985. Women's gender consciousness. *The Public Opinion Quarterly* 49:143–163.

Gurin, Patricia, and Edgar Epps. 1975. *Black consciousness, identity, and achievement: A study of students in historically black colleges.* New York: John Wiley & Sons.

Gurin, Patricia, Arthur H. Miller, and Gerald Gurin. 1980. Stratum identification and consciousness. *Social Psychology Quarterly* 43:30–47.

Hamilton, Alexander, James Madison, and John Jay. [1788] 1961. *The Federalist papers.* New York: New American Library.

Hamilton, David L., ed. 1981. *Cognitive processes in stereotyping and intergroup behavior.* Hillsdale, N.J.: L. Erlbaum Associates.

Harris, Charles W. 1989. Federal and local interests in the nation's capital: Congress and District of Columbia appropriations. *Public Budgeting and Finance* 9, no. 4 (winter):66–82.

Hochschild, Jennifer L. 1981. *What's fair? American beliefs about distributive justice.* Cambridge: Harvard University Press.

Hochschild, Jennifer L., and Monica Herk. 1990. "Yes, but . . .": Principles and caveats in American racial attitudes. In *Majorities and minorities*, ed. John W. Chapman and Alan Wertheimer. New York: New York University Press.

Huber, Joan, and William H. Form. 1973 *Income and ideology: An analysis of the American political formula.* New York: Free Press.

Huntington, Samuel P. 1981. *American politics: The promise of disharmony.* Cambridge, Mass.: Belknap Press.

Iyengar, Shanto, and Donald R. Kinder. 1987. *News that matters.* Chicago: University of Chicago Press.

Jackson, Bryan O. 1987. The effects of racial consciousness on political mobilization in American cities. *The Western Political Quarterly* 40:631–46.

Jackson, Rev. Jesse L. 1990. Foreword: The state of New Columbia—A call for justice and freedom. *Catholic University Law Review* 39, no. 2 (winter):307–10.

_______. 1994. *Hearing on policy alternatives to D.C. statehood.* U.S. Congress. Senate Committee on Government Affairs (4 Aug.).

_______. 1991. *Hearing and markup on admission of state of New Columbia into the Union.* U.S. Congress. House. Committee on the District of Columbia. Subcommittee on Judiciary and Education, 102d Cong., 1st sess. 14 Nov.

Jaffe, Harry S., and Tom Sherwood. 1994. *Dream city: Race, power, and the decline of Washington, D.C.* New York: Simon & Schuster.

Jenkins, Kent, Jr. 1993. The long road to New Columbia. *The Washington Post Magazine*, 4 July.

Jennings, M. Kent, and Gregory B. Markus. 1988. Political involvement in the later years: A longitudinal survey. *American Journal of Political Science* 32:302–16.

Johnson, Janet Buttolph, and Richard A. Joslyn. 1986. *Political science research methods.* Washington, D.C.: CQ Press.

Jones, Bryan D. 1994. *Reconceiving decision-making in democratic politics: Attention, choice, and public policy.* Chicago: The University of Chicago Press.

Judd, C. M., and J. A. Kulik. 1980. Schematic effects of social attitudes on information processing and recall. *Journal of Personality and Social Psychology* 38:569–78.

Kahneman, Daniel, and Amos Tversky. 1982. The simulation heuristic. In *Judgment under uncertainty: Heuristics and biases,* eds. D. Kahneman, P. Slovic, and A. Tversky. New York: Cambridge University Press.

Kernell, Samuel. 1986. *Going public: New strategies of presidential leadership.* Washington, D.C.: CQ Press.

Key, V. O., Jr. 1961. *Public opinion and American democracy.* New York: Alfred A. Knopf.

Kinder, Donald R. 1983. Diversity and complexity in American public opinion. In *Political science: The state of the discipline,* ed. Ada W. Finifter. Washington, D.C.: American Political Science Association.

Kinder, Donald R., and D. Roderick Kiewiet. 1981. Sociotropic politics: The American case. *British Journal of Political Science* 11:129–61.

King, Martin Luther, Jr. [1963] 1976. Letter from Birmingham Jail. In *Martin Luther King, Jr., a documentary: Montgomery to Memphis,* ed. F. Schulke. New York: W.W. Norton.

Kirschten, Dirk. 1990. Capital electioneering. *National Journal* 22:948–51.

Kluegel, James R., and Eliot R. Smith. 1986. *Beliefs about inequality: Americans' views of what is and what ought to be.* New York: Aldine DeGruyter.

Krueger, Richard A. 1988. *Focus groups: A practical guide for applied research.* Newbury Park, Calif.: Sage Publications.

Kuklinski, James H., Robert C. Luskin, and John Bolland. 1991. Where is the schema? Going beyond the "s" word in political psychology. *American Political Science Review* 85:1341–56.

Kurland, Adam Harris. 1993. *Hearings, H.R. 51, to provide for the admission of the State of New Columbia into the Union.* U.S. Congress. House. Committee on the District of Columbia. Subcommittee on Judiciary and Education, 103d Congress, 1st sess. (July 28).

Ladd, Everett Carll. 1989. *The American polity: The people and their government.* 3d. ed. New York: W.W. Norton.

Ladd, Everett Carll, and Seymour Martin Lipset. 1980. Anatomy of a decade. *Public Opinion* 3:2–9.

Lamb, Karl A. 1974. *As Orange goes.* New York: W.W. Norton.

Laney, Garrine P. 1991. *Shadow representatives in Congress: History and current developments.* Report prepared for Congress by Congressional Research Service. Washington, D.C.: CRS.

Langer, Judith. 1991. Focus groups. *American Demographics,* 13:38–39.

Lowery, Bill. 1991. *Hearing and markup on admission of state of New Columbia into the Union.* U.S. Congress. House Committee on the District of Columbia. Subcommittee on Judiciary and Education, 102d Cong., 1st sess. 14 Nov.

Mathews, David. 1988. *The promise of democracy: A source book for use with national issues forums.* Dayton, Ohio: Kettering Foundation.

McCombs, Maxwell E., and Donald L. Shaw. 1976. Structuring the "unseen environment." *Journal of Communication* 26, no. 2:13.

McCracken, Grant. 1988. *The long interview.* Qualitative Research Methods, vol. 13. Newbury Park, Calif.: Sage Publications.

McDonald, Forrest. 1992. *Hearing and markup on admission of state of New Columbia into the Union.* U.S. Congress. House. Committee on the District of Columbia. Subcommittee on Judiciary and Education, 102d Cong., 2d sess. (March).

McKinsey & Co., Inc. 1994. *Assessing the District of Columbia's financial future.* In collaboration with the Urban Institute. Washington, D.C.: Federal City Council.

Medish, Mark C. 1993. *Hearings, H.R. 51, to provide for the admission of the State of New Columbia into the Union.* U.S. Congress. House. Committee on the District of Columbia. Subcommittee on Judiciary and Education, 103d Congress, 1st sess. (July 28).

Melendez, Edgardo. 1988. *Puerto Rico's statehood movement.* New York: Greenwood Press.

Merton, Robert K., and Patricia L. Kendall. 1946. The focused interview. *American Journal of Sociology* 51:541–57.

Merton, Robert K. 1987. The focussed interview and focus groups: Continuities and discontinuities. *Public Opinion Quarterly* 51:550–66.

Merton, Robert K., Marjorie Fiske, and Patricia L. Kendall. 1956. *The focused interview.* Glencoe, Ill.: Free Press.

Metropolitan Washington Council of Governments. 1993. Tabulation of commuting modes for federal civilian workers by jurisdiction from 1990 Census of Population and Housing. Washington, D.C.

Meyers, Edward M. 1986. *Rebuilding America's cities.* Cambridge, Mass.: Ballinger Publishing Co.

_______. 1990. External factors affecting District of Columbia budgets. Paper submitted to D.C. Commission on Budget and Financial Priorities ["Rivlin Commission"]. Washington, D.C.

_______. 1989. They don't have to work in D.C., but they choose to: The residency requirement works. *The Washington Post,* op-ed column, 11 October.

Miller, Arthur H., Patricia Gurin, and Gerald Gurin. 1980. Age consciousness and political mobilization of older Americans. *The Gerontologist* 20:691–700.

Miller, Arthur H., Patricia Gurin, Gerald Gurin, and Oksana Malanchuck. 1981. Group consciousness and political anticipation. *American Journal of Political Science* 25:494–511.

Miller, James C., III. 1992. *Hearings and markup on admission of state of New Columbia into Union.* U.S. Congress. House. Subcommittee on Judiciary and Education, 102d Cong., 2nd sess. 24 Mar.

Mink, Patsy T. 1987. *Hearings to provide for the admission of the state of New Columbia into the Union.* U.S. Congress. House. Committee on the District of Columbia. Subcommittee on Fiscal Affairs and Health, 100th Cong., 1st sess. 17 Mar.

Morgan, David L. 1988. *Focus groups as qualitative research.* Vol. 16 of Qualitative Research Methods. Newbury Park, Calif.: Sage Publications.

Morgan, David L., and Margaret T. Spanish. 1985. Social interaction and the cognitive organization of health-relevant behavior. *Sociology of Health and Illness* 7:401–22.

Nelson, Dale C. 1979. Ethnicity and socioeconomic status as sources of participation: The case of ethnic political culture. *American Political Science Review* 73:1024–38.

Nie, Norman H., Sidney Verba, and John R. Petrocik. 1976. *The changing American voter.* Cambridge: Harvard University Press.

Noyes, Theodore W. 1951. *Our nation's capital and its un-Americanized Americans.* Washington, D.C.: self-published.

Phillips, Kevin P. 1969. *The emerging Republican majority.* New Rochelle, N.Y.: Arlington House.

Population Reference Bureau. 1992. *The challenge of change: What the 1990 census tells us about children.* Washington, D.C.: Center for the Study of Social Policy.

Ragland, James. 1993. The Jackson factor. *The Washington Post Magazine*, 4 July.

Raskin, Jamin B. 1990. Commentary: Domination, democracy and the District; the statehood position. *Catholic University Law Review* 39:417–40.

________. 1994. *Hearing on policy alternatives to D.C. statehood.* U.S. Congress. Senate Committee on Governmental Affairs (Aug. 4).

________. 1991. Liberate the District: Now that we've freed Kuwait. *Nation*, no. 252:371–74.

________. 1993. *Hearings, H.R. 51, to provide for the admission of the State of New Columbia into the Union.* U.S. Congress. House. Committee on the District of Columbia. Subcommittee on Judiciary and Education, 103d Congress, 1st sess. 28 July.

Raven-Hansen, Peter. 1991. The constitutionality of D.C. statehood. *The George Washington University Law Review* 60, no. 1:160–93.

________. 1992. *Hearing and markup on admission of state of New Columbia into the Union.* U.S. Congress. House. Committee on the District of Columbia. Subcommittee on Judiciary and Education, 102d Cong., 2d sess. 24 Mar.

Rohrabacher, Dana. 1991. *Hearing and markup on admission of New Columbia into the Union.* U.S. Congress. House. Committee on the District of Columbia. Subcommittee on Judiciary and Education, 102d Cong., 1st sess. 14 Nov.

Roper Center for Public Opinion Research. 1994. Print-out of Survey results, 20 April.

Rusk, David. 1993. *Cities without suburbs.* Washington, D.C.: Woodrow Wilson Center Press.

Schrag, Philip G. 1985. *Behind the scenes: The politics of a constitutional convention.* Washington, D.C.: Georgetown University Press.

________. 1990. The future of District of Columbia home rule. *Catholic University Law Review* 39:311–72.

Schuman, Howard, Charlotte Steeh, and Lawrence Bobo. 1985. *Racial attitudes in America: Trends and interpretations.* Cambridge, Mass.: Harvard University Press.

Sears, David O., and Jack Citrin. 1982. *Tax revolt: Something for nothing in California.* Cambridge, Mass.: Harvard University Press.

Sears, David O., Carl P. Hensler, and Leslie K. Speer. 1979. Whites' opposition to "busing": Self-interest or symbolic politics? *American Political Science Review* 73:369–84.

Sears, David O., and Rick Kosterman. 1991. Is it really racism? The origins and dynamics of symbolic racism. Presentation at the Annual Meeting of the Midwestern Political Science Association. Chicago

Seidman, I. E. 1991. *Interviewing as qualitative research: A guide for research.* New York: Teachers College Press.

Shingles, Richard D. 1981. Black consciousness and political participation: The missing link. *American Political Science Review* 75:76–91.

Siedman, Louis Michael. 1990. The preconditions for home rule. *Catholic University Law Review* 39:373–416.

Simon, Senator Paul. 1993. Remarks at the Rebuild America National Leadership Summit, Washington Hilton, Washington, D.C., 10 June.

Singer, Eleanor. 1988. Presidential address: Pushing back the limits to surveys. *Public Opinion Quarterly* 52:416–26.

Skene, Neil. 1990. The Madison perception and D.C. statehood. *Congressional Quarterly Weekly Report* 48:630.

Smith, Sam. 1974. *Captive capital: Colonial life in modern Washington.* Bloomington, Indiana: Indiana University Press.

________. 1991. *The statehood papers: Articles on D.C. statehood, 1970–1991.* Washington, D.C.: Progressive Review.

Sniderman, Paul M., Michael G. Hagen, Philip E. Tetlock, and Henry E. Brady. 1986. Reasoning chains: Causal models of policy reasoning in mass public. *British Journal of Political Science* 16:405–30.

Standard & Poor's. 1993. *Creditweek municipal*, February 8.

Standen, Jeffrey. 1992. *Hearing on markup on admission of state of New Columbia into the Union.* U.S. Congress. House. Committee on the District of Columbia. Subcommittee on Judiciary and Education, 102d Cong., 2d sess. 24 Mar.

Stewart, David W., and Prem N. Shamdasani. 1990. *Focus groups: Theory and practice.* Vol. 20 of Applied Social Research Methods Series. Newbury Park, Calif.: Sage Publications.

Templeton, Jane Farley. 1987. *Focus groups: A guide for marketing and advertising professionals.* Chicago: Probus Publishing.

Tooley, Jo Ann. 1991. Database. *U.S. News & World Report*, 18 February, 10.

Tucker, Sterling. 1978. *Hearings, joint resolution to amend the Constitution to provide for representation of the District of Columbia in the Congress.* U.S. Congress. Senate. Committee on the Judiciary. Subcommittee on the Constitution, 95th Cong., 2d sess. 27 Apr.

Twomey, Steve. 1993. The 51st state. *The Washington Post Magazine*, 4 July.

United States Constitutional Convention. [1787] 1966. *Notes of debates in the federal convention of 1787.* Athens, Ohio: Ohio University Press.

U.S. Bureau of the Census. 1975. *Public employment in 1974.* GE 74, no. 1. Washington, D.C.: GPO. May.

________. 1982. *Special tabulations on government employment levels in the District of Columbia and seven other selected cities.* Governments Division. Transmittal letter to E.M. Meyers, 3 February.

________. 1984. *Census of the population, 1980,* Vol. 2 of Subjectreports: Journey to work; characteristics of workers in metropolitan areas, table one. Washington, D.C.: GPO.

________. 1991. *Census of population and housing.* Summary tape file 3A.

________. 1991. *Statistical abstract of the United States* (110th ed.). Washington, D.C.: GPO.

________. 1992a. *Money income of households, families, and persons in the United States: 1991.* Current Population Reports, series P–60, no. 180. Washington, D.C.: GPO.

________. 1992b. *Poverty in the United States: 1991* Current Population Reports, series P–60, no. 181. Washington, D.C.: GPO.

________. 1993. *1990 census of the population, general population characteristics, metropolitan areas.* Series CP–1–1B. Washington, D.C.: GPO.

________. 1994a. Population projections for states, by age, sex, race, and Hispanic origin: 1993 to 2020. Current Population Reports, P–25–1111. Washington, D.C.: GPO.

________. 1994b. *Statistical abstract of the United States: 1994* 114th ed. Washington, D.C.: GPO.

________. 1995. *Income, poverty, and valuation of non-cash benefits: 1993.* Current Population Reports, P–60–188. Washington, D.C.: GPO

U.S. Conference of Mayors. 1984. *Homelessness in American cities: Ten case studies.* Washington, D.C.

U.S. Congress. 1957. *Alaska—admission into Union.* House. Committee on Interior and Insular Affairs, 79th Cong., 1st sess. House Report no. 624 (June 25).

________. 1959. *Report on statehood for Hawaii.* Senate. Committee on Interior and Insular Affairs. 80th Cong., 1st. sess. Senate Report no. 80.

________. 1987. *New Columbia Admission Act.* House. Committee on the District of Columbia, 100th Cong., 1st sess. House Report no. 100–305 (Sept. 17).

U.S. Department of Commerce. Economics and Statistics Administration. 1991. Summary tape file 1A, Table 6A, July.

U.S. Department of Labor. 1991. *Geographic profile of employment and unemployment.* Washington, D.C.: GPO.

U.S. General Accounting Office. 1980. *Experiences of past territories can assist Puerto Rico status deliberations.* Report to Congress, GGD–80–26, 7 March. Washington, D.C.: GAO.

U.S. General Accounting Office. 1994. *Financial status: District of Columbia finances.* Briefing report to congressional requesters, 22 June. Washington, D.C.: GAO.

Valentine, Steven R., U.S. Department of Justice. 1992. *Hearing and markup on admission of state of New Columbia into the union.* U.S. Congress. House. Committee on the District of Columbia, Subcommittee on Judiciary and Education, 102d Cong., 2d sess. 24 Mar.

Verba, Sidney, and Gary R. Orren. 1985. *Equality in America: The view from the top.* Cambridge, Mass.: Harvard University Press.

Verba, Sidney, and Norman H. Nie. 1972. *Participation in America: Political democracy and social equality.* New York: Harper & Row.

Wadlington, Claire H. 1992. *Hearing and markup on admission of state of New Columbia into the Union.* U.S. Congress. House. Committee on the District of Columbia. Subcommittee on Judiciary and Education, 102d Cong., 2d sess. 24 Mar.

Walden, Graham R. 1990. *Public opinion polls and survey research: A selective annotated bibliography of U.S. guides and studies from the 1980s.* New York: Garland Publishing.

Watson, Tom. 1987. House panel approves D.C. statehood bill. *Congressional Quarterly Weekly Report* 45:1192.

Weaver, R. Kent, and Charles W. Harris. 1989. Who's in charge here?: Congress and the nation's capital. *The Brookings Review* 7, no. 3 (summer):39–46.

Weisberg, Jacob. 1991. Shadow boxing. *The New Republic,* no. 204:16.

Welch, Susan, John Comer, and Michael Steinman. 1975. Ethnic differences in social and political participation: A comparison of some Anglo and Mexican Americans. *Pacific Sociological Review* 18:361–83.

Westin, Peter. 1990. *Speaking on equality: An analysis of the rhetorical force of "equality" in moral and legal discourse.* Princeton, N.J.: Princeton University Press.

Williams, Juan. 1993. History lessons. *The Washington Post Magazine,* 4 July.

Wilson, James Q., and Edward C. Banfield. 1964. Public regardingness as a value premise in voting behavior. *American Political Science Review* 58:876–87.

Wirthlin Group. 1995. *Public attitudes toward issues facing Washington, D.C.* Prepared for the Federal City Council. Washington, D.C.: Wirthlin Group.

Yankelovich, Peter. 1991. *Coming to public judgment: Making democracy work in a complex world.* Syracuse, N.Y.: Syracuse University Press.

Zandonade, Tarcisio. 1992. Phone conversation by author with representative of Brazilian embassy, 20 March.

Interviews

Interviews by the author were held with dozens of people involved with the District. Below is a partial listing:

Barry, Marion. 1994. Then mayor-elect, 29 November.

Chavous, Kevin. 1993. D.C. councilmember and chair, Council Committee on Self-Determination, 14 April.

Davis, Thomas M. III. 1995. Representative, U.S. House, and chair, Subcommittee of the District of Columbia,11 May.

Demczuk, Bernard. 1993. Director, D.C. Office of Intergovernmental Relations, 8 May.

Grier, George. 1993. Demographer, 14 January.

Hill, John W., Jr. 1995. Director, audit support and analysis, U.S. General Accounting Office, 17 May.

Jackson, Jesse. 1993. Elected lobbyist for D.C. statehood, 8 July.

Kelly, Sharon Pratt. 1993. Mayor of the District of Columbia, 9 July.

Norton, Eleanor Holmes. 1993. The District's delegate, U.S. House, 11 July.

Rivlin, Alice. 1993. Deputy director, U.S. Office of Management and Budget and former chair, D.C. Commission on Budget and Financial Priorities, 27 May.

Sloan, E. Ned. 1993. Chair, D.C. Statehood Commission, 13 November.

Smith, Sam. 1993. Cofounder, D.C. Statehood Party, 27 April.

Walsh, James. 1995. Representative, U.S. House, and chair, Subcommittee on D.C. Appropriations, 2 May.

Wilson, John A. 1993. Chairman, Council of the District of Columbia, 13 May.

Index